Regional Economies as Knowledge Laboratories

Regional Economies as Knowledge Laboratories

Edited by
Philip Cooke

University Research Professor in Regional Development and Director, Centre for Advanced Studies, University of Wales, Cardiff, UK

and

Andrea Piccaluga

Associate Professor of Business Administration, University of Lecce and Research Associate, Laboratory of Economics and Management, St Anna School of Advanced Studies, Pisa, Italy

Edward Elgar
Cheltenham, UK • Northampton, MA, USA

Published by
Edward Elgar Publishing Limited
Glensanda House
Montpellier Parade
Cheltenham
Glos GL50 1UA
UK

Edward Elgar Publishing, Inc.
136 West Street
Suite 202
Northampton
Massachusetts 01060
USA

A catalogue record for this book
is available from the British Library

ISBN 1 84376 821 6

Typeset by Manton Typesetters, Louth, Lincolnshire, UK.
Printed and bound in Great Britain by MPG Books Ltd, Bodmin, Cornwall.

Contents

Figures

Tables

Contributors

Heidi Wiig Aslesen
Step-Group, Centre for Innovation Studies
SINTEF Technology Management
Hammersborg Torg 3
NO-0179 Oslo
Norway

Frans Boekema
Faculty of Economics and Business Administration
University of Tilberg
5000 LE Tilburg
The Netherlands

Philip Cooke
Centre for Advanced Studies
Cardiff University
44–45 Park Place
Cardiff
CF10 3BB
UK

Goio Etxebarria
Department of Applied Economics
University of the Basque Country
48015 Bilbao
Spain

Koen Frenken
Urban and Regional Research Centre Utrecht (URU)
Faculty of Geosciences
Utrecht University
The Netherlands

Seamus Grimes
Centre for Innovation and Structural Change
National University of Ireland
Galway
Republic of Ireland

Dr Fumi Kitagawa
Research Co-ordinator
Research and Development Centre for Higher Education
Hitotsubashi University
2-1, Naka, Kunitachi-shi, Tokyo
186-8601, Japan

Kati-Jasmin Kosonen
University of Tampere
Research Unit for Urban and Regional Development Studies (Sente)
Tampere
Finland

Mark Lorenzen
Research Center on Dynamic Market Organization (DYNAMO)
Danish Research Unit on Industrial Dynamics (DRUID)
Department of Industrial Economics and Strategy
Copenhagen Business School
Copenhagen
Denmark

Peter Maskell
Research Center on Dynamic Market Organization (DYNAMO)
Danish Research Unit on Industrial Dynamics (DRUID)
Department of Industrial Economics and Strategy
Copenhagen Business School
Copenhagen
Denmark

Frank G. van Oort
Urban and Regional Research Centre Utrecht (URU)
Faculty of Geosciences, Utrecht University
The Netherlands
and
The Netherlands Institute for Spatial Research (RPB)
The Netherlands

Andrea Piccaluga
Scuola Superiore Sant'Anna
Pisa
Italy

Lucio Poma
Università degli Studi di Ferrara – Facoltà di Economia
Ciras – International Research Centre for Environment and Development
Via del Gregorio 13 - 44 100 Ferrara
Italy
and Antares – Research Centre for Industrial and Territorial Economics

Roel Rutten
Faculty of Economics and Business Administration
University of Tilberg
5000 LE Tilburg
The Netherlands

Silvia Sacchetti
Università degli Studi di Ferrara - Facoltà di Economia
Institute for Industrial Development Policy (L'institute)
Via del Gregoria 13 - 44 100 Ferrara
Italy
and Antares – Research Centre for Industrial and Territorial Economics

Martin Sokol
Research Fellow
Urban Institute Ireland,
University College Dublin
UCD - Richview Campus
Clonskeagh Drive, Dublin 14
Republic of Ireland

Markku Sotarauta
University of Tampere
Research Unit for Urban and Regional Development Studies (Sente)
Tampere
Finland

Ernesto Tavoletti
Department of Economics and Management of Enterprises and Local Systems
Facoltà di Economia
Università di Firenze
Florence
Italy

Mikel Gómez Uranga
Department of Applied Economics
University of the Basque Country
48015 Bilbao
Spain

Mark C. White
Centre for Innovation and Structural Change
National University of Ireland
Galway
Republic of Ireland

Kerstin Wolter
Institute for International and Regional Economic Relations
University Duisburg-Essen
Duisburg Campus
Lotharstr. 65, LB 319a; 47048 Duisburg
Germany

Introduction: the scale question in knowledge creation, capture and commercialization

Philip Cooke

INTRODUCTION: TOWARDS THE KNOWLEDGE ECONOMY

This book seeks to navigate the sometimes rocky shoals and reefs of the knowledge economy. After the concept was first elucidated by Machlup (1962), progress in developing and operationalizing it was slow. This is partly because of an evolving interest in and study of the role of *information* in the economy. This can be traced back at least to the pioneering research at Bell Laboratories of engineer Claude Shannon (1948, 379–80) who defined information as messages possessing *meaning* for sender and recipient. We might term this the 'train timetable' theory, not least as Shannon said that communication's 'significant aspect is that the actual message is one *selected from a set* of possible messages' (1948, 379 original emphasis). This then fuelled research leading to consistent observations that, in the second half of the twentieth century an 'information explosion' could be observed, with associated 'information overload' (Miller, 1978) from the exponential growth in messages, increasingly diffused by 'information technology' (IT, later ICT in recognition of communications technologies; Seely Brown and Duguid, 2002; Lievrouw and Livingstone, 2002) within what was perceived to have become an 'Information Society' or the 'Information Age' (Castells, 1996; 1997; 1998).

The key question Machlup (1962; see also, 1980) raised long before this began in earnest was as follows: which are the key economic sectors in which such assets are concentrated, and how can a serious attempt be made to map out the production and distribution of knowledge sectors in the (United States) economy, showing where their significance lies? Machlup classified knowledge production into six major sectors: education, R&D, artistic creation, communications media, information services, and information technologies. He showed that these accounted for the largest share in the economy, and predicted that knowledge production was destined to grow absolutely and relatively over time. A more detailed analytical account emerged with the contribution of Eliasson et al. (1990), not only capturing the shift in intellectual focus in its title (*The Knowledge Based Information Economy*) but bringing an operational measurement method to fruition for economies other than the US. This study was a forerunner leading to adoption by OECD (1996) of the *knowledge economy* concept which was important and useful for its future economic analysis, and for its operationalization into a method for measurement of knowledge economy densities or magnitudes in economies (OECD, 1999).

THE KNOWLEDGE ECONOMY TODAY

However, Eliasson et al. (1990) did not come down clearly on the side of a statistically useful definition of the 'knowledge economy'. Their analysis was experimental, hedged around greatly by trying simultaneously to capture measurement of the 'information economy' by analysis of service sector metrics, the measurement of telecommunication services as part of company and organizational expenditure, and, importantly, discussing measurements based on the labour content of information economy activities. This latter approach was taken up and developed much later by Burton-Jones (1999) who took a strongly labour market and occupational position on how the knowledge economy was to be defined. However, it is difficult to do this nationally across countries, and currently it is largely impossible to do it regionally in a comparatively meaningful way, mainly because of definitional and categorization problems. Hence, while paying lip-service to such elements as qualification density and equipment intensity, OECD (1999) adopted for reasons of practicality a definition that is based on two macro-sectors: 'high technology manufacturing' and 'knowledge intensive services'. The former includes, categories such as: aerospace, computers, communication and office equipment, pharmaceuticals, radio and TV equipment, while knowledge intensive services are communications, software, R&D, financial services, welfare and public administration services. Efforts are being made by OECD to weight such sectors according to Burton-Jones' occupational emphasis to produce a more refined yet practicable measure, albeit still fundamentally sector-based.

Looking at the question not so much cross-sectionally as longitudinally, from an accounting perspective, intangible goods such as knowledge now account for both a greater share by value of corporate assets than hitherto and a greater share than the value of tangible assets. The shift since 1950 is 20:80 to 70:30, at least in the USA, according to Dunning (2000). This, along with huge rises in intellectual labour and patent registration in the last half century, leads most observers of economic evolution to assert with confidence that a 'knowledge economy' is present and active in most advanced economies. However, in addition to definitional issues, this also raises others key to the focus of the succeeding chapters of this book. One of these relates to a geographical question that is scale-related.

By *scale*-related is meant, primarily, distinctions between the supranational, national and sub-national, including the meso-level and below. This is of course germane to the content of a book the focus of which is *regional economies*. While this is clearly a governance issue (in Europe, this means the EU, member state, regional and local levels of governance), it is also, importantly, an industrial organization issue such as that outlined in the economic integration literature which analyses interactions among 'global value networks' and 'local clusters' as a specific form of globalization (Gereffi, 1999; UNIDO, 2002; Henderson et al., 2002). It is necessary, therefore, to situate the meaning of *regional economies* in an at least partial relationship to a 'debate' that has arisen in economic geography to define clearly what is meant here, in contradistinction to aspects of the debate that, in tune with a conservative political economy tradition (for example List, 1841) asserted that only national economies matter.

REGIONAL ECONOMIES AND THE QUESTION OF 'SCALE'

As with many things, such as a historic failure to provide a convincing theory of location and city formation (on this, and a solution, see Krugman, 1995) there has been since the dawning of modern geography an inability by its practitioners to carve out a core area of theoretical competence of the status of, say 'class' or 'structuration' in sociology, the 'Phillips curve' explanation of the relation between unemployment and inflation in economics, or 'multi-level governance' in political science. The last-named is of direct relevance to issues tackled in this book, so what do its leading propositions say? First that different levels of governance relate not in a linear, power-imposing manner, but by evolving spheres of capability among which interactions occur by negotiation between parties of consequence to specific competence areas. Study then focuses on change or evolution, including devolution, of such competences and capabilities as political systems mature. This allows contrasts of the following kind to be drawn with confidence by exponents of multi-level governance, in this case referring to the relations between national and regional electoral outcomes. Germany demonstrates a predictable relationship between regional and national outcomes since strong regional differentiation in voting is exceptional. Spain's relationship of regional to national elections is complex due to distinctive regional electoral dynamics arising from historical, cultural and linguistic expressions of difference in specific regions. Canada's regional and national electoral dynamics are mostly decoupled because of historical, cultural and linguistic expressions of difference (Hough and Jeffery, 2003). The explanation is that there is geographical variation in what counts as first and second order political issues for the electorate. In other words, the larger 'scale' does not always, or indeed ever, impose its will on the lesser. For how, as an abstraction, could it?

Contrast this with an eclectic mixture of critique, comment and conceptualization on the issue of 'scale' emanating from contemporary economic geography. Already attacked by Dicken et al. (1997) for a conservative, linear determinism that sees 'globalization' as a totalizing, relentless and inevitable power, it proceeds in an all-encompassing way to deny capability to other 'scales'. Trying to escape this we see, for example, Bunnell and Coe (2001) and Mackinnon et al. (2002) saying it is both wrong to emphasize the regional level and wrong to overlook regional specificity. Scale clearly does not exclude presence of fences for sitting on. This is an improvement upon Listian positions such as that of Bathelt (2003) writing in the same journal that only nations have specificity and that they may also be *closed* systems, which in a world of liberal free trade and widespread immigration may serve only to unite in scepticism the 'glocalists' (for example Swyngedouw, 1997), with those whose interests are expressed in this book. This latter commentary on *closure*, albeit moderated in ways that still privilege the national over any other scale, is especially curious, for it manages both to advocate a nineteenth century view of the contemporary relation of the nation (state) to its regions that equates, in effect, to annihilation, and attack for inattention to scale issues, authors who have empirically demonstrated precisely the presence of regional governance capabilities. These exist even where regional 'government' is absent, and display accomplishment at managing economic development and innovation support actions where national governments may have been inactive in such spheres (for example Asheim and Isaksen, 2002).

REASSERTING THE REGIONAL ECONOMY AS A SPATIAL CONSTRUCT

So, to be clear, in this book we do not align with the geographical perspective that stresses linear hierarchy as the power vector for innovation. We are closer to the multi-level governance school of thought, taking our definition of 'region' as a governance level above the local and beneath the national. This also rejects a weak usage of 'regional' that crops up journalistically to describe, for example, the Middle East, the Baltic States or South East Asia (which increasingly incorporates China – some region!). We advocate for geopolitical usage the term 'georegion' instead. Nor, it will be clear, does this book support the linear, hierarchical determinism of the 'scalar envelope' approach with its weak grasp upon 'agency'. For this flies in the face of research that shows sub-national policy mobilization regarding shaping of innovation capabilities to be common, if not yet ubiquitous (for a progenitor of spatial 'enveloping', see Brenner, 2001).

But we go further in reasserting the relevance of the 'regional', as denoted above, to the study of innovation and recent extensions of analysis of the processes involved, backwards along the knowledge value change into knowledge exploration and production itself, by speaking of 'regional economies'. This contested term is considered an artifice principally by those wedded to an increasingly questionable notion that economies are only characteristic of a national scalar envelope (for example Brenner, 2001; Bathelt, 2003; for a penetrative critique, see Nielsen and Simonsen, 2003). However, we have seen how the now settled 'globalization' debate undermined that comforting presumption by demonstrating the significance of the greater extensive and intensive integration of global value chains and industry organization occasioned by the intersection of multinational firms and local–regional clusters on a worldwide basis (see, for example, Gereffi, 1999; Henderson et al., 2002; UNIDO, 2002). Thus, it is unexceptional to conceive of the global economy, and more exceptional than it was to conceive of economies as only national phenomena. Thus what is an economy? Of the innumerable definitions, the two that follow, one from the Collins (2000) dictionary, the other from the Internet investment glossary service investorwords.com, are as useful as any:

> the complex of human activities concerned with the production, distribution and consumption of goods and services. (Collins, 2000)

and, perhaps surprisingly:

> activities related to the production and distribution of goods and services in a particular geographic region. (http:www.investorwords.com/1652/economy.html)

Clearly, the Collins definition is preferable given the argument above, but the key point is that it contains no scalar restrictions, unlike the second definition. In statistical terms, if measures of the variables are available, as they are in many accounting frameworks based on, say, regional input–output tables, the key elements of the regional, or even urban or county economy can be apprehended. Of course this does not imply any 'containerized' notion of economic flows. For example, we disagree with Bathelt (2003) that: 'only a few regions can be characterised as being economically self-sufficient hosting a full ensemble of related industries and services which could serve as a basis for the establishment of an innovation system.'(Bathelt, 2003, 796) because it is impossible, in a globalized world economy, to envisage a *country*, including, for example, the USA, in that happy position, let alone a region as defined here as a sub-national governance entity. In January 2002 the US began running, for the first time, a monthly trade deficit in advanced technology products like biotechnology and other leading edge technologies (Library of Congress, 2003). It has, of course, imported a massive amount of intellectual capital since time immemorial (Saxenian, 2000). Hence, to complete this part of the justification for treating regional economies as conceptual and real open systems with meaning for governance relations, we propose to combine those given above in a definition of regional economy as:

> the complex of human activities concerned with the production, distribution and consumption of goods and services in a particular geographic region.

This now leaves us the task of defining and justifying the second key term in our title 'knowledge laboratories'. To begin, recall our earlier discussion of the knowledge economy. We said this refers to an economy and its sectors in relation to the intensity of human knowledge capital employed and of technological inputs purchased. At the present unsatisfactory stage of statistical refinement, this was shown to comprise defined International Standard Industrial Statistical categories denoted by the OECD definition of 'high technology manufacturing' and 'knowledge intensive services'. Now we will make a further elaboration on this in light of the foregoing discussion of 'regional economies'. That is by *knowledge economy* as utilized here, we now mean two things: first, industries that embody significant intellectual capital and high value-added, in manufacturing (high technology) and services (knowledge intensive; OECD, 1999); and, second, places (largely lower scale, for example regions, localities) with at least 40 per cent of employment in such economic activities. The reason for selecting 40 per cent is explained in Cooke and De Laurentis (2002). In brief, examining such data for European Union regions, it captures most EU regions not in receipt of EU Regional Policy Structural Funds and contains very few that thus qualify. In that respect, it is a reasonably precise measure of regional development. Hence we shall occasionally refer to regions of that kind as already displaying the characteristics of 'knowledge economies' (for further discussion, see Cooke, 2002).

KNOWLEDGE LABORATORIES

But what about 'knowledge laboratories'? This is perhaps a neologism in the economic geography literature, although such institutes exist with that name, notably that in the University of South Denmark at Odense where it combines literary criticism and new media research. In Stanford University, it conducts research in the key Artificial Intelligence fields of 'knowledge representation' and 'knowledge reasoning'. In Harvard Medical School, it is the name of the Countaway Medicinal Library. In New Zealand, it is an innovation service and place for experimentation in theory and practice of innovation in a firm or organization, facilitated by the service provider known by the name in question. In the regional science field, the idea was mooted in relevant language by Sabel (1995). He wrote of the desirability in experimental policy of 'decentralized co-ordination', later referred to by economic theorists as 'autopoesis' and complexity theorists as 'self-organizing systems' or 'complex adaptive systems' (see Curzio and Fortis, 2002). Sabel himself developed aspects of this theorization in his discussion of the use by epistemic scientific communities (Haas, 1992) exchanging knowledge across disciplinary boundaries, of informally developing hybrid or 'pidgin' vocabularies (Sabel, 2002 after Galison, 1997). Galison (1997) refers to these as 'contact languages' occurring in what Nowotny et al. (2001) call 'trading zones' and 'transaction spaces'. This demands high levels of cognitive reflexivity, monitoring and learning to cross boundaries while avoiding conflict with valued potential partners.

There is a clear connection here to literature recognizing interdisciplinary interaction as a key feature perceived to characterize emergent 'Mode 2' knowledge production (Gibbons et al., 1994). Traditional scholastic disciplines rooted in large-scale teaching departments of universities (Mode 1) were observed to be breaking down with the growth of funded academic research. Diversification of knowledge production in specialist Research Centres that were at arm's length from normal pedagogic activity, capable of bridging industry–academe boundaries, as occurred most fully in the Stanford University model described by Gibbons (2000), but also closely in touch with problem-focused researchers from other disciplines, characterized Mode 2 'transdisciplinarity'. Further ingredients included also reflexivity, and networking to tackle knowledge 'heterogeneity'. This influential and somewhat prescient perspective was criticized later, not least by some of its authors (in Nowotny et al., 2001) because it remained rather lofty and science-centric whereas the socioeconomic context is rather seen to be causing science and society to 'co-evolve' in their development. Thus, for example, as society turned against nuclear physics because of its unsolved pollution problems, and sought greater resource attention for healthcare, so science policy shifted from physics and chemistry to biosciences. Thus in this context *a knowledge laboratory is a process with institutional and organizational presence that integrates transdisciplinary communities of practice to form knowledge for policy learning and innovation.*

Examples of this way of thinking and operating are touched upon at various points in this book, most notably in Sotarauta's in-depth study of knowledge laboratory exploration for purposes of regional development in rural Finland. Thus *Epanet* in Finland's Vaasa-Suomi region connects 20 new Chairs and Research Centres in collaborating counties, *none of which has a university*. This *Filial* model affiliates professors and centres to at least six universities elsewhere, thus negating the sunk costs, inertia and vested interests of traditional 'bricks and mortar' academe. In Italy, disappointment with traditional universities as regional development engines has led to diffusion of the *Pisa* model of *Scuoli Superiore*, or Advanced Study Institutes, to five 'laboratory' regions (Puglia, Umbria, Marche, Lombardia and Campania) to emulate Pisa's Institute–Corporate–Spinout system that has been judged a success (OECD, 2001). These new approaches recognize the weakness of universities per se as knowledge transceivers, but the centrality of research knowledge to future regional development potential. Tavoletti's study in this book also addresses certain failures of the university *qua* developmental institution in its own right by reference to the low marketability of doctoral 'talent' where boundaries between scholarship and the labour market are unusually severe, as they are in Italy.

REGIONAL ECONOMY AS KNOWLEDGE LABORATORY

So we may think of the regional economy that embraces a 'knowledge laboratory' capability as one that is more highly evolved than, for example, a 'learning region', the key functionaries in which seek to capture knowledge and information from more accomplished institutional settings and try to apply it, not always appropriately and probably not swiftly, to problems of development, 'lock-in' and path dependence currently confronting them. The 'knowledge laboratory' epithet denotes exploration, the quest for new knowledge, the testing of that knowledge, reflection upon it and practical application suitably shaped to enhance the capabilities of institutions and organizations, especially firms in that region. This implies making optimal use of 'Constructed Advantage' (Foray and Freeman, 1993; de la Mothe and Mallory, 2003) from collaboration and networking across institutional boundaries that exist in the transdisciplinary mix of communities of practice. This further implies the presence of institutional innovation networks integrating regional institutions to each other and beyond to other regions, national systems and globally located knowledge network nodes:

> 'Knowledge' refers not only to research and development in the natural sciences and engineering, but also to related scientific activities (surveys, statistics, mapping, etc.) as well as a full range of technical, managerial, and social skills and cultural contexts… The way in which institutions can identify, appropriate, apply and disseminate knowledge is by acting as part of an innovation system. These systems include knowledge producers (such as laboratories), knowledge users and appliers (such as firms), knowledge regulators (such as food and drug inspection agencies, intellectual property agencies), knowledge diffusers (including such smart infrastructure as information highways), knowledge funders (such as granting agencies), and so on. (de la Mothe, 2003)

Knowledge laboratory functions become the key elements of regional innovation systems in formation or already formed. This suggests new kinds of benchmarking and indicator measurement in order for regional knowledge laboratories to know more about their internal capabilities and the relations of capable knowledge teams in science, management and culture with such teams elsewhere in the world. The chapter in this book by Frenken and van Oort represents a first research effort to discuss 'hybrid' 'transaction space' collaborations and measure regional and urban capabilities in terms of specific knowledge generation (here biotechnology) measured in the publications of authors recorded in the Science Citation Index.

That knowledge and those that explore, examine and exploit it in ways that are of consequence to regional economic development is not confined to scientific knowledge is testified to in the chapter by Aslesen. This looks thoroughly into Knowledge Intensive Business Services, asking how and for what kinds of firms such capabilities contribute to regional development. The focus is on consultants' economic activity and competence generating processes and the evidence is from a survey of both consultancy firms and consultancy users in the largest city regions in Norway. Consultants are found to be key to innovation since they diffuse capabilities through markets globally and locally. They are 'light institutions' operating with contact languages in innovative transaction spaces.

This opens up a question regarding such transaction spaces or milieux. This is whether it is the relational space in which such actors and others in a putative innovation system combine to create the knowledge surpluses that arise from 'localized knowledge spillovers', or the firms displaying capabilities in regard to the exploitation of localized knowledge spillovers that cluster in proximity to gain from this 'constructed advantage'. This is the subject of the chapters by Lorenzen and Maskell and by Poma and Sacchetti. Basically two positions have emerged, represented to a considerable degree in these chapters. The first and strongest is that of Jaffe et al. (1993), Audretsch and Feldman (1996) and Malmberg and Maskell (2002) who argue in favour of the power of localized knowledge spillovers as drivers of innovation, especially in knowledge-based clusters. Breschi and Lissoni (2001) have argued that there is no convincing evidence that non-pecuniary spillovers have displaced Marshallian pecuniary (market) advantages. Interestingly both sides argue their cases in respect of the meso-level of analysis.

The critique (well-represented in work by Caniëls and Romijn, 2004) is thus of both sides for ascribing too much influence to regional *milieux* and too little to firm *capabilities* or what may also be referred to as *entrepreneurship* (on firm resources as capabilities see Penrose, 1959; on *dynamic* capabilities, see Teece and Pisano, 1994). The current position in regard to the development of clearer understanding of regional accomplishment, at least in so far as externalities (static or dynamic) are concerned, is that what is needed is more penetrative analysis of the firm-level contribution to regional *capabilities*. The default conclusion, itself a series of hypotheses, is that further work is required on types of agglomeration advantage, ranging from static to dynamic spillovers, pecuniary to non-pecuniary, and pure versus impure knowledge spillovers at the firm level but aggregated up to at least the regional level.

Lorenzen and Maskell explore this new space and suggest that the industrial cluster firm is efficient compared to single, integrated firms because different simultaneous knowledge creation spillovers occur allowing for both knowledge exploitation and exploration. Exemplifying this suggestion with case studies of the popular music and furniture industries, the chapter concludes that proximity works for firms in clusters through weak ties, low information cost and trust advantages. Poma and Sacchetti also address these key knowledge processes within firms and territories. The study balances knowledge dynamics between firms and local economic systems with knowledge dynamics inside firms. Poma and Sacchetti introduce a concept of *knowledge life cycles*, addressing fluctuation in flows of knowledge. Survey work in two Italian regions reveals knowledge decay as a source of lock-in only to be defended against by constant renewal.

WHATEVER HAPPENED TO CLUSTERS?

Moving on, these lines of reasoning and research arrive at another interesting question. It is whether the newly realized importance, not so much of macro-institutional functionalism as represented by 'Triple Helix' thinking as inspired by Etkowitz and Leydesdorff (1997; but see Etkowitz, 2003 for a more nuanced view that highlights Research and Centres of Excellence as key bridging entities) but of refinements to it that take us forward. That is, we now recognize that, for instance, it is particular research 'stars' and/or types of graduate 'talent' that are important direct factors in economic added value and 'constructed advantage'. Along with more closely focused study of firm capabilities and interactions within and beyond market exchange, such as that conducted in this book by Wolter, again investigating biotechnology, this leads to an inversion, to some extent, of the intellectual primacy in policy and, less, academe of the Porterian notion of the cluster as the driving force of growth through competitiveness, productivity and innovation (otherwise known as 'The Washington Consensus'; Capra, 2002; Kay, 2003).

Recently, recognition has grown among academic specialists and policy advocates that cluster policy as proposed by the likes of Porter (1998) isn't working. On the surface this is because of economic downturn (scarcer venture capital, fewer spinouts), but the dominant approach to analysis of past successes was both superficial and time-discounted. It has proven superficial because its underlying notion of competitiveness is that of markets, something Wolter highlights as a weakness for science-driven industry analysis, and pays little or no attention to sources of advantage that arise from investment in *capabilities* such as those not susceptible to 'markets' but arising from large scale, increasingly public investments in research – of the kind that is increasingly conducted not even in typical university departments, but in specialized Centres of Excellence or Expertise.

The cluster approach also tends to discount time in its accumulation and representation of cases (wine clusters, agricultural implements clusters, carpet clusters). Some of these began in the nineteenth century or earlier and some are in decline. Nevertheless they are bracketed alongside newer, high technology clusters (venture capital in Boston, electronics in San Francisco) whose origins may also often be traced back half a century or even longer in the case of Silicon Valley (Kenney and Florida, 2000; Sturgeon, 2000) as if they were identical, generic and instant. Hence after a decade of studies during which a few market-driven clusters like Silicon Valley soared Icarus-like before crashing and burning, leaving the wreckage of 400 000 job-losses, national and regional cluster-building strategies are under critical review or are being superseded.

Creating more systemic networks amongst key 'transaction space' institutions and organizations like firms, incubators, research centres, investors and consultants at the regional level is a process explored in fine detail in Kitagawa's chapter on industry–science relationships in Japan and the UK from a comparative institutional perspective, highlighting different processes of *regionalization* in the two countries. This study particularly highlights the role of universities as part of national 'industry–science relationships' in which substantial resources are being invested in enhancing regional knowledge economies. Recognition of multi-level interactions among organizations and institutions of different capabilities in such systems is a valuable finding, as is recognition of invisible but nevertheless real boundaries that persist between distinct corporate forms, like universities, compared to their lesser prominence among inter-personal networks competent in contact languages. Carlsson (2004) has shown that empirical research into regional innovation systems had outpaced that by other innovation systems approaches together by 2000. The importance of this concept following an 'open systems' operational existence is testified to in White and Grimes' chapter, which shows how a combination of endogenous and exogenous influences secured Ireland's emerging knowledge economy. Thus although Ireland is not on a par with the world's most advanced knowledge economies, subsequent policy investments in support of more intensive knowledge-driven activities have followed.

CRITIQUE

We come finally to three papers that ask fundamental questions about the key assumptions which much of the foregoing discussion and supporting chapters tend to take for granted. The first is the chapter by Rutten and Boekema who argue and demonstrate that regions may be important for reasons given in the above review, but we must always be conscious that 'scalar envelopers' will inevitably accuse work that is interested in the field of ignoring the fact that many innovations do not take place in regional networks. They remind us that many companies do not think in terms of region when they innovate, but they do they think in terms of networks, sometimes regional ones. Why? The chapter aims to explain when proximity occurs in inter-firm knowledge transfer and when not. This leads to a conceptualization of the relation between learning and proximity in which the region is not always helpful in explaining the role of proximity in inter-firm learning.

The second corrective to a perspective that can be misinterpreted in facile ways to caricature a 'regional container' view of innovation, knowledge generation, or economic development is provided in the chapter by Etxebarria. Pointing out that knowledge management is centrally concerned with management of human relationships, a view is developed to focus on stakeholders to gain understanding of how a company based on relationships with its environment works. Relationships may be embedded in a specific, non-reproducible social framework imbued with specific, historically formed values (trust, collaboration, solidarity; Uzzi, 1996). Hence, relationships among stakeholders and social responsibility of firms suffer less 'noise' in transmission than normal and accordingly have the same meaning for firms and communities. However, this is not permanent; again Poma and Sacchetti's observations about fluctuations in knowledege and meanings, their decay and renewal, perhaps through system shocks, comes to mind. These questions are pursued by reference to one of the world's most localized industrial systems, Mondragon, whose long-term success has pulled its key economic activities out into the wider Spanish, European and world markets with fascinating implications arising from the clash in codes between a social production ethic and one rooted in market exchange, entrepreneurship and profit.

In this vein, the final chapter acts as a further corrective to over-rosy views about the synergetic surpluses presumed to arise from consensual interactions, whether between macro-institutions with divergent perspectives, core competencies and missions or more localized forms of benign collaboration among networks of innovators. The chapter by Sokol is a critique of the notion of a 'knowledge economy' and the various conceptual appurtenances that attend regional science research and scholarship in relation to it. Sokol thus first critically examines the concepts associated with the argument that there is a macroeconomic transformation towards the 'knowledge economy'. In the process, he justifiably raises questions about the problematic nature of such a transformation, particularly its implications for social and economic cohesion. He suggests strongly that within the constraints of the current profit-driven political economy, knowledge processing and accumulation will stimulate the process of reproducing existing inequalities. Finally he suggests that an analysis rooted in the ideas of global socio-spatial divisions of labour and value networks may be a superior and preferable way to conceptualize whatever socioeconomic transformation may be ongoing.

CONCLUSIONS

It will be evident that the contributors to this book, many representing a new generation of regional scientists, have written stimulating and challenging accounts of the current condition of regional and supra-regional economic interactions as they affect many parts of the contemporary space economy. There are new accounts of policy interventions, methodologies for measuring, detailed analyses of local–regional inter-firm, intra-firm and transaction space interactions mainly around knowledge generation, transformation and commercialization in the form of innovations that should meet the appreciation of a wide audience. There are also critical perspectives that warn of the importance of maintaining a balanced perspective in trying to assess the depth and reach of the presently upward slope of change that revalues the role of knowledge in market competition. Once more, not all members of society participate equally, and institutions that were founded to secure a more egalitarian society are under severe strain. Nevertheless, in delineating the key features of contemporary thinking about regional economies and introducing the idea of knowledge laboratories, the intention behind the book is to supply an alternative way of thinking and acting upon the regional problem. This means fostering an appreciation of the importance, not of borrowing yesterday's tired development recipes, but of creating relevant futures from the transdisciplinary interaction of local and global knowledges, embracing the key idea of modern regional analysis and policy being guided metaphorically by an image perhaps inspiring the institutionalization of laboratory experimentation of an open, social scientific kind.

ACKNOWLEDGEMENTS

Thanks to Sally Hardy and the Regional Studies Association (RSA) for inviting me to be a gatekeeper for the 'Knowledge Economy' track at the RSA Pisa Conference in April, 2003. Thanks also to Andrea Piccaluga for sharing the burden of running the track and editing this book. Nicola Bellini and Daphne Kooistra were fine hosts on my arrival in Pisa. I was personally delighted to meet so many old friends and make some new ones at the conference. Finally, I'd like to thank Roel Rutten for sending improving comments on this introductory chapter.

BIBLIOGRAPHY

Asheim, B., and A. Isaksen (2002), 'Regional innovation systems: the integration of local "sticky" and global "ubiquitous" knowledge', *Journal of Technology Transfer*, **27**, 77–86.

Audretsch, D., and M. Feldman (1996), 'Knowledge spillovers and the geography of innovation and production', *American Economic Review*, **86**, 630–40.

Bathelt, H. (2003), 'Growth regimes in spatial perspective 1: innovation, institutions and social systems', *Progress in Human Geography*, **27**, 789–804.

Brenner, N. (2001), 'The limits to scale? Methodological reflections on scalar structuration', *Progress in Human Geography*, **25**, 591–614.

Breschi, S., and F. Lissoni (2001), 'Knowledge spillovers and local innovation systems: a critical survey', *Industrial and Corporate Change*, **10**, 975–1005.

Bunnell, T., and N. Coe (2001), 'Spaces and scales of innovation', *Progress in Human Geography*, **25**, 569–89.

Burton-Jones, A. (1999), *Knowledge Capitalism*, Oxford: Oxford University Press.

Caniëls, M., and H. Romijn (2004), 'What drives innovativeness in industrial clusters? Transcending the debate', *Cambridge Journal of Economics* (forthcoming).

Capra, F. (2002), *The Hidden Connections*, London: HarperCollins.

Carlsson, B. (2004), 'Innovation systems: a survey of the literature from a Schumpeterian perspective', in Horst Hanusch and Andreas Pyka (eds), *The Companion to Neo-Schumpeterian Economics*, Cheltenham, UK and Northampton, MA, USA: Edward Elgar.

Castells, M. (1996), *The Information Age: Economy, Society and Culture Vol.I: The Rise of the Network Society*, Oxford: Blackwell.

Castells, M. (1997), *The Information Age: Economy, Society and Culture Vol. II: The Power of Identity*, Oxford: Blackwell.

Castells, M. (1998), *The Information Age: Economy, Society and Culture Vol. III: End of Millennium*, Oxford: Blackwell.
Collins & Co. (2000), *The Collins English Dictionary*, London: HarperCollins.
Cooke, P. (2002), *Knowledge Economies*, London: Routledge.
Cooke, P., and C. De Laurentis (2002), *EU Knowledge Economy Index*, Cardiff: Centre for Advanced Studies.
Curzio, A., and M. Fortis (eds) (2002), *Complexity and Industrial Clusters*, Heidelberg: Physica-Verlag.
De la Mothe, J. (2003), 'Re-thinking policy in the new republic of knowledge', University of Ottawa Program of Research in Innovation Management and Economy discussion paper 02-01.
De la Mothe, J., and G. Mallory (2003), 'Industry–government relations in a knowledge-based economy: the role of constructed advantage', University of Ottawa Program of Research in Innovation Management and Economy discussion paper 02-03.
Dicken, P., J. Peck, and A. Tickell (1997), 'Unpacking the global', in R. Lee and J. Wills (eds) *Geographies of Economies*, London: Arnold.
Dunning, J. (ed.) (2000), *Regions, Globalisation and the Knowledge-Based Economy*, Oxford: Oxford University Press.
Eliasson, G., S. Fölster, S. Lindberg, T. Pousette, and E. Taymaz (1990), *The Knowledge Based Information Economy*, Stockholm: The Industrial Institute for Economic and Social Research.
Etkowitz, H. (2003), 'Research groups as "quasi-firms": the invention of the entrepreneurial university', *Research Policy*, **32**, 109–21.
Etkowitz, H., and L. Leydesdorff (1997), *Universities and the Global Knowledge Economy*, London: Pinter.
Foray, D., and C. Freeman (1993), *Technology and the Wealth of Nations: The Dynamics of Constructed Advantage*, London: Pinter.
Galison, P. (1997), *Image and Logic: A Material Culture of Micro-Physics*, London: University of Chicago Press.
Gereffi, G. (1999), 'International trade and industrial upgrading in the apparel commodity chain', *Journal of International Economics*, **48**, 37–70.
Gibbons, J.(2000), 'The role of Stanford University: a dean's reflection', in C. Lee, W. Miller, M. Hancock, and H. Rowen (eds), *The Silicon Valley Edge*, Stanford, CA: Stanford University Press.
Gibbons, M., C. Limoges, H. Nowotny, S. Schwartzman, P. Scott, and M. Trow (1994), *The New Production of Knowledge: the Dynamics of Science and Research in Contemporary Societies*, London: Sage.
Haas, P. (1992), 'Introduction: epistemic communities and international policy coordination', *International Organisation*, **46**, 1–37.
Henderson, J., P. Dicken, M. Hess, N. Coe, and H. Yeung (2002), 'Global production networks and the analysis of economic development', *Review of International Political Economy*, **9**, 436–64.
Hough, D., and C. Jeffery (2003), 'Elections in multi-level systems: lessons for the UK from abroad', in R. Hazell (ed.), *The State of the Nations 2003*, London: The Constitution Unit and Imprint Academia.
Jaffe, A., M. Trajtenberg, and R. Henderson (1993), 'Geographic localisation of knowledge spillovers as evidenced by patent citations', *Quarterly Journal of Economics*, **108**, 577–98.
Kay, J. (2003), *The Truth About Markets*, London: Allen Lane.

Kenney, M., and R. Florida (2000), 'Venture capital in Silicon valley: fuelling new firm formation', in M. Kenney (ed.), *Understanding Silicon Valley*, Stanford, CA: Stanford University Press.
Krugman, P. (1995), *Development, Geography and Economic Theory*, Cambridge, MA: MIT Press.
Library of Congress (2003), *International Trade: Data and Forecasts (Issue Brief to Congress)*, Washington, DC: The Library of Congress.
Lievrouw, L., and S. Livingstone (eds) (2002), *The Handbook of New Media*, London: Sage.
List, F. (1841), *The National System of Political Economy*, Basel: Kyklos-Verlag and New York: A.M. Kelley.
Mackinnon, D., A. Cumbers and K. Chapman (2002), 'Learning, innovation and regional development: a critical appraisal of recent debates', *Progress in Human Geography*, **26**, 293–311.
Machlup, F. (1962), *The Production and Distribution of Knowledge in the United States*, Princeton, NJ: Princeton University Press.
Machlup, F. (1980), *Knowledge: Its Creation, Distribution and Economic Significance Vol. I: Knowledge and Knowledge Production*, Princeton, NJ: Princeton University Press.
Malmberg, A., and P. Maskell (2002), 'The elusive concept of localisation economies: towards a knowledge-based theory of spatial clustering', *Environment and Planning A*, **34**, 429–49.
Miller, J. (1978), *Living Systems*, New York: McGraw-Hill.
Nielsen, E., and K. Simonsen (2003), 'Scaling from "below": practices, strategies and urban spaces', *European Planning Studies*, **11**, 911–28.
Nowotny, H., P. Scott, and M. Gibbons (2001), *Re-Thinking Science*, Cambridge: Polity.
OECD (1996), *The Knowledege-Based Economy*, Paris: OECD.
OECD (1999), *S&T Indicators: Benchmarking the Knowledge-Based Economy*, Paris: OECD.
OECD (2001), *The Pisa Model*, Paris: OECD.
Penrose, E. (1959), *The Theory of the Growth of the Firm*, Oxford: Oxford University Press.
Porter, M. (1998), *On Competition*, Boston, MA: Harvard Business School Press.
Sabel, C. (1995), 'Experimental regionalism and the dilemmas of regional economic policy in Europe', paper for seminar Local Systems of Small Firms and Job Creation, Paris: OECD.
Sabel, C. (2002), 'Diversity, not specialisation: the ties that bind the (new) industrial district', in A. Curzio and M. Fortis (eds), *Complexity and Industrial Clusters*, Heidelberg: Physica-Verlag.
Saxenian, A. (2000), 'Networks of immigrant entrepreneurs', in C. Lee, W. Miller, M. Hancock and H. Rowen (eds) *The Silicon Valley Edge*, Stanford, CA: Stanford University Press.
Seely Brown, J., and P. Duguid (2002), *The Social Life of Information*, Boston, MA: Harvard Business School Press.
Shannon, C. (1948), 'A mathematical theory of communication', *Bell System Technical Journal*, **27**, 379–423 and 623–56.
Sturgeon, T. (2000), 'How Silicon Valley came to be', in M. Kenney (ed.) *Understanding Silicon Valley*, Stanford, CA: Stanford University Press.

Swyngedouw, E. (1997), 'Neither global nor local: "glocalisation" and the politics of scale', in K. Cox (ed.) *Spaces of Globalisation*, New York: Guilford Press.
Teece, D., and Pisano, G. (1994), 'The dynamic capabilities of firms: an introduction', *Industrial and Corporate Change*, **3**, 537–56.
UNIDO (2002), *Industrial Development Report 2002/2003: Competing Through Innovation and Learning*, Vienna: United Nations Industrial Development Organization.
Uzzi, B. (1996), 'Social structure and competition in interfirm networks: the paradox of embeddedness', *American Science Quarterly*, **61**, 674–98.

1. Strategic adaptation to the knowledge economy in less favoured regions: a South Ostrobothnian University network as a case in point

Markku Sotarauta and Kati-Jasmin Kosonen

1. INTRODUCTION

The knowledge economy, as it is defined in this volume, is a challenging environment for regional development agencies. In an industrial society, tangible resources and borders between nations, institutions, organizations and regions largely determined the destiny of regional economies and societies. In a knowledge economy, however, borders still exist and matter, of course, but they are fuzzier than before. Now the positions of both organizations and regions are more determined by their own competencies and skills to learn and develop in a continuous process. Consequently, local initiatives and an enterprising disposition are becoming more and more important in regional development. Institutional and innovative capabilities of regions are crucial. Scarce resources need to be channelled and allocated more efficiently than before, and new operational models need to be created to achieve a sustainable, competitive position in global economy. For, as Cooke (1995, 19) points out, one of the key policy recommendations is that the regional and local competitive edge rests on a successful interlinking of local and regional networks with global networks.

In Finland, mainly large university cities and/or smaller towns specialized in the electronics industry have been able to meet the challenges of the knowledge economy and have been able to prosper economically in the global economy (see Antikainen and Vartiainen, 1999; Antikainen, 2001; Huovari et al., 2001). People and firms have migrated to those city regions where they believe that future opportunities are situated (see Raunio, 2001; Kostiainen, 1999).

Less favoured regions (LFR) often have little or no qualified human capital on which they can build or with which they can attract innovative activities to cope with the challenges of the knowledge economy. In a knowledge economy less favoured regions face three major challenges: a) how to increase institutional capacity; b) how to mobilize scarce resources and competencies; and c) how to forge beyond many lock-ins hindering development efforts. These questions cannot be answered only by trying to find new policies; new ways to organize policy-making and to manage policy processes are needed in addition. Therefore, we are after a more profound understanding of the way policy processes are launched and led in the knowledge economy.

This chapter examines a key knowledge economy institution – the modern university – in the face of these conditions by asking 'how can universities respond to the challenges faced in less favoured regions in a global, informational and networked knowledge economy?', 'how is it possible to cross the many barriers between academia, business and public administration?' and 'what are key factors in a successful development process?'. We are therefore interested in how less favoured regions can strategically adapt to the demands of a changing economy. Strategic adaptation refers to a process in which adaptation both to a changing environment and to the strategic choices of agents plays a significant role.

The research reported in this chapter is based on 30 thematic interviews, seven workshops focused on building university networks (72 people involved altogether), statistics, other relevant research reports, strategy and development programmes and on other written material about the innovation support work done in South Ostrobothnia, an LFR in western Finland. Interviews can be divided into four different groups according to the parent organization of the interviewee:

- Policy-makers in development agencies responsible for the promotion of economic development of the whole of South Ostrobothnia and Seinäjoki town (4 representatives)
- Representatives of firms (8)
- Representatives of the Seinäjoki Science Park, Centre of Expertise Programme and Technology Development Fund (Tekes) (8 representatives)
- University, polytechnic and other higher education personnel (10 representatives)

The lead author of this chapter also acts as chairman of the steering group of the University Network of South Ostrobothnia, and was actively involved in creating the network. His experiences are also used in writing this article, but being aware of the importance of a distancing perspective on the crucial issues, the chapter is largely based on other data, with his expertise mainly used in designing rigorous research questions for the study.

2. SOUTH OSTROBOTHNIA AND ITS CENTRE, SEINÄJOKI TOWN: THE CHALLENGE FACED

Located in western Finland, South Ostrobothnia is a region with a population of approximately 200 000, and the regional centre Seinäjoki is a town with a population of approximately 30 000. The region's strengths and development potential are in a traditional spirit of enterprise and in a large number of small and medium-sized enterprises, the food industry, mechanical wood-processing, metal processing, and strong 'social capital' expressed in regional identity and cultural heritage. Weaknesses include resistance to change, minimal network cooperation, the dominance of primary production in the economy, a low degree of processing of goods and a low volume of exports. In addition, the region suffers a low level of higher education and research, brain drain characteristics, and cut-backs in educational and research resources (see Regional Development Plan, 1994 and 2002). In comparison to the regions of Europe, South Ostrobothnia is clearly a less favoured region; if regional GDP per capita is 100 for the EU15, in South Ostrobothnia it is 72.3 (Regional Development Plan, 2002).

In South Ostrobothnia, the levels of education, income and exports are among the lowest in the country, and the region is more dominated by primary production than the rest of Finland. Concentrations of various types of industry (furniture, farm machinery, carpet making and fur farming) are typical for the region too. Most of the region's firms are micro firms employing fewer than three people, and most of the micro firms and even the larger ones are not particularly well suited to meet the challenges of a knowledge economy (see Kautonen and Sotarauta, 1999). In South Ostrobothnia the quantity of R&D expenditure in total (see Figure 1.1), and R&D both in the firms and public institutions is one of the lowest in Finland. Also the number of patent applications is very low in South Ostrobothnia; in 2001 there were only 19 applications, equalling 1.1 per cent of the patents of the whole country. The educational level is the second lowest among Finnish regions. The innovation support structures and innovation culture are weak, and most of the firms in the region are operating on short time horizons. Their development and innovation activities focus mainly on pragmatic problem-solving. Long term R&D does not have a significant role in the majority of the region's firms. The best firms in the region, however, are at a high level technologically, but their numbers are estimated to be very low (Swot Consulting Finland Ltd., 2003). It can be concluded that South Ostrobothnia is not very well equipped to meet the challenges of a knowledge economy.

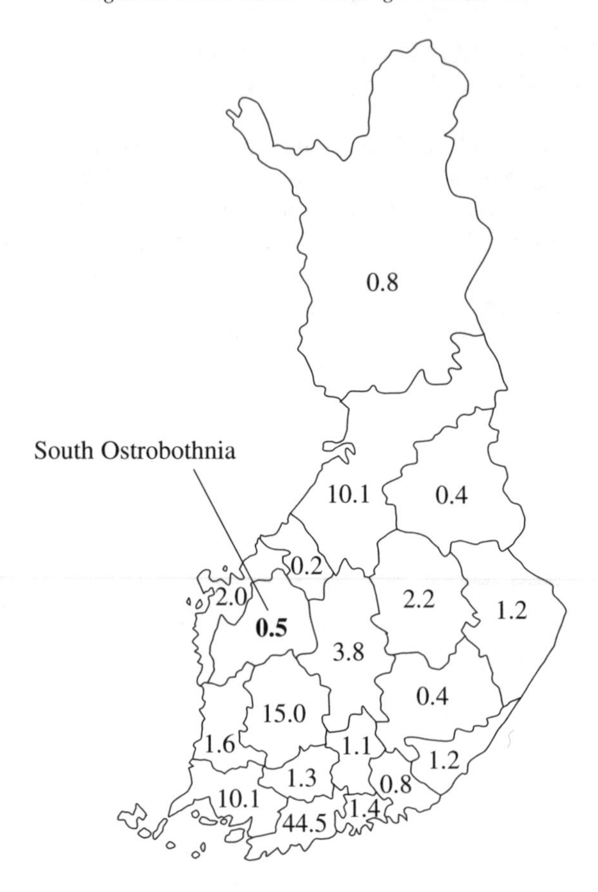

Figure 1.1 The share of Finnish R&D expenditures by region: 2001 (%)

2.1 The Response: Increasing Institutional Thickness as a Main Strategy

In the 1990s the dominant mood in South Ostrobothnia can be described as frustration and fear that the region has been left out of the recent innovation and technology oriented development. This was thought to imply a serious danger that South Ostrobothnia would end up being some kind of 'peripheral pocket' in an otherwise well developed national knowledge economy called Finland. Therefore most of the regional, sub-regional and local development programmes and strategy documents are directed to solve this issue.

The general policy discussions in various forums (such as media, seminars, conferences, and strategic planning processes) about the development of South Ostrobothnia and its challenges often culminated in the observations regarding the lack of a local university. Even though the policy discussions often result in a shared mourning at not having 'the most important resource of a knowledge economy' South Ostrobothnia was already in the 1980s and especially in the 1990s active in building the institutions of a knowledge economy. The main development lines in strengthening the institutional base of South Ostrobothnia can be summarized as follows:

- Raising institutional capacity by inducing universities to open branch units in Seinäjoki
  - University Association of South Ostrobothnia (11 employees in 2003) – founded 1960
  - University of Tampere, Institute for Extension Studies in Seinäjoki (approx. 25 employees) – founded 1981
  - University of Helsinki, Institute for Rural Research and Training in Seinäjoki (approx. 35) – founded 1988
  - Sibelius Music Academy Training Centre in Seinäjoki (approx. 5) – founded 1991
  - University of Vaasa, Seinäjoki Unit (approx. 10) founded 1998
  - Tampere University of Technology/ Digital Media Institute DMI/ Telemedicine Laboratory – Medical Information Technology research unit in Seinäjoki (7+5 employees) – founded in 2003
- To found and strengthen Seinäjoki Polytechnic as the only locally owned and independent higher education institute in the region (reached permanent polytechnic status in 1996, it was put together from earlier independent colleges)
  - A total of 21 undergraduate and 2 graduate degree programmes
  - Approximately 3200 students and 275 staff members
  - Seinäjoki Polytechnic annual R&D expenses are almost 2 500 000 euros (in 2001) and the share of external funding of its total R&D expenditures is 85 per cent.
- Raising institutional capacity by founding new specialized development agencies
  - Seinäjoki Technology Centre Ltd, (owned by the town of Seinäjoki and the Seinäjoki Polytechnic). The Seinäjoki Technology Centre Ltd has incubator-, facilitator-, and business-development services for knowledge and technology intensive start-ups and/ or spin-offs.
  - Foodwest Ltd, (owned by municipalities and foodstuff companies), specializes in product and process development in the foodstuff sector. Founded in 1995.
  - Mechanical wood-processing marketing office South Bothnia Wood Innovation Centre Wincent (Coordinated by the University of Helsinki). Founded in 1997.

  - Life IT Ltd specializes in the R&D activities of the medical information technology field. Originally founded as an association in 1998, company established in 2000.
  - Tietoraitti Ltd specializes in telecommunications network management and network support services. Founded in 1989.
- Building infrastructure in Seinäjoki
  - TRIANO Seinäjoki Science Park (built during the years 2000–2003) includes Mediwest technology park, Frami and Foodwest Ltd
  - The investors are local municipalities, Seinäjoki Polytechnic, South Ostrobothnia Hospital District (hospitals and municipalities), private companies, and a German investment bank. Investments total 43 million euros for Mediwest and Frami between years 2001–2003 (Frami 25 million euros).
- General and targeted development programmes (only a few examples mentioned)
  - Centre of Expertise Programme – The Centre of Expertise Programme is an objective programme created in accordance with the Regional Development Act and the result of the programme is a network of centres of expertise around Finland. Seinäjoki has had the Seinäjoki Centre of Expertise in Food since 1998. From the beginning of 2002 Seinäjoki was nominated a centre of expertise in intelligent products and systems.
  - The ePohjanmaa Programme is part of the national 'Regional Centre Programme' in the Seinäjoki region. At national level the aim is to strengthen town regions, and at local level in Seinäjoki the programme focuses on information and communication technology aiming to build wide regional cooperation and public–private partnership in the development of a local innovation environment.
  - Research and Innovation Development Programme for the years 2000–2006 is one of the 12 thematic regional development programmes of South Ostrobothnia.
  - EU Structural Fund Development Programmes – South Ostrobothnia does not form a unified entity concerning EU structural fund area classification. Therefore three types of development programme are implemented: Objective 2 (a) with municipalities and sub-regions under a restructuring process; objective 2 (c) with municipalities and sub-regions under a restructuring process, but performing relatively well and in transition to non-funded status, and finally Objective 3 programmes for social restructuring projects.

In South Ostrobothnia and especially in Seinäjoki Town the strategy has been to increase institutional capacity, and a significant change has happened during the last 20 years, especially in the 1990s. It may be summarized that in South Ostrobothnia there are now institutions of a knowledge economy, but that they are still quite small and fragile, and at the early stages of development. Regional activity in themes related to knowledge and innovation has significantly increased during the last ten years, but in comparison to major city-regions in Finland it is still quite low. The cognitive patterns of policy-makers and firms have changed considerably in ten years. Moreover, channels to global and national sources of information and knowledge have developed but they are still very weak and scarce, and in addition quantity and quality of research has remained one of the lowest in Finland.

It is also worth mentioning that before renewal of the Finnish regional governance system in the mid-1990s, the most important development agencies were located in Vaasa, while in Seinäjoki there were only branch units. Thus reform has meant most of the decisions concerning promotion of economic development can now be made in the region instead of in Vaasa.

3. THE EMERGENCE OF THE SOUTH OSTROBOTHNIAN UNIVERSITY NETWORK: EPANET

With the turn of the millennium South Ostrobothnia had taken many small, yet from a regional perspective large and integrated steps towards engagement in the knowledge economy. The infrastructure and organizational base of an innovation system was developed. In spite of new developments and significantly changed perceptions among policy-makers, most of the firms in the region did not see the need to integrate themselves with the knowledge economy and its operational models. By national standards the innovation culture among firms was undeveloped, but firms have shown some signs of awakening.

> Many firm[s] have realised that they need to put more effort into process development, flexibility and quality, and stuff like that. This has raised the question, also here, if firms can cope with the new challenges alone, and this has forced firms to rethink their relationship to the research world, and they have asked more often than before, where to find help in this kind of development work. Now there is [a] lot of demand for new pieces of information and new knowledge, and for organisations who can produce this kind of knowledge. (Representative of Tekes)

In 'the Development Programme for Research in South Ostrobothnia – 1998', founding a university network was raised as a means to strengthen the quantity and quality of research in South Ostrobothnia, and opening new pipelines to new knowledge created elsewhere. A university network, however, was not the only solution presented in the policy discourse. Especially during the national parliamentary elections (1999), many kinds of initiatives in the air were presented by parliamentary candidates; the choices ranged from the foundation of a local university – University of Seinäjoki – to a specific faculty of foodstuffs at the University of Vaasa but located in Seinäjoki, to founding a research centre of Tampere University of Technology in Seinäjoki, to integration of existing university filials, the idea being to have one large unit instead of many small ones. Initiatives focusing on reorganization of existing structures and founding new ones tended to freeze the discussion, and it was clear that a new way of seeing the issue of strengthening research, and especially founding the mystical university network, was needed. Eventually official opinion was mobilized and in four years the concept of a 'university network' was created and implemented.

What happened?

3.1 Phase I: Preparatory Analysis and Commencement of Discussion 'Roundabout'

In the late 1990s there was a huge gap between the goals of regional development strategies, plans and programmes, that is the wishes of policy-makers, and the actual outcomes, resources and realities of the region; a network university, a new faculty, Seinäjoki's 'own university' or integration of filials were not materializing. Universities and their filials saw the discussion as a normal 'policy rhetoric full of nice ideas but nothing to take seriously'.

In this kind of environment the Research Unit for Urban and Regional Development Studies (Sente) of the University of Tampere made a proposal to the Regional Council of South Ostrobothnia for a project to create a 'University Network of South Ostrobothnia' concept in 1999 in collaboration with the University Association and other interested partners. The 'hidden aim' was to thrash out the matter of a university network and if possible to create an implementable concept for it, or if that was not possible to reach consensus that it is a far fetched utopia, to forget the whole idea, and in that way to get more space to focus more on other things.

The actual project began with analyses of the previous discussions on the issue in the media, development programmes, reports and various studies. In addition, analyses focused on the roles of universities in regional development and different models of organization in the research literature. The analysis was done by a 'core group', that is, two researchers from the University of Tampere and one official from the University Association of South Ostrobothnia. In the analysis the core group identified five different models of possible 'knowledge laboratories', from which four were based on earlier initiatives and discussions and the fifth was a new one. The five models were:

- Strengthening the network – increasing quantity and improving quality of cooperation between existing university branch units
- Founding a new research centre – preferably focusing on some specific technology and related to the Tampere University of Technology
- Strength from merger – incorporation of existing university branch units and thus having one 'big player' (in practice it would have still been a small unit in national comparison and especially in international comparison).
- Focus on education – creating unique masters programme(s) specifically for South Ostrobothnia
- Focus on creating an attractive milieu to competitive academic individuals – founding 12 new research professorships for 5-year terms in cooperation with interested universities, the aim being to have a new interdisciplinary research community of 40–60 researchers, professors being the core.

3.2 Phase II: Communication 'Roundabout'

After identifying five possible models, introduced briefly above, a series of workshops was organized for regional development agencies, firms, business associations, university filials, the executive group of Seinäjoki Polytechnic, and for the universities of Helsinki, Vaasa and Tampere. Workshops and further informal discussions included much face-to-face discussion with key persons – the number of people involved in different forums is 72.

At the workshops the five models, and the analysis of their strengths and weaknesses, were introduced. The discussions mainly focused on the potential of the five models to achieve desired policy objectives. It was also evident that the models were not mutually exclusive but in many ways overlapping. In the discussions 'the 12 research professor' model attracted most of the attention and raised a lot of surprised, enthusiastic and/or cautious reactions. The most frequent reactions were: 'Crazy idea – 12 professors, here, in an academic wasteland? There are none here now!'; 'it is expensive, isn't it'; 'we'll be never able to recruit professors to Seinäjoki, there is no academic tradition here'; and 'who wants to destroy his/her university career by coming to Seinäjoki, the periphery of academe'; 'after the five-year term, they will leave this place and then we'll be in the same situation again'; 'they will not work here, they will be suitcase-professors'; and finally 'sounds interesting; where is this model adopted from, where has this been done earlier?'.

In discussions, formal and informal, the cautious and surprised first reactions began step by step to become more enthusiastic, and a certain kind of excitement began to spread among key policy-makers and university people. The 12 research professor model was perceived to be both challenging and radical but at the same time realistic so that key players began to see it as a concrete opportunity to do 'something big' and 'to get back into the game'.

> I believe that we, here in South Ostrobothnia, will be able to create something genuinely new and surprising, and hence we'll be more credible also in the national and international scientific community. (Representative of university filial)

> We realised that we were totally out of the Finnish R&D funding circles. I mean 100% out. And that money is not applied for by regions or organisations but people in them, and the same goes with the networks, it is people. It is not some university unit that plunges into R&D networks but nationally and internationally well-known researchers. (Representative of university filial)

Through the many-faceted discussions and a report of the core group, the '12 research professorships' model gained approval and finally emerged as the core of a South Ostrobothnian University network known as Epanet. The most important realization was that the low quantity and quality of research in South Ostrobothnia was not a problem as such, but the true problem lay in the fact that there were not enough competent individuals who could compete for national and international research funding and who were respected and credible actors in wider circles. The whole innovation system and R&D climate was distinctively regional and thus rather introverted in nature. Based on this kind of reasoning, an objective to create a multidisciplinary research community of 40–60 researchers formed by more than one university was set. The central idea was to found 12 new research professorships as the core of a new community, and professors themselves were supposed attract funds for their own research groups.

Founding professorships was seen as a good way of creating attractive opportunities for talented and competitive individuals. In Finland, there is a fixed number of professorships at the universities, and in many fields the competition in professorships is quite fierce. Therefore the assumption was that there are plenty of young and hungry academics preparing themselves for the competition of permanent professorships in their fields, and thus an opportunity to have a fixed term professorship for five years might later turn out to be a crucial factor in their future aspirations. Based on this kind of reasoning it was believed that it might be possible to attract competent academic people to the 'periphery of Finnish academe' to build their own competitiveness.

> One can sacrifice five years of his/her life in Seinäjoki, and hence be more competitive in Helsinki, Tampere or abroad, it's not a bad deal. It is not a bad deal for Seinäjoki either, we'll have [a] bunch of hungry people here for five years wanting to show the world how good they are, and then they leave, and we'll get [a] new group of them, and thus we always have active professors here, and our

> ties to universities deepen after their departure – we'll be connected to them afterwards too. (Representative of university filial)

As Seinäjoki did not have the reputation of being an academic town there was a danger that there might be a nationwide discussion about 'Seinäjoki professors' referring to lower standards and quality, and therefore it was decided at the beginning that every professor must be recruited by using the standard procedures of respective universities, and that they must meet all the same criteria as any other professor in Finland. In addition it was decided that each new professorship to be founded must be new in Finland; they should add new resources and fields of research not only to South Ostrobothnia but to the whole of Finland too. This was seen as important for anticipated criticism of deconcentrating Finnish research resources 'all over the fields and forests' could be met by the counter argument that all the new professors are faculty of respective universities even though they constitute an interdisciplinary research community in Seinäjoki. Therefore they contribute not only to the innovation system of South Ostrobothnia but to the scientific research of Finland as a whole (Sotarauta et al. 1999) and at the same time they are a link between an emerging new research community and already established and strong communities.

3.3 Phase III: Communication 'Roundabout' Continues and Becomes more Focused Management

In autumn 2000, a press conference was organized and the idea of recruiting 12 research professors to Seinäjoki was made public. The press conference highlighted the discussion around the Epanet model throughout South Ostrobothnia and beyond, with media commentary welcoming this 'new bold initiative'. The press conference was, in a sense, an open invitation to participate in discussion about the network itself, its focus and finance. The invitation was widely accepted and after the press conference there were signs of 'a snowball effect'. Concrete developments began to happen; initiatives for the professorships and funding began to emerge from several, also quite surprising directions. Outside the region the general feeling was disbelief; firstly it was not believed that South Ostrobothnians would be able to raise enough funding for 12 professorships, and secondly it was not believed that enough qualified researchers would apply for the positions.

If the first phases were characterized by the creation of a new interpretation of research and university network and to some extent of their contents too, and also of giving birth to creative tension and hence mobilizing people and resources, now there was an immediate need to institutionalize the management of the rapidly emerging network and a public discussion about the model, its prospects and realities. After further negotiations and new rounds of discussions, the University Association of South Ostrobothnia was given the management of the Epanet network by universities and other key actors. Being a small independent association employing only a few people without big ambitions to develop Epanet to benefit itself, the university association was seen as a neutral and objective organization that everybody could trust.

> This (Epanet) was organised through such an organisation that does not have money or power. Suddenly an organisation that is used to organising summer university courses is in the core of the regional development here. It is, however, so that this kind of endeavour cannot be given to the universities only, they are so easily tempted to cash the profits. And I wouldn't like to see the co-ordination in the hands of some of the regional development agencies either. This must not end up being some bureaucratic development process. University association is just right in between universities and regional development agencies. (Representative of university filial).

By the end of 2003 there were 12 full-time and three part-time professors already in work and the objective had been met and exceeded. In addition there were six professorships in the process of being founded, and when writing this chapter, it seems that there will be altogether 21 professors operating in South Ostrobothnia. The fields of research and universities of the first 15 are as follows:

- Information technology applications
  - Research professorship in Health Care Information Technology – Tampere University of Technology.
  - Research professorship in Electronic Business with a particular focus on the development of new kinds of business activities and forms of service – University of Tampere
  - Research professorship in Virtual Technology with a particular focus on mechatronics and embedded systems applications – Tampere University of Technology
  - Research professorship in Logistic Systems – University of Vaasa
- Economics and business administration
  - Research professorship in Consumer Behaviour with food industry as the field of research – University of Vaasa.
  - Research professorship in Rural Enterpreneurship – University of Helsinki
  - Research professorship in Entrepreneurship, with a particular focus on the growth and management of SMEs – University of Vaasa.
  - Research professorship in Concept Management, with special focus on the furniture industry as the field of application – University of Vaasa

- Regions and welfare
  - Research professorship in Regional Development, with a special focus on urban competitiveness and promotion of strategic regional development – University of Tampere
  - Research professorship in Popular Music, with focus on Musicology, Art Management and New Technologies – Sibelius Academy.
  - Research professorship in Laboratory Medicine, with a particular focus on addiction medicine – University of Tampere
  - Part-time professorships in the field of health care: rehabilitation and nursing science – University of Lapland and University of Tampere
- Industry-specific topics
  - Research professorship in Food Chains and Food Safety – University of Helsinki
  - Research professorship in Plastic Composite Technology – Tampere University of Technology
  - Management of the research and development of Aluminium Technology – in collaboration with University of Vaasa

The complexity of the funding of Epanet can be illustrated by following figures: there are altogether 85 funding organizations (including 58 firms and 27 municipalities); approximately 200 contracts between a donor and the University Association of South Ostrobothnia that channels the funds to the involved universities (see Table 1.1).

Table 1.1 *The funding of the Epanet network in September 2003 (each professorship is an individual project and thus division of funding bodies varies significantly between professorships)*

	Euro	%
European Union and state of Finland	3 038 000	43.4
Municipalities	2 429 000	34.7
Firms	1 127 000	16.1
Other public sector funding (universities and polytechnic)	406 000	5.8
Total	7 000 000	100.0

Source: University Association of South Ostrobothnia/Epanet co-ordination office)

3.4 Epanet as an Organizational Innovation

Epanet is an *organizational innovation*; through Epanet many difficult borders and barriers between universities, between universities and polytechnic, and between business and universities have been overcome. The Epanet network has been built up together with universities that have their main campuses elsewhere, and the professors comprise the faculty of the host universities but work mostly in and/or for Seinäjoki region. Epanet has thus been able to induce five prominent universities to be more actively involved in the activities of South Ostrobothnia. In addition Epanet has been able to transcend disciplinary borders by creating a research community of researchers from different disciplines and universities.

> It (Epanet) was able to overcome some of the characteristic problems of the Finnish universities: the dominance of disciplines, the hobby-like nature in interdisciplinary studies, and thirdly a fear of founding new institutions to compete with old university departments. (Representative of university filial)

The Epanet network is funded by many national, regional and local organizations, and through Epanet South Ostrobothnians have been able to utilize many kinds of funding resources in implementing a shared strategy, and thus have also been able, through partnership, to transcend borders between funding bodies. Epanet has also been able to persuade important firms of the region to fund the research professorships and therefore also to participate more deeply in the discussion about knowledge, innovation, applying new technologies, and so on.

> One of the most positive things has been the new activity between firms and these professors ... there are already now some projects in which firms have actively raised research questions, and firms have also made initiatives for the professorships, and their disciplines. (Representative of Seinäjoki Technology Centre Ltd)

In spite of the obvious success in creating and putting together the Epanet concept and network, and getting funding for it, three issues are frequently raised: a) Is Epanet a project of definite duration or is it a long-lasting institution? b) Is it contributing to business and regional development in the long or short run? And c) Should the professors carry out more basic and applied research or should they become pragmatic problem-solvers for firms? There are significant expectations of Epanet professors ranging from pragmatic problem-solving for industry through contract research and consulting, to bridging research in South Ostrobothnia to national and global top-level research, and the creation of a new research and innovation culture.

> A professor has an academic freedom and therefore his/her interests of course determine what will be studied. We should be able to recruit people who understand firms, and who are interested in taking their needs into account. Hopefully both professors and firms will be active in creating new forms of interaction. (Representative of firms)

Most notably the first issue is whether Epanet is a series of projects or an institution. Will it become a permanent part of the research and innovation system of South Ostrobothnia or fade away after five or perhaps seven years? In its early phases Epanet is based on contracts of definite duration, and the desire in the region is to get permanent funding for Epanet, and thus institutionalize it. It seems to be evident that the whole Epanet network will not be funded through the state budget. Therefore the question is also about how well the Epanet professors (and their research groups) will succeed in their research and other activities, and so receive further funding after the first term.

Second, many policy-makers and firm representatives are expecting quick solutions to daily problems of regional development and innovation in firms. The idea, however, is that the Epanet professors are to strengthen applied research in the region and draw also on research carried out elsewhere, and they are not supposed to end up being practical problem-solvers, or varieties of consulting professors. So, third, Epanet professors and their research groups are also expected to bridge the 'academic wasteland of Finland' (Seinäjoki) to the main scientific centres of Finland and beyond, and in that way channel information to and from South Ostrobothnia. It is too early to say anything definite about the outcome of the activities of the Epanet network; only time will tell, but so far through Epanet, and by other related processes, a) the belief in the future has been strengthened, b) an enormous discussion about research and innovation in firms has been raised, c) positive curiosity towards South Ostrobothnia in Finland has been aroused, and thus the image of the region has improved, and d) universities are more committed to the region, and a new interdisciplinary and inter-university research community has been born.

4. CONCLUSION

South Ostrobothnia has consciously made efforts to free itself from past path dependence and to branch out by creating new institutions, by seeking out new human capital to draw on, and by creating a new perception of the region, its current state and future prospects. The developments in South Ostrobothnia raise questions about how it was able to be pulled together; are there any general messages for management of regional development?

First, the swiftly emerging organizational innovation focused upon *the spirit of the time* in Finland was the soil in which the seeds of the new path were rooted. It made a more collective interpretation of 'South Ostrobothnia in the knowledge economy' possible. When the knowledge economy and related issues were discussed everywhere, such as in the media, conferences, literature, and so on, and when the national bodies began to channel resources into it, also the local 'inspirers', the champions of development efforts, were thus able to utilize general societal discourse in their own argumentation.

Secondly, *intensive collaboration* among firms, the public sector and educational institutes made it possible to launch a new flagship process. However, it should be remembered that in Finland, in the 1990s a common strategy for all public efforts to promote regional development was building networks for policy-making and implementation. The experiences of South Ostrobothnia, and other Nordic regions too (see Linnamaa, 2002; Bruun, 2002a; 2002b and 2002c; Kostiainen and Sotarauta, 2003), show that those authorities that themselves invest financial and/or temporal resources in the development processes have more success as network builders than those who do not. In contrast, authorities that enter network building without such investments face considerable scepticism and will probably have little chance of making the most of the network strategy.

Thirdly, *individuals* and *coalitions* formed by local actors have played a decisive role in the crucial phases of development. In strengthening institutional capacity and creating the Epanet network, the combination of enthusiasm and authority that the key actors embodied transmitted a positive and regionally anchored view of new prospects to other development agents, firms and the general public. Fourthly, in mobilizing people and resources the role of an *ambitious but believable story* was of utmost importance in a world that is full of information, development programmes, projects and other development efforts. In one of its dimensions regional development is about competing ideas and interpretations, and by a believable story it is possible to link fragmented pieces of information together, and in the emergence of Epanet, an *inductive and inducing strategy* was applied that was wrapped in a constantly emerging story line. The whole process was based on a collective sense-making of the knowledge economy and its reflections in South Ostrobothnia, and thus collective interpretation and conceptualization formed a core in the strategy process. The story about a less favoured region in the global knowledge economy with its own identity, strong pipelines and stubborn resistance to give up in front of 'big changes' and to adapt strategically formed the plot of the Epanet story. It is also worth noticing that it was not a question of a ready made plot, but a constantly emerging and ongoing discussion that bounced back and forth between vision and practical issues, and between many organizations. This is how a 'knowledge laboratory' approach to regional development must operate.

Fifth, *the capacity to bring forth a vision* of a different future for the region was important in the emerging story line. The mechanical formulation of a vision and strategies was not sufficient but the skills and abilities of key actors to use visions and strategies as tools in creating the story and its implications are more important than a strategic plan with well formulated and documented visions. To be truly functional in the development work, vision should be communicable, challenging and appealing. Vision is not an outcome of a planning process but a long process itself.

Sixth, in an inductive and inducing strategy process it is important to create a *sense of urgency*, because often the formulation of a vision or development programme and, for example, receiving EU funding provide a development network with a false sense of security (Sotarauta and Lakso 2000). Development efforts need the sense of drama that in South Ostrobothnia was found in a combination of crisis, a believable story, credible individuals and a desire to show rest of the Finland that 'our region is not out of the game yet'. In creating a sense of urgency the role of the media as a forum of critical discussion is important in making the discussion public and people aware of the challenges and opportunities.

Seventh, a strong message is that *institutions* provide inducing and inductive processes with a general framework, and they have a major directing effect on processes. Institutions frame the stories and actions of individuals, and prevent them getting out of hand. At their best, institutions open new opportunities for individuals and small active groups of people but do not to trap them in bureaucracy and thus lock the whole region in the past. South Ostrobothnia was in the 1990s able to increase institutional capacity in strategically important sectors through the creation of new institutions and hence open opportunities for new processes like Epanet to be launched.

Based on the South Ostrobothnian case, it can be concluded that in strategic adaptation, first of all, the sensitivity to identify various changes is important, but especially crucial is to create the region's own perception of a new phase of development, as well as its own 'story of the future' and its support. Also the capacity for bold and fast decisions in the community is important. If successful, this capacity may be institutionalized in the community and become an object of local pride and an important part of local culture. This experimental process of strategic adaptation is not a mechanical policy-making process but a complex and emergent set of interactions which crosses many borders and administrative levels.

BIBLIOGRAPHY

Antikainen, J. (2001), *Kaupunkiverkkotutkimus 2001* (Urban Network Study 2001), Aluekeskus- ja kaupunkipolitiikan yhteistyöryhmän julkaisu 1/2001, Helsinki: Sisäasiainministeriö (publication of the Urban Policy Group, the Ministry of the Interior).

Antikainen, J., and P. Vartiainen (1999), 'Framing the urban network in Finland – the urban network study 1998', in *A Portrait of Finnish Cities, Towns and Functional Urban Regions*, Helsinki: Ministry of Interior, Committee for Urban Policy, pp. 15–22.

Bruun, H. (2002a), 'The emergence of a regional innovation network. A process analysis of the local bio grouping in Turku, Finland', in M. Sotarauta and H. Bruun (eds) *Nordic Perspectives on Process-Based Regional Development Policy*, Nordregio Report (3), Stockholm: Nordregio, pp. 79–124.

Bruun, H. (2002b), 'Mobilising a regional lighthouse. A study of the digital North Denmark programme', in M. Sotarauta and H. Bruun (eds) *Nordic Perspectives on Process-Based Regional Development Policy*, Nordregio Report (3), Stockholm: Nordregio, pp. 125–56.

Bruun, H. (2002c), 'Building policy networks. A comparative study of public attempts to create, coordinate, and stimulate high technology in Turku, Finland, and in Trondheim, Norway', in M. Sotarauta and H. Bruun (eds) *Nordic Perspectives on Process-Based Regional Development Policy*, Nordregio Report (3), Stockholm: Nordregio, pp. 157–84.

Cooke, P. (1995), 'Planet Europa: network approaches to regional innovation and technology management', *Technology Management*, **2**, 18–30.

Swot Consulting Finland Ltd. (2003), *Etelä-Pohjanmaan alueellinen teknologiastrategia* (The technology strategy of South Ostrobothnia) TEKES Teknologiastrategiat.

Etelä-Pohjanmaan korkea-asteen tutkimuksen ja koulutuksen aluestrategia 2003–2006 (Higher education and research strategy of South Ostrobothnia 2003–2006) (2003), Seinäjoen kaupunki.

Huovari, J., A. Kangasharju, and A. Alanen (2001), 'Alueiden kilpailukyky (The competitiveness of regions)', Pellervon taloudellisen tutkimuslaitoksen raportteja (the reports of the Pellervo Economic Research Centre) no. 176, Helsinki.

Kautonen, M., and M. Sotarauta (1999), *Seinänaapurien innovaatio-ohjelma* (The Innovation Programme of Seinäjoki Sub-region), Seinänaapurit. Seinänaapurien kumppanuusyhteisö (the Partnership Community of Seinäjoki sub-region), Seinäjoki.

Kostiainen, J. (1999), 'Kaupunkiseudun kilpailukyky ja elinkeinopolitiikka tietoyhteiskunnassa (The comptitiveness of city-regions and UED-policy in information society)', in M. Sotarauta (ed.) *Kaupunkiseutujen kilpailukyky ja johtaminen tietoyhteiskunnassa*, Helsinki: The Finnish Association of Local Authorities. Acta 106.

Kostiainen, J., and M. Sotarauta (2003), 'Great leap or long march to knowledge economy: institutions, actors and resources in the development of Tampere, Finland', *European Planning Studies*, **10** (5).

Linnamaa, R. (2002), 'Development process of the ICT cluster in the Jyväskylä Urban Region', in M. Sotarauta and H. Bruun (eds) *Nordic Perspectives on Process Based Regional Development Policy*, Nordregio Report (3), Stockholm: Nordregio.

Morgan, K. (1997), 'The learning region: institutions, innovation and regional renewal', *Regional Studies*, **31** (5), 491–503.

Raunio, M. (2001), 'Osaajat valintojen kentällä: Helsingin, Tampereen, Turun, Jyväskylän, Porin ja Seinäjoen seutujen vetovoimaisuus virtaavassa maailmassa (Experts in the field of choices: The attractiveness of Helsinki, Tampere, Turku, Jyväskylä, Pori and Seinäjoki in the flowing world', Tampere: Research Unit for Urban and Regional Development Studies. Sente publications 11 / 2001.

Regional Development Plan for South Ostrobothnia 2020 (2002), Regional Council of South-Ostrobothnia (in Finnish).

Regional Development Programme for South Ostrobothnia: Rural Area Programme – objective 5 B (1994), Regional Council of South-Ostrobothnia (in Finnish).

Sotarauta, M., and T. Lakso (2000), *Muutoksen johtaminen ja luova jännite: Tutkimus Kainuun kehittämistoiminnasta* (Change managenment and creative tension: A study of promotion of development in Kainuun region), Helsinki: Suomen Kuntaliitto Acta-sarja 132 (the Finnish Association of Local and Regional Authorities, Acta-series 132).

Sotarauta, M., T. Lakso, and S. Kurki (1999), *Alueellisen osaamisympäristön vahvistaminen: Etelä-Pohjanmaan korkeakouluverkoston toimintamalli* (Strengthening the regional expertise base: The network-concept of higher education and research in South-Ostrobothnia), Tampere: Tampereen yliopisto, Alueellisen johtamisen tutkimusyksikkö. Sente-julkaisuja 4/1999 (University of Tampere, Research Unit for Urban and Regional Development Studies. Sente-publications 4.1999).

2. Higher education and high intellectual unemployment: does education matter? An interpretation and some critical perspectives

Ernesto Tavoletti

1. INTRODUCTION: GLOBALIZATION AND THE KNOWLEDGE DRIVEN ECONOMY

What is the nature of the link between 'globalization' and the so-called 'knowledge economy'? Why has globalization made knowledge such an important ingredient for economic performance, according to widespread belief? In other words, is globalization the cause of the great attention paid to knowledge and is this attention justified? We believe these questions have far less easy answers than expected.

In some ways, 'globalization' does not seem to be anything new in a capitalistic economy. In this sense we do not agree with M. Castells (Castells, 1993) and M. Carnoy's (Carnoy, 1998) belief, indeed quite representative of the dominant doctrine, that what is special about the 'global economy' is that 'strategic core activity, including innovation, finance and corporate management, function on a planetary scale in real time and that this globality became possible only recently because of the technological infrastructure provided by telecommunications, information systems, microelectronics machinery, and computer-based transportation' (Carnoy, 1998, 21).

On the contrary, the innovations of the last two or three decades in high tech industry have been large and substantial in improving quality and speed of information provision. However, the fact is that they are not the main point in explaining the current attention paid to knowledge as the key for improving economic growth. Therefore, we want to suggest that it is not recent high tech innovations that have made knowledge fundamental for economic performance.

Indeed it can be hypothesized that the high tech 'revolution' has made information a far less important and strategic ingredient than in the past, because it is available much more quickly and cheaply, and for many more people than in the past; in many cases it is no longer a rare and inaccessible resource. The current importance paid to knowledge and information derives not from high tech innovations but from some structural changes in the composition of the world economy that provoked a major change in the 'general view'.

2. KNOWLEDGE AS ABILITY TO GENERATE EFFECTIVE ACTION

According to rationalist epistemology there is a definitional difference between 'knowledge' and 'information'. 'Knowledge' is what an individual receiving a message already has and what changes as a result of receiving information. 'Information' is the message that is transferred. So, *strictu sensu*, rationalist epistemology assumes that only information can be transferred, knowledge being something belonging to the individualistic sphere. What makes this difference almost irrelevant in the rationalist tradition, at least from a practical point of view, is that, as a rule, all knowledge can be translated into information.

The Cartesian tradition assumes, in fact, a dualism between an objective world of physical reality and a subjective mental world of an individual. Rationalist thinking can either reduce the physical reality to mental states and processes ('idealism') or reduce the mental world to physical states and processes ('materialism'). In both cases *knowledge* is a collection of representations that can be translated into language, *thinking* is their manipulation process and *communication* is the transfer of *information* (Lakoff, 1987). Language and sentences can deliver a representation of the world that can be true or false, coherent or not coherent, but their ultimate grounding is in their *correspondence* with the state of affairs they represent (Winograd and Flores, 1986). It is the *correspondence theorem*, between representation and physical reality, that allows in principle that all knowledge can be translated into information.

The consequence of mainstream economic growth theory, as expressed for example in Romer's endogenous growth model (Romer, 1986), is that growth stands for the accumulation of codified objective knowledge. The rationalist epistemology and the *correspondence theorem* means Romer assumes that 'knowledge' is like a blueprint that has a separate existence from that of any individual. According to this doctrine, the enormous accumulation of information (and so knowledge), allowed by recent high tech innovations, provides a major and historically unprecedented boost to productivity and economic growth. Romer argues, correctly, that in the long run economic growth is a function of knowledge but we agree neither with Romer's definition of knowledge nor with his view about the high tech role in accumulating it.

The concept of knowledge developed in the self-organizing approach (Maturana et al., 1986), described as well by Robert A. te Velde (te Velde, 1999), is much more useful in explaining the relation between knowledge and economic growth and the possible impact of high tech innovations.

In 1968, Maturana's neurophysical research on colour vision showed that physical reality had only a triggering role in the generation of the colour space of the observer (Maturana and Varela, 1980): the nervous system acts as a generator of phenomena, rather than as a filter in mapping reality. Living systems live in their own mental world, that is, they refer to some 'external' environment (a system at a higher scale) that they have created themselves, as in Heisenberg's phenomenological theorem where the interpreted and the interpreter do not exist independently (te Velde, 1999, 5). According to Maturana's view the main feature of living systems is *autopoiesis* ('self-creation'). They are open to information but closed to knowledge, which is rooted in personal history, personal features and previous knowledge. The main difference with 'idealism' is that the *correspondence theorem* is not true any more. But if the *correspondence theorem* is not true and we live in a world of *autopoietic* systems in which each one is just a source of perturbation to the others or, in other words, we have a different world for each single *autopoietic* system, how is it possible that we have valuable interactions? Maturana speaks of 'structural coupling' or mutual co-adaptation of two independent systems.

> An autopoietic system will by necessity evolve in such a way that its activities are properly coupled to its medium. Its structure must change so that it generates appropriate changes of state triggered by specific perturbing changes in its medium; otherwise it will disintegrate – it dies. The structural coupling generated by the demands of autopoiesis plays the role that the rationalistic tradition naively attributes to having a representation of the world (Winograd and Flores, 1986).

So two agents interacting repeatedly with each other might become structurally coupled. 'Structural coupling occurs when the agents develop behaviours that reciprocally trigger complementary behaviours. As a result, their actions become coordinated so as to contribute to the continued autopoiesis of each other … . These interlocked patterns of behaviour form the so-called *consensual domains*' (te Velde, 1999, 5). Maturana refers to behaviour in a *consensual domain* as *linguistic behaviour*; when the nervous system has developed in such a way that it can interact with its own symbolic descriptions we have *language*. The main function of language is not the transmission of information about an external physical reality but the establishment and consolidation of a *consensual domain* through continuous interaction with other autopoietic systems. Agents are not in a physical reality but in a *consensual domain*: 'reality only exists within a consensual domain and is a construct of the agents within that domain. Reality is therefore neither objective nor individual but essentially social in nature'.[1]

On the one hand, these epistemological premises imply that 'information' cannot be translated into 'knowledge' by the simple use of a codified language, and knowledge is no more a storable good that can be accumulated. On the other hand, 'knowledge' is always associated with action: you cannot attain knowledge without concrete, specified cognitive processes operating on experiences obtained through concrete interactions between agents (Arthur et al., 1997). Already established consensual domains allow meaningful interactions and coordinated actions between agents. Moreover, the point is that the consensual domain is always local and social in nature. The individual possibility to attain knowledge is strictly linked to the social system and consensual domains in which one acts, whether this is a department, a firm, a local system or a region.

The difference between information and knowledge becomes sharp. Information is an amount of symbolic descriptions produced by individuals, which is storable and can exist by itself: it is an evolution of the behaviour in a *consensual domain*, in which individuals can interact with their own symbolic descriptions. We called this evolved behaviour *linguistic behaviour*. The main function of information and language is to improve interactions between individuals and, through interactions, knowledge. There is no direct link between the accumulation of information and the increase of knowledge. Knowledge does not exist by itself but only inside a community of individuals and is continually regenerated and given existence through linguistic and non-linguistic activity, and the structural coupling generated by that activity. Breakdowns may occur at any moment at the individual as at the social level. This brings us very far from the neoclassic growth model, in which knowledge is individually and steadily accumulated, almost like a sort of capital. Knowledge becomes a very fragile social product, inseparable by the evolutionary process of actions and interactions inside a 'local' community of individuals.

If we assume this concept of knowledge it is at least doubtful that the new technologies made knowledge more important than it was in the past, or even that they significantly enhanced the exchange of knowledge between people.

The adoption of information technology might greatly improve the transfer of information but the critical elements of the 'converter' role are the human-specific qualities to deal with breakdowns and to create consensual domains (Brown and Duguid, 1998). These technologies could play a role in the coordination of action but are at best a supplement to the delicate and complicated processes of inter-human communication. If the share of non-substitutable informal communication is high, the introduction of information technologies could even damage the existing communication processes and patterns. This is understood well by Robert A. te Velde: 'what marks the rise of a *knowledge society* is the fact that economic value is explicitly attributed to the ability to generate effective action. Effective linguistic behaviour and good language skills are the cornerstones of such a *knowledge society*, not massive databases and 'intelligent' expert systems' (te Velde, 1999, 8).

3. THE CULTURAL SHIFT FROM PHYSICAL ASSETS TO KNOWLEDGE

So, if it is not information technology that made 'knowledge' (as ability to generate effective action) so important in the present economy, what did produce such a major shift in the western interpretation of economic growth, paying much more attention to knowledge in respect to tangible assets? The confusion between information and knowledge, and the consequent consideration of a database as accumulated knowledge, certainly played a role in focusing so much academic and political attention on the supposedly amazing potential of information technology in increasing knowledge.

Nonetheless, we agree that knowledge has become a more and more important 'raw material' in the past two or three decades. Here follows our 'non IT' explanation.

First, after World War Two reconstruction and satisfaction of basic needs through mass standardized production, economic activity in the major industrialized countries shifted from material goods to services and information-processing activity. Services, involving in general a much higher level of interaction between human beings, require more complex consensual domains, language skills and abilities to overcome breakdowns in relations: so, higher levels of knowledge are needed.

Second, changes from mass standardized production to flexible customized production, and from vertically integrated large firms to vertically disintegrated networks between small–medium firms and clusters of firms, have produced a 'spreading of knowledge' from the centre to the outskirts. Analysing the reasons for this change in production would bring us too far from our purposes but, for certain, this new structure requires a much larger diffusion of knowledge between a much greater number of economic agents than does vertical integration (Lorenzoni, 1990).

Third, economic activity, in industry, agriculture and services, is increasingly science-based. As we saw in previous sections, behaviour in a *consensual domain* is a *linguistic behaviour* when the nervous system has developed in such a way that it can interact with its own symbolic descriptions (*language*).

Development has gone so far and scientific language has proved so useful in economic activity that this knowledge is now extremely complex and must be provided to everyone through that special social activity that we call education and training. Certain levels of education and training prove unavoidable in providing every kind of knowledge but it is in science that they seem to be more effective. Science and knowledge in general have long been important for economic growth but as economies evolved and became more complex, under increasing competition, they became critical, together with the activity of education and training to provide them.

Fourth, increased global competition, initially between the USA and Japan, during the 1980s, gave clear evidence of the importance of 'knowledge'. During the 1980s the fear that Japan could overtake the United States in international competition even produced new research to understand the roots of Japan's competitive advantage. This research started to highlight the new importance of 'knowledge' in the competitive advantage of a nation.

What is special about Japan is that its thought never experienced the Western and Cartesian dichotomy between mind and physical reality that we discussed extensively in previous sections. As Nonaka and Takeuchi explain, the

> Japanese have a tendency to stay in their own world of experience without appealing to any abstract or metaphysical theory in order to determine the relationship between human thought and nature. Such a basic attitude of the *oneness of human and nature* is one of the most important characteristics of the Japanese intellectual tradition (Nonaka and Takeuchi, 1995, 29).

'Moreover, the natural tendency for the Japanese is to realize themselves in their relationship to others' (Nonaka and Takeuchi, 1995, 31).

If we recall our definition of 'knowledge' as the ability to do something in a *consensual* domain nurtured and sustained through continuous social interactions, we realize that the three philosophical pillars of the Japanese tradition, *oneness of human and nature*, *oneness of body and mind*, *oneness of self and other* have produced a much more modern concept of 'knowledge' than the West.

Many observers agree in considering this 'knowledge' to be the key of Japan's success. Nonaka and Takeuchi hold that the success of Japanese companies is not due to their manufacturing prowess; access to cheap capital; close and cooperative relationships with customers, suppliers and government agencies; or lifetime employment, seniority systems and other human resources management practices – although they consider all these factors to be important. Instead, they make the claim that Japanese companies have been successful because of their skills and expertise at 'organizational knowledge creation'. By this they mean the capability of a company as a whole to create new knowledge, disseminate it through the organization, and embody it in products, services and systems. Organizational knowledge creation therefore becomes the key to the distinctive ways that Japanese companies innovate.

As we will see later on, the problem is that in many countries, such as Italy and even Japan itself, this newly discovered concept of 'knowledge' did not extend to the management and teaching methods of higher education.

4. KNOWLEDGE AND EDUCATION

The increasing importance of knowledge produced, as a consequence, an increasing importance for education in policy-making, because of the high level of complexity reached by *linguistic behaviour*.

In addition, the old Western concept of 'knowledge' was a major boost for formal education and training policies. As far as the policies of single Western countries are concerned, both at the national[2] and regional[3] levels, higher education has received increasing financial, legislative and 'associative' efforts (Cooke and Morgan, 1998).

The problem is that education and higher education are not enough to produce economic growth and, in their traditional methods, they are not enough to produce even 'knowledge', according to our new definition of knowledge. In the Republic of Georgia, for example,[4] half of school leavers now go straight into higher education and another third enter tertiary vocational training (largely as a possible back door into university); since 1991 over 200 new degree-offering institutions have sprung into life alongside the old state university (Wolf, 2002). With half the registered adult unemployed holding degrees, Georgia is a living example that education is, at least, not enough to produce economic growth.

5. HIGHER EDUCATION AND HIGH INTELLECTUAL UNEMPLOYMENT

What is surprising in this entire scenario is that even some Western countries, like Italy, experienced the highest level of unemployment between young and highly educated individuals. So, on the one hand, national and regional governments are making so much effort to improve higher education, on the basis that 'knowledge' is the key for economic growth. On the other hand, these highly educated individuals seem to be the most affected by unemployment! There is also a great need for workers for positions that require a very low level of education, as immigration flows from poor countries and requests for more immigration by firms suggest. Table 2.1 shows data for the

Table 2.1 Unemployment rates for geographic areas and qualifications

	North-West	North-East	Centre	South
Degree and doctorate	5.6	7.9	14.1	28.0
High School	3.8	3.6	9.8	27.3
Professional training	4.1	3.2	8.3	26.6
Secondary school	5.9	4.0	10.5	24.7
Primary or no school at all	11.1	5.8	14.5	35.6
Total	5.0	4.3	10.6	26.8

Italian case from the National Institute of Statistics (ISTAT, 2001), for individuals from 25 to 34 years old.

According to these official data from the Italian National Institute of Statistics (ISTAT), in every Italian region, people with a High School diploma or even just professional training have a better chance of getting a job than people with a university degree, assuming they are from 25 to 34 years old.

In Central Italy, the level of unemployment amongst young people with primary or no schooling is practically the same as that among individuals with university degrees (14.1 per cent and 14.5 per cent respectively). According to an investigation by the Marche Region (1998), 'the difficulties of young Italian individuals with high qualifications to enter the labour market are great and they are revealed by the long time that is needed to get a job,[5] that is often disappointing and unstable'.[6]

Even if, according to the Italian National Institute of Statistics (ISTAT), the scenario improves, analysing data for individuals from 34 to 64, that is really a very small consolation for the 'young' generation of a 'knowledge economy'.

Italy has the lowest 'comprehensive private internal rate of return to tertiary education',[7] for males, among OECD countries: 6.5 per cent (Italian data for females is not available) (see Table 2.2).

Italy's 'expenditure on instruction, research and development (R&D) and ancillary services in tertiary education institutions as a percentage of GDP' is 0.83 per cent, the lowest among OECD countries. It is 1.03 per cent for Turkey, 1.11 per cent for Mexico, 1.07 per cent for Hungary, 1.10 per cent for Spain, 1.07 per cent for the United Kingdom, 1.13 per cent for France, 1.06 per cent for Germany; the country mean is 1.32 per cent (OECD, 2002, 207). Only Mexico, Poland, Korea and Slovak Republic among the 30 OECD countries have a lower level than Italy of foreign students enrolled (OECD, 2002, 236).

It is well known that employment-to-population ratios among young adults who are not in education provide information on the effectiveness of transi-

Table 2.2 Comprehensive private internal rate of return to tertiary education. OECD countries 2002, males

United Kingdom	17.3%
United States	14.9%
Denmark	13.9%
France	12.2%
The Netherlands	12%
Sweden	11.4%
Italy	6.5%
OECD country mean	11.8%

tion frameworks. Employment-to-population ratios for 20 to 24-year-olds generally exceed 70 per cent with the exception of some OECD countries such as Greece, Italy, Poland and Turkey. For the 25 to 29 age group, most OECD countries have ratios of between 70 to 80 per cent, with the exception, again, of Greece, Italy, Poland and Turkey (OECD, 2002, 255).

According to OECD data,

> in a few OECD countries, even young people who have completed tertiary-level education, probably a first degree given the age band involved, are subject to considerable unemployment when they enter the labour market. The ratio of unemployed non-students to the total youth population among this age group is up to 16 per cent or more in Greece, Italy, the Slovak Republic and Turkey, and higher than 13 per cent for 25 to 29-year-olds in Greece and Italy (OECD, 2002, 257).

The country mean among the 30 countries joining the OECD is 5.2 per cent for the 20 to 24 age group and 3.9 per cent for 25 to 29-year-olds. Moreover, by comparing work status for the 20 to 24 age group, Italy shows a remarkably small gap (in comparison to other OECD countries and the country mean) between those who have obtained upper secondary education and above and those who have not. These data for Italy, especially the ones from ISTAT, are so abnormal as to require a critical analysis.

Certainly, much could be done to improve legislation and coordination between the higher education system and firms. However, we believe that the main cause of these numbers, at least in the Italian case, is a fundamental contradiction in the educational system. This logical contradiction can be summarized as follows: we make the claim that relying on the traditional Western concept of 'knowledge', as we explained it in the previous sections, the Italian system of higher education was built to provide higher education as a 'positional good', and to provide it to as many as possible. This claim requires a full explanation.

The political economy of education markets classifies two broad types of commodity produced in education: *student goods* and *knowledge goods*. Student goods are what are acquired by students during their course of study. Knowledge goods are tradable intellectual property, such as copyrighted books, research data, patented scientific discoveries. Student goods divide into *self-goods* and *training goods*. Self-goods are purchased by the student or her family in order to enhance attributes of that student. Training goods are purchased by employers in order to enhance the value-creating skills of their employees. Self-goods are further divided into *positional goods*, which are status goods that provide social advantage, and *other goods of self-improvement*.

In the United States, Japan and most industrialized countries, the most desired forms of positional goods are places in elite schools and the professional faculties of leading universities. In Japan it is normal that a high school student would attend an expensive evening school to prepare admission examinations to prestigious universities, and it is not so rare that a student would spend some years, after ending high school, just in the effort to be admitted to the University of Tokyo, Faculty of Law. Admittance to this or other elite schools means a high probability of achieving the highest and best-paid positions in public administration and private corporations (Dore, 1965). The struggle among students to get a degree from prestigious institutions is no less intense in the United States (Duke, 1986).

What is special about Japan, in particular, is that its tradition and philosophy developed a concept of knowledge very similar to our new definition of 'knowledge', and its most innovative firms pioneered the introduction of this new knowledge into production (also described by Ikujiro Nonaka and Hirotaka Takeuchi in the *The Knowledge-Creating Company*), whereas its educational system has remained stuck to the traditional Western concept of knowledge. The reason is that the Japanese educational system has always been a Western one in its main framework. When Japan underwent the catch-up phase of its historical development, that was a political choice of imitation of Western models by the central government (Duke, 1986). During the USA military occupation a strong Western policy for education was enforced (Hall, 1949). So, today, this ancient Western origin of the educational system is well established in the Japanese tradition of higher education (Duke, 1986). In our opinion, the fact that firms were not managed by the government, as education was, allowed them to preserve the concept of 'knowledge' typical of the Japanese tradition.

Coming back to 'positional goods', the problem about them, in education as elsewhere, is that they are *hierarchical* in character (by definition some are more valuable than others). They are not just 'scarce', like all economic commodities, but *scarce in absolute terms*, in the sense that total supply is fixed. According to Marginson (Marginson, 1997, 27–50), positions of social leadership are finite and cannot be expanded through changes in education, and there cannot be universal or equal access to such positions, except when education has no positional value. In Hirsch's words, 'positional competition, in the language of game theory, is a zero-sum game: what winners win, losers lose' (Hirsch, 1976, 52), and when the number of educated people with a given level of credentials increases, the value of these credentials must decline. Education may provide knowledge, skills and social experiences without limitations, but as long as it is employed as a screening device for social positions 'advance for everyone' is an illusion:

> At any moment in time, and for any one person, standing on tiptoe gives a better view, or at least prevents a worse one. Equally, getting ahead of the crowd is an effective and feasible means of improving one's welfare, a means available to any one individual. It yields a benefit, in this sense, and the measure of the benefit is what individuals pay to secure it. The individual benefit from the isolated action is clear-cut. The sum of the benefits of all the actions taken together is nonetheless zero (Hirsch 1976, 7).

This phenomenon, even if obvious as it appears, is very tricky for neoclassical tools and methodological individualism as they tend to miss the interdependence between individuals and the negative externalities resulting from education: as a consequence, the full costs of education may be underestimated. The methodological individualist assumes, in fact, the social good is the arithmetical aggregate of all of the individual goods. But, as we can see, this methodology lacks any sense for individual benefits of positional investment in education.

The big difference between Italy and, for example, Japan and the United States concerns positional goods. In Italy places and degrees in prestigious universities are almost irrelevant because of extremely egalitarian policies between universities, the result being that a simple and ordinary degree is the main positional good available in education.

The importance that the labour market has traditionally attached to degrees from different Italian universities is not comparable to the importance that is given in Japan or the United States. Some Italian universities are better than others but the traditional social screening devices (apart from non-academic ones that have always played a major role in Italy, such as wealth and parents' education) have always been the level of qualification (primary, secondary, university) more than the universities where they have been obtained. As proof of that, until a very few years ago there was free access to almost every Italian public university to every Italian student holding any high school diploma or professional training whatsoever; exceptions were so few as to be almost irrelevant. The effect of this policy was that the positional good 'university degree' lost much of its 'positional rent', with all of the typical consequences that the political economy of education suggests: 1) individual investment in education falls short of expectations; 2) 'credentialism': the growth of educational credentials reduces the positional information conveyed by each credential and individuals look for more credentials; 3) the employer intensifies the screening process, raising the required level of credentials and forcing ever higher levels of investment in education; 4) professional groups require increasing levels of qualification to enter the profession; 5) 'the race gets longer for the same prize'; 6) education becomes a 'defensive necessity'; 7) as living standards rise, more people can invest in positional goods, and positional competition is intensified, especially during economic stagnation when the scramble for the remaining positional goods increases; 8) the value of positional goods falls and their price rises; 9) individuals suffer disappointment, frustration and 'deadweight' social costs.

The logical contradiction implied by a policy whose objective is to provide the same positional good to everyone, combined with a concept of knowledge provided by the educational system, that is merely instrumental to positional competition and far from the needs of production and society, result in a high level of unemployment and dissatisfaction among highly educated people. Here are two possible, not mutually exclusive, ways out for the Italian and similar cases:

1. Assuming that positional goods are probably the most important goods produced in the educational market, the higher education system should reject any utopian purpose of egalitarianism and, once it is aware of the characteristics and limits of positional goods, introduce a hierarchy between universities, making the system coherent with the existence of positional goods. Shifting positional goods competition from levels of qualification to universities would allow a modern and widespread policy for higher education without its present logical contradiction (this in effect is what is happening currently in the UK).
2. Remove the old Western concept of 'knowledge' as information that can be indefinitely and individualistically accumulated without action, and introduce in the educational system the concept of knowledge we defined in previous sections. This new concept, if not able by itself to reduce the positional value of education, would imply a closer relation between formal education, action, interactions with other individuals, local community and work, and would avoid a mere production of positional goods. This 'new knowledge' is not just instrumental to positional competition but also useful to economic activity and society. In this new circumstance, if positional competition goes wrong due to logical contradictions in policy or for some other reason, the result is not 'a positional

> good, *education*, that doesn't have a position any more' (and so is valueless on the labour market) but a creation of knowledge that is economically valuable. Indeed, this 'new knowledge' does not need a positional framework at all.

The second solution is the most interesting as it would reduce the socially expensive zero-sum game for positional goods, and would produce a kind of knowledge and education more relevant to the needs of modern firms. Its democratic and more egalitarian nature is a bonus. Figure 2.1 synthesizes the conceptual framework and the two possible policies. On the vertical axis is the kind of knowledge that the educational system provides: 'traditional/individualistic' (at the top) or 'social' (at the bottom) according to our definitions. On the horizontal axis is the degree of positional competition: 'non-active' on the left (because of logical incoherence in the system, like in Italy, or because not intended, like in the Netherlands), active on the right. The square high on the left is the only one, according to our definitions, that produces a high level of unemployment among highly educated people. The

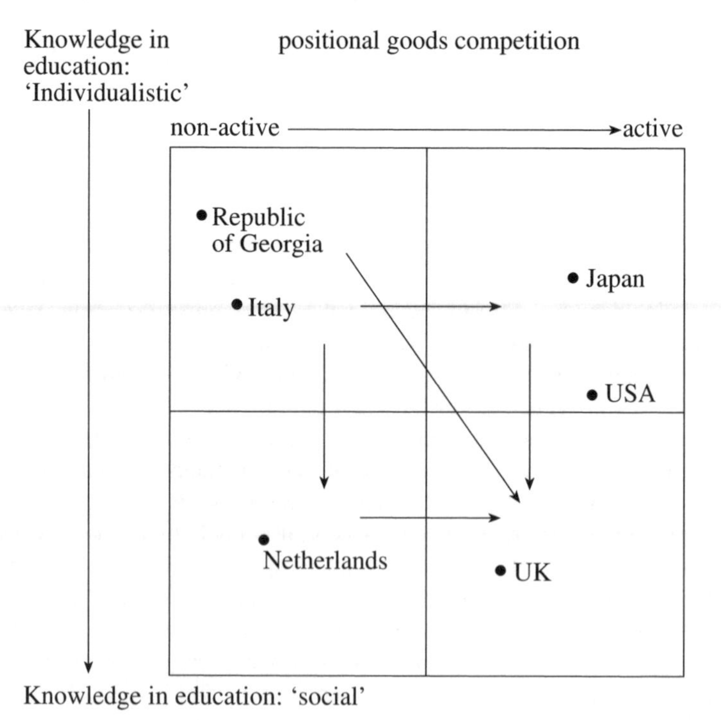

Figure 2.1 The conceptual framework

arrows going out of this square indicate the two, not mutually exclusive, policies to solve the problem. Even if the co-location of countries in the figure is only an example to clarify the conceptual framework, the UK may well be a case in which both the policies are active.

If we accept the epistemological view of the previous sections and agree: 1) on a definition of 'knowledge' as ability to produce effective action in a social context; 2) that the educational system must help in producing this kind of 'knowledge'; 3) that knowledge is the key factor in economic growth; 4) that in the present economy the most widely requested forms of knowledge are individual competences such as *problem* solving, relational skills, professional communication, team work and cooperation; then we understand why firms pay increasingly less attention to positional goods such as university degrees, obtained through individualistic accumulation of 'traditional knowledge', and pay increasing attention to expensive psychometric tests (Jenkins, 1999).

It is also possible to argue that a coherent system of 'positional goods competition' could work more effectively when the major employers are large firms. In this case, because of the great asymmetries in information between employer and possible employee, firms could be compelled to rely more heavily on educational 'credentials'. When firms are very small, or on a family basis, and embedded in a local network of relations based on trust, which reduces asymmetric information, such as is found in typical industrial districts of Central Italy, even a coherent system of 'positional goods competition' could not work, let alone the incoherent one that seems to exist just now.

The problem of eliminating the 'mismatch' between present academic knowledge and knowledge requested by firms is too great to be treated here and would require a complex system of policy measures such as: 1) shifting from a passive to an 'active' way of teaching, to develop the newly requested competencies and link the concept of knowledge to the concept of 'ability to produce effective action in a social context' (Leoni and Mazzoni, 2002); 2) introducing 'stages' and partnerships to allow firms and students to know and interact repeatedly with each other through project-based working, so that they may become structurally coupled, remembering that 'structural coupling occurs when the agents develop behaviours that reciprocally trigger complementary behaviours. As a result, their actions become coordinated so as to contribute to the continued autopoiesis of each other' (te Velde, 1999) and would build their relation on effective interaction, more than through 'credentialism' and socially expensive 'positional goods competition'; 3) reforming universities' funding structure to promote devolution and a development of knowledge not just 'publishable' but that is linked to the surrounding social community, according to our concept of 'knowledge' as a 'social behaviour':

> the concentration of effort in achieving published research … can result in high opportunity costs in terms of the contributions institutions can make to local economic development. There is a need to modify the funding system, so that both the contribution universities are making … to social reproduction, social capital and social inclusion, and the potential they have for applied research, are recognized and encouraged (Morgan, 2002, 68).

6. CONCLUSION

This chapter does not seek to propose a general policy framework, rather its aim was to show that every effective policy framework for filling the 'mismatch' between higher education and the real economy requires embracing a new concept of 'knowledge', as outlined in previous sections.

This concept, well developed from a philosophical point of view, is not yet ordinarily held in the educational systems of industrialized countries. Its adoption would help in explaining phenomena like high unemployment among highly educated people and would have highly social implications for local communities.

It would contribute to avoiding the *global auction* for investment, technology and jobs operating like a 'Dutch auction' (Brown and Lauder, 1997, 173), in which corporate investors are able to play off nations, communities and workers as a way of increasing their profit margins, and downward bidding spirals impoverishing local communities and workers by forcing concessions on wage levels, rents and taxes in exchange for investment in local jobs.

If the higher education system is, in fact, going to provide this new form of knowledge, together and in full coordination with surrounding communities, instead of involving itself in the expensive and deteriorating fight for positional goods, systems would no longer have an excess of highly educated people, nor would they have the more subtle and invisible general downsizing in positional competition. People would gradually and mentally involve themselves, during and inside their university courses, with the economic activities carried on in the communities in which they live, and would not just present themselves one day on the market, to sell the educational positional goods that they have laboriously obtained through individualistic accumulation of 'knowledge'.

We should probably go back to the classics and the founding father of the socioeconomic concept of 'industrial district', Alfred Marshall, who had a very different view from the following mechanical and formalized neoclassical tradition: his 'educational principles transcend the school-room and highlight the need to ensure young people have contact with real life quite early, when their mental elasticity is greater. There is more to learn in the workshop than in technical schools, where "*imitation has to yield the first place to formal instruction*"' (Marshall, *Industry and Trade*, 1919, 351). 'Education is also a process of socialization, in which "*sympathies*" are developed by personal contacts "*on the river and in the football field*"' (Marshall, 1919, 822–3).[8]

That is probably the best answer to 'the new international division of labour' (Carnoy, 1995, 211–17) for industrial districts and local communities: to invest in education to develop this new 'social knowledge', in order to accelerate the evolution of their own social environment, because 'reality is therefore neither objective nor individual but essentially social in nature' (te Velde, 1999). The world would be no more 'a representation of mine' (Schopenhauer, 1819), rather it would be 'a creation of us' as social community.

NOTES

1. Te Velde (1999), p. 6. See also, for a fundamental critique on the autopoietic model Roth and Schwegler (1990), 'Self-organizing and the unity of the world'. We may summarize the main difference between 'autopoiesis' and 'rationalistic thinking' as follows. *Rationalist thinking has two forms; it can either reduce the physical reality to mental states and processes ('idealism') or reduce the mental world to physical states and processes ('materialism'). In both cases the 'correspondence theorem',* between representation and physical reality, *is true, and* language and sentences can deliver a representation of the world that can be true or false, coherent or not coherent, but their ultimate grounding is in their correspondence with the state of affairs they represent. On the other hand, 'autopoiesis' assumes that the *'correspondence theorem' is not true any more: 'physical reality' becomes a product of social interactions among individuals and so a 'consensual domain'.*
2. See, for an extensive treatment, Slaughter (1998), 'National higher education policies in a global economy'.
3. See, for an extensive treatment, Cooke and Morgan (1998), *The Associational Economy*.
4. Its population is 5.4 million, it is number 139 in the world in GDP per inhabitant at purchasing-power parity and number 16 in the world in unemployment rate.
5. In 1993 individuals looking for a job for more than 12 months were 59.4 per cent. In 1996 they increased to 66.4 per cent.
6. Organismo Bilaterale Marche (1998), *Disoccupazione, offerta di lavoro giovanile e domanda di professionalità delle imprese nelle Marche*, p. 51.
7. The rate of return represents a measure of returns obtained, over time, relative to the cost of the initial investment in education (the costs equal tuition fees, foregone earnings net of taxes adjusted for the probability of being in employment less the resources made available to students in the form of grants and loans; benefits are the gain in post-tax earnings adjusted for higher employment probability less the repayment, if any, of public support during the period of study) (OECD, 2002, 126–34).
8. In Raffaelli (2003), *Marshall's Evolutionary Economics*, p. 64.

BIBLIOGRAPHY

Arthur W.B., S. Duralauf and D. Lane (1997), 'Introduction: process and emergence in the economy', in W.B. Arthur, S. Duralauf and D. Lane (eds), *The Economy as an Evolving Complex System II*, Addison-Wesley.

Becattini, G. (1979), 'Dal "settore" industriale al "distretto" industriale. Alcune considerazioni dull'inità di indagine dell'economia industriale', *Rivista di Economia e Politica Industriale*, 1.

Brown, J.S. and P. Duguid (1998), 'Organizing knowledge', *California Management Review*, **40**, 90–111.

Brown, P. and H. Lauder (1997), 'Education globalisation and economic development', in A.H. Halsey, H. Lauder et al. (eds), *Education: Culture, Economy and Society*, Oxford and New York: Oxford University Press, pp. 156–223.

Carnoy, M. (1995), 'Education and the new international division of labour', in *International Encyclopedia of Economics of Education*, Oxford: Pergamon.

Carnoy, M. (1998), 'Globalisation and educational restructuring', *Melbourne Studies in Education*, no. 39.

Castells, M. (1993), 'The informational economy and the new international division of labour', in Martin Carnoy, M. Castells, S.S.Cohen and F.H. Cardoso (eds), *The New Global Economy in the Information Age: Reflections on Our Changing World*, University Park, PA: Pennsylvania State University Press.

Cooke, P. and K. Morgan (1998), *The Associational Economy*, Oxford: Oxford University Press.

Dore, P. Ronald (1965), *Talent Training and Social Order*, Berkeley, CA: University of California Press.

Duke, B. (1986), *The Japanese School. Lessons for Industrial America*, Westport, CT: Praeger Publishers.

Hall, R. King (1949), *Education for a New Japan*, Ch. 1: 'Ashes or Opportunity', Yale: Yale University Press.

Hirsch, F. (1976), *Social Limits to Growth*, Twentieth century fund, Cambridge, MA: Harvard University Press.

ISTAT (2001), *Unemployment rates for year 2001*, accessed at www.istat.it.

Jenkins, A. (1999), 'Companies use of psychometric testing and the changing demand for skills: a review of the literature', London School of Economics, Centre for the Economics of Education discussion paper no. 12, London.

Lakoff, G. (1987), *Women, Fire, and Dangerous Things: What Categories Reveal about the Mind*, Chicago: The University of Chicago Press.

Leoni, R. and N. Mazzoni (2002), 'Saperi accademici e competenze richieste nei luoghi di lavoro: verso una riduzione del mismatch?', Economia Politica, 1.

Lorenzoni, G. (1990), 'L'architettura di sviluppo delle imprese minori. Costellazioni e piccoli gruppi', Bologna: il Mulino.

Marginson, S. (1997), *Markets in Education*, Sydney: Allen & Unwin.

Marshall, A. (1919), *Industry and Trade*, London: McGraw-Hill.

Maturana, H.R. and F.J. Varela (1980), *Autopoiesis and Cognition: The Realization of the Living*, Dordrecht: D. Reidel Publishing Company.

Maturana, H.R., G. Uribe and S. Frenk (1986), 'A biological theory of relativistic colour coding in the primate retina', *Arch. Biologia y Med. Exp.*, (supplement 1).

Morgan, B. (2002), 'Higher education and regional economic development in Wales: an opportunity for demonstrating the efficacy of devolution in economic development', *Regional Studies*, **36**(1).

Nonaka, I. and H. Takeuchi (1995), *The Knowledge-Creating Company*, Oxford: Oxford University Press.

OECD (2002), *Education at a Glance: OECD Indicators*, Paris: OECD.

Organismo Bilaterale Marche (1998), *Disoccupazione, offerta di lavoro giovanile e domanda di professionalità delle imprese nelle Marche*, A. Merloni Foundation on behalf of the Marche region.

Raffaelli, T. (2003), *Marshall's Evolutionary Economics*, London: Routledge.

Romer, P. (1986), 'Increasing returns and long-run growth', *Journal of Political Economy*, **94**, 1002–37.

Roth, G. and H. Schwegler (1990), 'Self-organizing and the unity of the world', in W. Krohn, G. Kuppers and H. Nowotny (eds), *Selforganization: Portrait of a scientific revolution*, Dordrecht: Kluwer Academic Press.

Schopenhauer, A. (1819 [1969]), 'The World as Will and Representation', edited by G. Riconda with translation by N. Palanga, Milan: Mursia.

Slaughter, S. (1998), 'National higher education policies in a global economy', in J. Currie and J. Newson (eds) (1998) *Universities and Globalization: Critical Perspectives*, London: Sage, pp. 45–70.

Te Velde, A.R. (1999), *Markets for knowledge – where minds do meet*, 26 August 1999, unpublished paper, Delft University of Technology, Economics of Infrastructures Group, The Netherlands; the published Dutch version is: Te Velde, R. (2002), 'Kennis maken en kennis hebben', in van Baalen P., M. Weggeman, A. Witteveen (eds), Kennis en management ('knowledge and management'), Schiedam: Scriptum, pp. 358–79.

Winograd, T. and F. Flores (1986), *Understanding Computers and Cognition: A New Foundation for Design*, Norwood: Ablex Publishing Corporation.

Wolf, A. (2002), *Does Education Matter? Myths About Education and Economic Growth*, London: Penguin Books.

3. The geography of research collaboration: theoretical considerations and stylized facts in biotechnology in Europe and the United States[1]

Koen Frenken and Frank G. van Oort

1. INTRODUCTION

Whereas the geography of innovation has established itself as a central subject in economic geography (Feldman, 1999), geography is still a largely neglected subject in science studies including scientometrics. In particular, as collaboration in scientific knowledge production has become a central (policy) issue, it is surprising that few researchers have tried to understand the geography of research collaborations. Little is known about the role of proximity in scientific collaboration and how this affects the probability and nature of networking among research institutions. In this chapter we set out a number of theoretical considerations about the role of geography in science in general and in research collaboration in particular. To this end, we approach the subject by first discussing theoretical concepts advanced in the field of the geography of innovation, as this field of inquiry has recently produced a number of valuable theoretical insights in the relationships between geography, knowledge production and innovation. We then ask the question regarding to what extent these insights are helpful in theorizing the geography of research collaboration in science (and conclude that they are so only to a limited extent). Next, we discuss a number of stylized facts about research collaboration in Europe and the United States in the field of biotechnology, based on comparative empirical research on both continents. Special emphasis will be given to the geography of 'hybrid' collaborations between universities with institutions outside academia, which appear to be geographically more localized than collaborations between universities and than collaborations between extra-academic institutions. Finally we post some important research questions and data requirements needed for the development of an adequate explanatory and theoretical framework, and for more comprehensive research on the geography of research collaboration in other disciplines.

2. THE GEOGRAPHY OF INNOVATION

Consensus has grown among economists and economic geographers that knowledge production and knowledge spillovers are to an important extent geographically localized (Jaffe, 1989; Audretsch and Feldman, 1996; Feldman, 1999). Economists point to agglomeration economies as a source of concentration of industrial activity and innovation. Agglomeration economies of various sorts arise when people and firms engaged in production are geographically concentrated. These 'Marshallian' externalities concern labour market pooling, access to specialized suppliers of intermediate goods and business services, and knowledge spillovers (Feser, 2002). The concept of agglomeration has not only led to renewed interest in economic geography, but has also been incorporated in the core of the 'new growth' theories in economics. Recent growth models stress that regional convergence in welfare may not occur due to geographically bounded knowledge spillovers. Persistence of regional differences can then be understood from the existence of geographically localized externalities related to R&D at the regional level. An important implication of new growth theories holds that, if regional differences through local knowledge spillovers are persistent, the fate of regions is not necessarily determined by favourable physical conditions and cost competitiveness, but rather by concentration of R&D and high-skilled labour. It is probably safe to say that the policy implications arising from this research are not fully compatible with today's regional policies (and in particular, in the European Union).

Though the factors contributing to agglomeration economies go back to Marshall's late nineteenth century writing, econometric evidence on agglomeration economies has only been accumulating recently. Only now has it become apparent that definitions of knowledge and knowledge spillovers are ambiguous, and the impact of positive externalities resulting from knowledge spillovers is possibly overestimated (Breschi and Lissoni, 2001; Caniels and Romijn, 2003). Furthermore, considerable debate has centred on the spatial scale of analysis most suitable for identifying agglomeration economies and spillover effects. Although the regional and urban levels of analysis theoretically forms the most appropriate looking glass, empirical research results identify significant agglomeration effects at more than one geographical level (Rosenthal and Strange, 2001; van Oort, 2002; 2003). Agglomeration effects are found at the zip code, county, city and state levels.

Irrespective of the spatial unit of analysis chosen, most scholars apply a knowledge production function approach to explain the regional production of patents or innovations as a result of public and private R&D inputs and a local spillover index. In more than one case, scholars have been able to indicate that such spillovers turn out to be statistically significant, that is, exert a significant and positive effect on knowledge output as measured by patents or innovations. In particular, the money spent on university research in a region is said to be very beneficial for innovation in that region (Jaffe, 1989). More in particular, local externalities tend to benefit SMEs more than large firms, as the latter primarily, but not exclusively, rely on in-house R&D (Acs, 2002).

Sectoral decomposition also shows quite different results for different industries. In short, it is primarily the ICT sector for which strong and robust effects of local knowledge spillovers are found (Acs, 2002). This result is important because it suggests that agglomeration effects are very much dependent on the structure of the industry, the stage of the life cycle of firms and sectors, and the underlying nature of the knowledge base. This underlines the importance of analysing innovation at the level of a sector or a technology, rather than at the level of the economy as a whole.

Empirical studies have not been confined to the localization of the production of knowledge as measured by knowledge output indicators, but studies also dealt with geographically localized knowledge diffusion. An important study in this context has been carried out by Jaffe et al. (1993), who found that the large majority of citations to US patents stem from the same state as the one from which the cited patent originated, even when corrected for differences in regional sector distributions. This means that not only is the production of knowledge spatially bounded, but the diffusion of knowledge is as well. A second important diffusion mechanism at the local level is the creation of spin-offs by firms or research institutions. Typically, spin-offs 'inherit' at least part of the knowledge and competencies of parent firms, and through the mechanism of spin-offs, knowledge and competencies are diffused throughout the economy. Given the stylized fact that the large majority of spin-offs locate geographically close to the parent company, the pattern of knowledge diffusion through spin-offs becomes spatially bounded (Klepper, 2001).

An aspect enhancing the concentration of innovative activity that is less well researched empirically, but omnipresent in all debates, concerns the idea that face-to-face contacts in networks are necessary for the *transfer* of tacit knowledge (Glaeser, 1999; Howells, 2002). In contrast to codified knowledge, which can be transmitted through media over a large distance at low costs, transmission of tacit knowledge requires face-to-face interaction on a repeated basis. Moreover, to interpret codified knowledge some tacit knowledge is usually required as well. Also note that in the codification process of knowledge, such as the writing of patents, benefits arise from proximate specialized service providers such as specialized law firms and patent offices. The *development* of new tacit knowledge is said typically to occur during close interaction between partners, for example, between firms and suppliers, or firms and research institutions. This interaction may take the form of formal collaborations, through mobility of persons, or through less formalized contacts.

Howells (2002), however, stresses that, although transfer and development of tacit knowledge is widely recognized as an important geographically localized phenomenon, little systematic empirical research has been carried out to support such a claim. A recent exception is the study by Breschi and Lissoni (2002) using Italian patent data of the European Patent Office to analyse the collaboration and mobility of inventors across companies and in space. The central idea behind their study holds that the tacit content of technological knowledge travels along with people who master it. This implies that knowledge flows, whether these are spillovers or traded services, are localized to the extent that research collaboration and labour mobility is. Using patent citations as in Jaffe et al. (1993), they found that network structure and mobility are both major factors explaining citation to patents. This result can be explained by the fact that collaboration networks and labour mobility are geographically localized phenomena, which, given their importance for the generation and diffusion of knowledge, render the knowledge spillovers localized as well. Their result thus questions whether spatial units are relevant units of knowledge diffusion analysis without taking into account the network structure between collaborating inventors as well as the mobility of inventors across companies and space and over time. Thus, only in so far as networks are geographically localized, can one expect knowledge production and diffusion to be geographically localized (compare Van Oort, 2002; 2003; Graham and Marvin, 2001).

The emphasis on the geography of collaborative networks rather than knowledge production, as the main vehicle of knowledge creation and diffusion, is also supported by the fact that collaboration itself is a proliferating phenomenon. The average number of organizations involved in research and innovation processing has increased substantially. Moreover, in some sectors societal functions that were traditionally 'assigned' to industry (commercializing technology) and academia (producing scientific knowledge) have become blurred. In these sectors, both academia and firms have become engaged in profit-seeking activities, and both academia and firms are active in scientific research, both fundamental and applied (Cohen and Levinthal, 1990; Rosenberg, 1990). As a result, a large variety of institutional arrangements for collaborative university–industry relationships have emerged in different territories and in different sectors (Etzkowitz and Leydesdorff, 2000). In this setting, success of collaboration often partly relies on complex formal contractual arrangements, partly on frequent face-to-face contacts and partly on the exchange of personnel, which is all facilitated when participants are geographically nearby and share an institutional environment. This provides an important explanation for the recent popularity of the concept of 'regional innovation systems', both in academia and in policy circles (for example, Cooke et al., 1997).

3. THE GEOGRAPHY OF SCIENCE

The above review of the geography of innovation provides theoretical rationales and empirical evidence of a strong (and sometimes even increasing) geographical concentration of innovative activity. From this, however, one should not automatically expect scientific research to be as localized geographically as industrial innovation, or to develop into a more localized activity over time. Scientific research is qualitatively different from industrial innovation (Dasgupta and David, 1994). Though in some disciplines the distinction between science and innovation has become less relevant, such as in biotechnology and informatics, scientific knowledge production generally differs from industrial knowledge production in at least two ways.

The first main difference between scientific and industrial knowledge production is the nature of the knowledge being produced and exchanged. The tacit component is expected to be much smaller in scientific knowledge production, which renders communication and collaboration at a distance much easier. However, it should be recognized that codified knowledge exchange also benefits from proximity, especially when the code itself is rapidly changing and is to be transferred to other scientists through training. The specificity of knowledge ('appliedness') is also expected to be much smaller in scientific research compared to industrial R&D. Consequently, problem definitions are to a lesser extent determined by the local context, but emerge from a global *discours*. If one accepts the claim that scientific knowledge production is typically characterized by a low degree of specificity and appropriability, this already suggests that scientific knowledge production is less localized geographically than industrial R&D. At the same time, though, it must be reminded that important differences in specificity and appropriability between scientific disciplines exist, and that, arguably, important fields such as biotechnology and IT are characterized by a relatively high degree of specificity and appropriability.

The second main difference between scientific and industrial knowledge production concerns the incentive structure. University scientists are explicitly oriented towards public diffusion of knowledge at the widest geographical scale possible, while investors in industrial R&D have an incentive to appropriate the results, whatever the mechanism used to achieve this. Thus, one should expect scientific knowledge production to be less localized than industrial innovation. When universities and industries collaborate in R&D, the differences in incentive structure give rise to complex institutional arrangements. The complexity of these collaborations renders it generally impossible to encode all contingencies in a contract, and, as a consequence, these networks have to rely at least partially on less formal institutions that reduce the risk of opportunism. One may therefore argue that in the case of university–industry relations, as stressed by the regional innovation system literature, proximity may be supportive to establish successful partnerships as less formal institutions rely on more frequent face-to-face contacts and a shared culture.

We conclude that the geography of science is different in at least those two respects from the geography of innovation. Nevertheless, the apparent robustness of localized externalities leading to regional agglomeration (discussed in the previous section on the geography of innovation) has not been tested with respect to scientific knowledge production systems. Scientometrics – the quantitative study of science – has paid relatively little attention to the geography of scientific knowledge production hitherto. The national level is dominant in scientometric analysis, which does not come as a surprise given that many studies are undertaken in the context of the evaluation of science policy (which in most countries is organized at the national level). Emphasis in scientometrics tends to be on collaboration and the phenomenon of internationalization of research networks (see Katz and Martin, 1997 for a review), while only a few studies address the regional dimension of scientific knowledge production (Katz, 1994; Liang and Zhu, 2002).

Collaboration in science has been increasing for a long time. The increase in research collaboration is a historically robust phenomenon starting at the beginning of the twentieth century when co-authorships accounted for less than 10 per cent of all publications, and continuing up to the end of the twentieth century with co-authorships accounting for over 50 per cent of all publications (Wagner-Doebler, 2001). Increased collaboration can be understood as the consequence of increased division of labour among scientists. In particular, collaboration has become the dominant form in applied and experimental sciences, where many pieces of knowledge and competencies are combined to produce a new piece of knowledge. Yet, collaboration has also quickly increased in less experimental sciences like mathematics (Wagner-Doebler, 2001). There is also evidence that the benefits for researchers engaged in collaboration are higher than average (Katz and Martin, 1997). For example, the citation impact of publications resulting from collaboration is substantially above average. The difference in citation impact is even higher for international collaboration. Furthermore, it has been found that the productivity of scientists is positively dependent on the frequency of collaboration. Collaboration tends to increase the level of personal productivity as measured by the number of publications produced per year. A further explanation of the rise in collaboration is the observation that costs have fallen substantially. Cheaper transport and communication, as well as qualitative advances in information and communication technology, have greatly facilitated collaboration in science over the past decades.

Within the literature on collaboration, there are some studies that link research collaboration to geography by looking at co-authored articles containing multiple addresses. Using this information, the geography of collaborating institutions can be mapped and analysed statistically. The results found so far are quite robust. As with many other types of human interaction, one should expect scientific collaboration to decrease exponentially with the distance separating partners. The first study that addressed this hypothesis has been Katz's (1994) study on collaboration between UK research institutions. Katz found that geographical proximity indeed provides a good predictor for the frequency of collaboration between research institutions. A study by Liang and Zhu (2002) on China also found that geographical proximity is one of the important factors determining the pattern of interregional collaboration. More recently, Danell and Persson (2003) analysed geographical patterns of R&D activities in Sweden using publications data and PhD careers, and Verbeek et al. (2003) analysed the geographical effects in citation patterns in patents to science.

Concerning internationalization, it has been estimated that the share of international collaborations doubled between 1987 and 1997 to account for 15 per cent of world publications in 1997 (Wagner, 2002). However, this in itself cannot be considered as a trend towards globalization, since the rise in international collaborations is to be compared to the rise in national (and local) collaborations to control for the structural phenomenon of increased networking. For example, Frenken (2002a) found that although the absolute number of European collaborations resulting in publications has risen rapidly during the 1990s, the number of collaborations at the national level increased rapidly as well. Comparing the bias to collaborate within national borders and with European partners over time, it was found that the bias to collaborate nationally remained strong and did not fall significantly over time (see also Frenken, 2002b). The main trend in scientific knowledge production, thus, has been not so much localization or globalization of science, but collaboration in science. It is through networks in 'communities of practice' that new knowledge is generated and shared, which may be or may not be strongly geographically localized. Concerning the geographical dimension of research collaboration, little is known.

The phenomenon of internationalization is well documented, yet does not provide in itself evidence of 'de-localization' when the rise in the number of collaborations at national and regional levels is not controlled for.

4. STYLIZED FACTS ON RESEARCH COLLABORATION IN BIOTECHNOLOGY

In the remainder of this study, we suggest how to address the geography of research collaboration empirically using biotechnology and applied microbiology as a case study. We refrain from theoretically informed hypothesis testing; rather, we propose a number of stylized facts that will require further generalization in other disciplines and theoretical explanation in future research. We will go into new data requirements that arise from our study as well, in particular, the need to regionalize the data on scientific publications to address sub-national levels of analysis.

The main data source in scientometrics in general (and used in our study) is the *Web of Science*, a product offered by the Institute of Scientific Information (ISI, http://www.isinet.com/). The Web of Science contains information on publications in all major journals in the world for 1988 onwards. It covers three databases: the Science Citation Index (SCI) including natural science journals, the Social Science Citation Index (SSCI) including social science journals, and the Arts and Humanities Citation Index (A&JCI) including journals belonging to the arts and humanities. Using the Web of Science, one can construct data on a specific discipline in a relatively straightforward way. Once a list of journals is obtained that is representative for the scientific discipline in question, publications belonging to a discipline can be simply retrieved by using the set of journals as a query. We analysed publications for the discipline of *biotechnology and applied microbiology* using a list available from the Institute for Scientific Information at the above-mentioned website (see the appendix for the list of journals).

An alternative approach is to define a scientific field by cluster analysis of journal–journal citation matrices, a procedure which defines a scientific discipline by cluster analysis based on most frequently occurring citing relationships between journals (Leydesdorff and Cozzens, 1993). On theoretical grounds, the latter procedure is to be preferred over the former, because scientific disciplines self-organize by means of citations. By means of clustering those journals that have dense citation relations among them, a scientific field can be delineated from neighbouring fields (using a threshold). However, the former procedure is less data-intensive and independent from the specific cluster procedure adopted. Other delineation strategies exist as well as other databases, both of which have been surveyed by Dalpé (2002).

Collaboration among research institutions is defined as the co-occurrence of two addresses in the same publication record. This means that a single-author paper with two or more affiliations is also counted as collaboration whereas a multi-authored paper with one address (that is an intra-organization collaboration) is not regarded as collaboration (Katz and Martin, 1997). The use of institutions rather than persons to indicate collaborations is necessary if one is interested in the geography of collaboration. Addresses refer to institutional affiliation and not to single persons per se.

Each address contains geographical information including country name, city name and, for the United States, the code referring to a US state. Unfortunately, the publication records kept in the Web of Science do not cover zip codes systematically. This means that only for the United States, can a regional analysis be carried out using the standard US state codes. For all other countries, the national level is the level of analysis, given the lack of codes for the regional level. In principle, one can carry out analyses on the city level (a level found appropriate in innovation and endogenous growth geographical research, see Glaeser et al. 1992) using the city names provided in the address field. However, cities provide a seemingly disturbing detailed spatial level of analysis if one would, ideally, control for neighbouring cities using spatial auto-correlation techniques (van Oort, 2002; 2003). This would require, for each municipality, information on all neighbouring municipalities. Obviously, this would render the data collection requirements more time consuming and complex, yet we intend to invest in this work in order to bring the research on the geography of science one step further.

In the following, we limit our analysis to the state level (for the United States) and the country level (for the EU15). We have selected all publications that contain at least two addresses. From this set, we constructed a dataset for the United States by selecting all publications that have at least one address originating from the United States. The United States dataset covers 14 years (1988–2001). Similarly, we constructed a dataset for the European Union by selecting all publications that have at least one address originating from one of the 15 member states of the EU. The European Union dataset covers 15 years (1988–2002). The total number of addresses originating from the EU and the US are given per year in Figure 3.1.

Limiting our analysis to the state level (for the United States) and the country level (for the EU15), we thus define areas at administrative levels, though we acknowledge this can be refined into more functional definitions in future research. Using these levels, we mean intra-state collaborations for the United States and intra-national collaborations for the EU. We further distinguish between 'federal' collaborations and international collaborations. Federal collaborations concern the co-occurrence of two addresses originating from different US states in the case of the United States, and two addresses

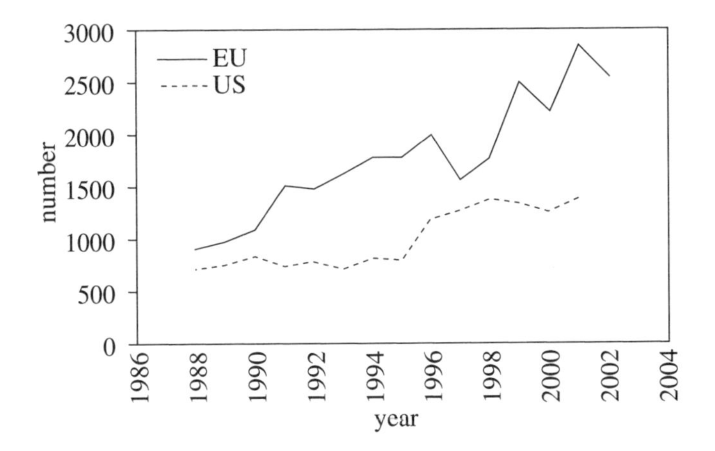

Figure 3.1 Growth of addresses originating from EU and US

originating from different EU countries in the case of the European Union. International collaborations concern the co-occurrence of one address in the United States and one address outside the United States. For the European Union, an international collaboration refers to a co-occurrence of an EU address and an address in a country outside the EU.

We further classified all collaborations except the international collaborations in one out of three categories called ACAD, NON ACAD and HYBRID. ACAD stands for collaboration between academic organizations, which involves universities, colleges, schools, and non-profit organizations with the advancement of science as its primary goal. NON ACAD stands for collaboration between non-academic organizations including firms, hospitals, and government research agencies that have primary goals other than advancing science (though very often pursue the advancement of science as a secondary goal).[2] HYBRID collaborations refer to the co-occurrence of an academic and a non-academic organization in one publication record.

Using the data on collaborations and the different classifications in which each collaboration is grouped, one can address a number of empirical questions leading to some stylized facts on research collaboration in biotechnology in both the EU and the US. We will go into (i) the importance of networking, (ii) the degree of internationalization of networks, (iii) the dominance of academia in collaboration, (iv) the degree of localization of hybrid collaborations, and (v) the existence of different institutional 'clubs' of countries in Europe.

Stylized Fact One: Networking as a Structural Trend

Is inter-organizational research collaboration important, and increasingly so? Figure 3.2 shows the average number of addresses per publication for both the EU and the US. It is clear that the number of addresses per publication has steadily risen in the past 15 years, approaching 1.8 addresses per publication in 2002 in the EU. This means that inter-organizational networks are proliferating rapidly in biotechnology. To compare the trend in Europe with the US, we notice a remarkable similarity both in the average number of authors per publication and the trend over time.

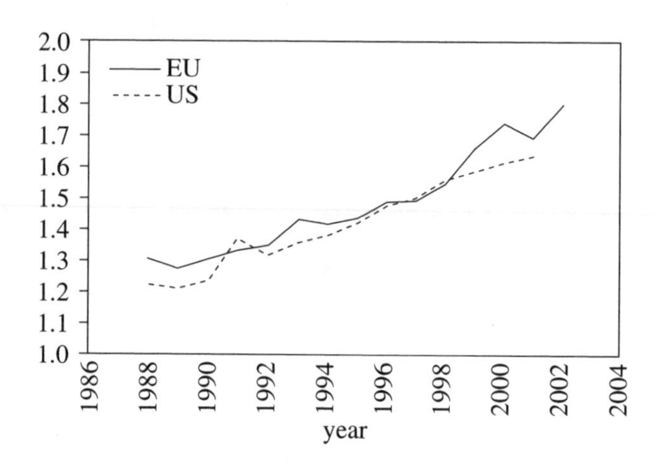

Figure 3.2 Number of addresses per publication for the European Union (1988–2002) and the United States (1988–2001)

Stylized Fact Two: Internationalization of Networks

Internationalization is a common trend in European countries and in the United States (Figures 3.3 and 3.4). For what concerns European countries, the share of international collaborations steadily increased until 1998 and decreased in most recent times, whereas the share of international collaborations involving an American organization stabilized in the mid-nineties but increased again from 1998 onwards. A tentative explanation for these trends may be that until recently, internationalization has been a structural phenomenon for the national biotechnology systems in biotechnology, yet from 1998, European collaboration has become more often a substitute for collaborations outside the European Union. For what concerns the United States, the trend in the long term is that of a rise in the share of international collaborations.

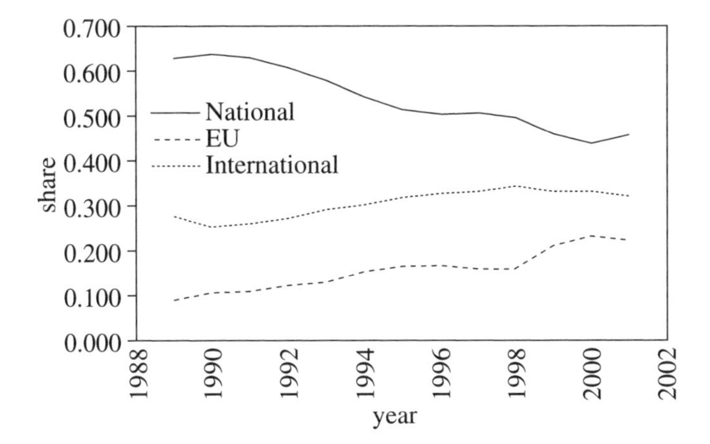

Figure 3.3 *Geography (EU): number of collaborations at different spatial levels of analysis (3-year moving average)*

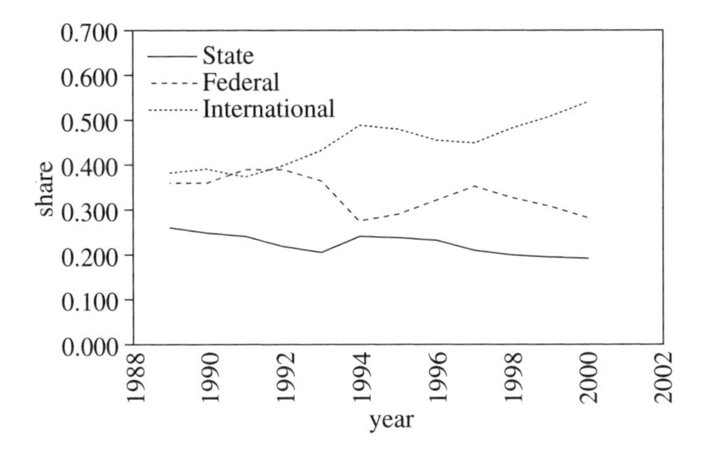

Figure 3.4 *Geography (US): number of collaborations at different spatial levels of analysis (3-year moving average)*

Stylized Fact Three: Academia Dominates in EU, less so in US

Figures 3.5 and 3.6 show the share of different types of relations in the EU and the US, respectively. Two major patterns appear. First, academia is dominant in collaboration (looking at the share of 'Academia and Hybrid'), which comes as no surprise. Second, the European system is dominated by collaborations among academic institutions, while hybrid collaborations occur much

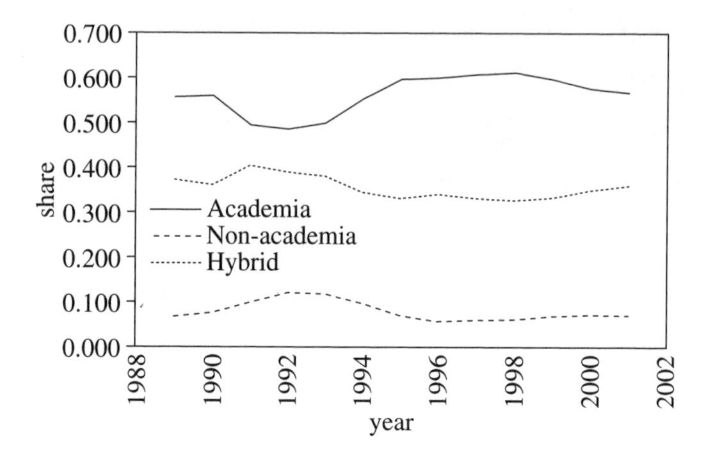

Figure 3.5 Collaboration patterns among academia and non-academic organizations (EU)

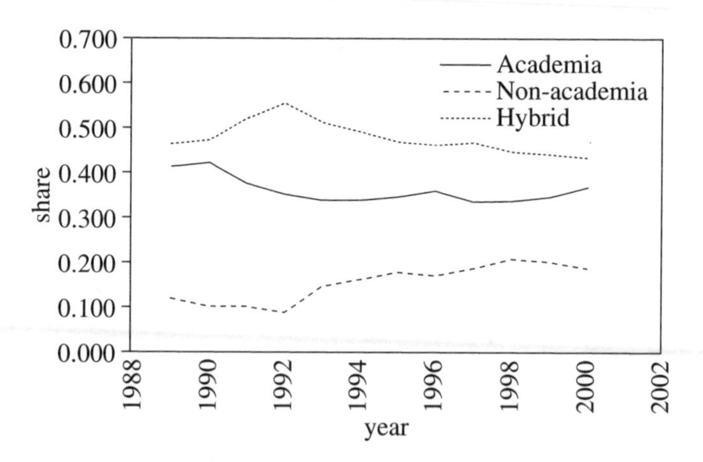

Figure 3.6 Collaboration types among academia and non-academic organizations (US)

more often in the Unites States. This confirms popular wisdom holding that more incentives in the US system exist for academia to collaborate with non-academic institutions, including firms. Possibly an important fraction of these collaborations is between academia and spin-off firms from academia (which, in principle, can be traced by looking at the mobility of persons over time).

Stylized Fact Four: Hybrid Collaborations Geographically most Localized

A recurrent theme in the geography of innovation holds that collaborations across societal subsystems generally, and university–industry relations in particular, are facilitated by geographical proximity. This would mean, in our classification, that hybrid collaborations occur relatively often at the lower geographical level. Since we did not classify research organizations into academic and non-academic when collaboration was international, we can only compare the two lower geographical levels, that is the nation and the EU level for Europe, and the state and federal level for the United States.

During the whole period considered, we counted in total 13634 collaborations within EU countries at the national level and 5525 collaborations at the EU level (involving two EU countries). This means that collaboration occurs 2.47 times more often nationally than at the European level. Looking at hybrid collaborations only, 4908 hybrid collaborations occurred nationally and only 1751 hybrid at the European level. This means that hybrid collaborations occur 2.80 times more often at the national level than at the European level, indicating that hybrid collaborations are indeed characterized by a higher degree of geographical localization than other types of collaborations.

In the United States, we counted 2910 collaborations at the state level and 4564 at the national (federal) level. Collaboration thus takes place 1.57 times more often at the federal level than at the state level. Looking at hybrid collaborations only, we counted 1446 such collaborations at the state level and 2044 collaborations at the national level. This means that hybrid collaborations occur only 1.41 more often at the federal level than at the state level, meaning that hybrid collaborations are relatively more localized geographically.

Stylized Fact Five: Institutional Clubs (Europe)

Looking at the geographical scope of countries' collaborations (Figure 3.7), we see a typical North–South divide with Latin countries being nationally oriented (Portugal, Spain, France and Italy) while other countries are more internationally oriented. Finland is an outlier as a Nordic country with a strong national orientation. Considering the EU, we obviously see smaller countries having more EU collaborations as fewer partners are available at the national level anyway (cf. Frenken, 2002a; b). In this respect, Belgium can be considered as a medium-size country with an outlier with an unexpectedly high number of EU collaborations (possibly reflecting the low propensity to collaborate nationally between northern and southern universities and the proximity effect of 'Brussels').

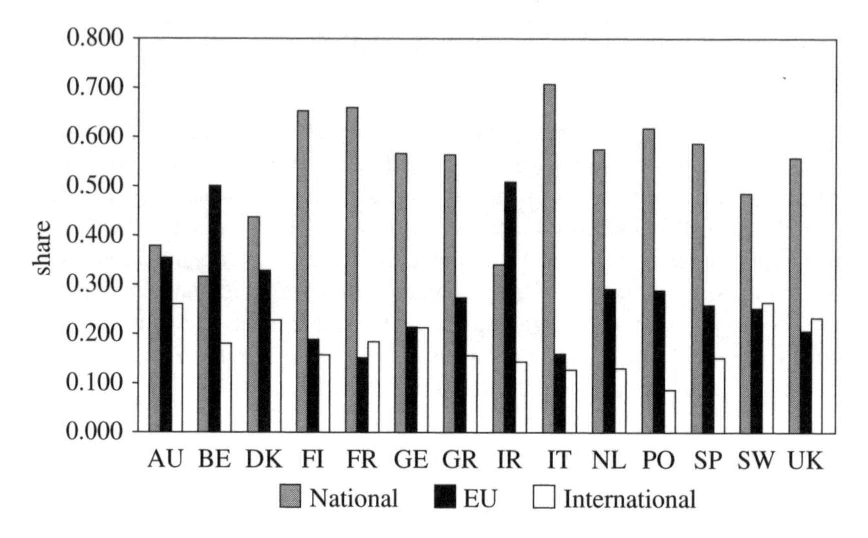

Figure 3.7 Geography of collaborations for all members of the European Union (all years)

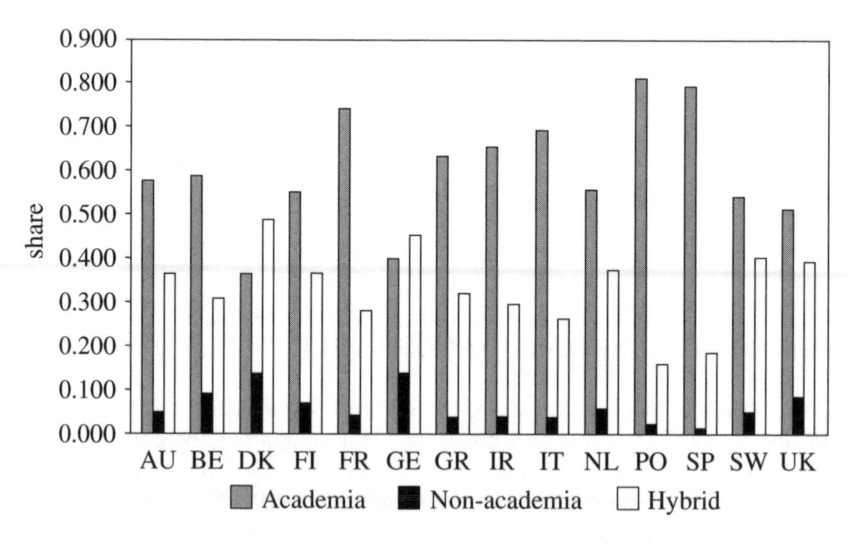

Figure 3.8 Collaboration types for all members of the European Union (all years)

Finally, with regard to the nature of national systems, the share of collaborations between different types of actors is especially informative (Figure 3.8). Again we see Portugal, Spain, France and Italy with a similar pattern. In these countries, the share of collaborations within academia is highest and little interaction exists with institutions outside academia. Germany, Denmark, UK, Sweden and the Netherlands have the largest involvement of non-academic institutions, which network often both with one another and with academia. This suggests that the national biotechnology systems in these countries perform relatively well in terms of organizing collaboration, and hereby, knowledge creation and diffusion.

5. SUMMARY AND DISCUSSION

We have shown how to characterize the geography of research collaboration at different spatial levels of analysis using data on the United States and the EU15. We conclude that the emphasis on the geography of collaborative networks rather than knowledge production, as the main vehicle of knowledge creation and diffusion, is supported by the fact that collaboration itself is a proliferating phenomenon. Using a number of indicators regarding the geography and nature of collaboration, we obtain an informative picture of the major similarities and differences between countries or groups of countries. A number of stylized facts have been collected including the increasing importance of internationalization, the dominance of academia in the EU compared to the US, the relatively localized nature of hybrid collaboration, and the existence of northern and southern clubs in Europe. These patterns probably confirm earlier expectations, yet these had never been shown to be true.

Unfortunately, we have been limited to analysing data on rather high levels of spatial aggregation in both the EU and the US. Given the lack of postal codes in the Web of Science database, the main data requirement for future research is to aggregate the addresses into low geographical unites (for example, NUTS 3 level regions). Only then can truly regional analysis be carried out.

Given the richness of the data available from the Web of Science, and the theoretical considerations that have been discussed above, one can think of a number of research questions to address in future research on the geography of research collaboration. First, one expects agglomeration economies to be present in regions hosting a high number of research organizations specialized in a particular discipline. Using the citation impact of publications at the state level in the United States, such effects have indeed been found (cf. Frenken and van Oort, 2003). However, from the recent, but by now robust literature on the geography of innovation literature we hypothesize that the relevant level of agglomeration and the economies that arise from it, is lower than the state or country in both the US and Europe. More research is needed on this topic, first of all rendering the data collection requirements to be more time-consuming and complex. Second, it needs to be addressed to what extent these economies can be explained by collaboration patterns between organizations rather than to proximity per se (Breschi and Lissoni, 2002). Thirdly, it needs to be assessed whether divergence or convergence between research inputs and output in regions occurs, and to what extent these patterns can be explained by institutional differences, agglomeration effects at local and regional levels or in (hierarchical, centrality-based) networks of research collaboration.

And, finally, we are in need of (quantitative) assessment of the impact of science and technology policies on the success of regional science systems. In particular, have the framework programmes of the European Union indeed led to a strengthening of the knowledge base of less favoured regions, being one of the objectives of the Commission? Or, possibly, has increased collaboration also led to increased mobility causing a brain-drain from less favoured regions towards the central European nodes of scientific knowledge production? These are some of the most urgent research questions that need to be addressed in current and future research.

NOTES

1. We would like to thank Hans van Amsterdam at the Netherlands Institute for Spatial Research (RPB) in The Hague for his valuable assistance in data handling, and Friso de Vor for his research assistance.
2. All entries have been manually checked.

BIBLIOGRAPHY

Acs, Z.J. (2002), *Innovation and the Growth of Cities*, Cheltenham, UK and Northampton, MA, USA: Edward Elgar.

Audretsch, D.B., and M.P. Feldman (1996), 'R&D spillovers and the geography of innovation and production', *American Economic Review*, **86** (3), 630–40.

Breschi, S., and F. Lissoni (2001), 'Knowledge spillovers and local innovation systems: a critical survey', *Industrial and Corporate Change*, **10**, 975–1005.

Breschi, S., and F. Lissoni (2002), 'Mobility and social networks: localised knowledge spillovers revisited', paper presented to the workshop Clusters in High-Technology: Aerospace, Biotechnology and Software Compared', Montreal, November.

Caniels, M.C.J., and H.A. Romijn (2003), 'What drives innovativeness in industrial clusters? Transcending the debate', paper presented at the Regional Studies Association conference, Pisa: 12–15 April.

Cohen, W.M., and D.A. Levinthal (1990), 'Absorptive capacity: a new perspective on learning and innovation', *Administrative Science Quarterly*, **35** (1), 128–52.

Cooke, P., M.G. Uranga, and G. Etxebarria (1997), 'Regional innovation systems: institutional and organisational dimensions', *Research Policy*, **26** (4–5), 475–91.
Dalpé, R. (2002), 'Bibliometric analysis of biotechnology', *Scientometrics*, **55** (2), 189–213.
Danell, R, and O. Persson (2003), 'Regional R&D activities and interactions in the Swedish triple helix', *Scientometrics*, **58** (2), 205–18.
Dasgupta, P., and P.A. David (1994), 'Toward a new economics of science', *Research Policy*, **23**, 487–521.
Etzkowitz, H., and L. Leydesdorff (2000), 'The dynamics of innovation: from national systems and "Mode 2" to a triple helix of university–industry–government relations', *Research Policy*, **29**, 109–23.
Feldman, M.P. (1999), 'The new economics of innovation, spillovers and agglomeration: a review of empirical studies', *Economics of Innovation and New Technology*, **8**, 5–25.
Feser, E.J. (2002), 'Tracing the sources of local external economies', *Urban Studies*, **39** (13), 2485–506.
Frenken, K. (2002a), 'A new indicator of European integration and an application to collaboration in scientific research', *Economic Systems Research*, **14** (4), 345–61.
Frenken, K. (2002b), 'Europeanisation of science', *Journal of Economic and Social Geography* (Tijdschrift voor Economische en Sociale Geografie), **93** (5), 561–68.
Frenken, K., and F.G. van Oort (2003), 'The geography of research collaboration in US aerospace engineering and US biotechnology and applied microbiology', paper presented at the third European Meeting on Applied Evolutionary Economics (EMAEE), University of Augsburg 9–12 April.
Glaeser, E.L. (1999), 'Learning in cities', *Journal of Urban Economics*, **46**, 254–77.
Glaeser, E.L., H.D. Kallal, J.A. Scheinkman, and A. Schleifer (1992), 'Growth in cities', *Journal of Political Economy*, **100**, 1126–52.
Graham, S., and S. Marvin (2001), *Splintering Urbanism. Networked Infrastructures, Technological Mobilities and the Urban Condition*, London: Routledge.
Howells, J.R.L. (2002), 'Tacit knowledge, innovation and economic geography', *Urban Studies*, **39** (5–6), 871–84.
Jaffe, A.B. (1989), 'Real effects of academic research', *American Economic Review*, **79** (5), 957–70.
Jaffe, A.B., M. Trajtenberg, and R. Henderson (1993), 'Geographic localization of knowledge spillovers as evidenced by patent citations', *Quarterly Journal of Economics*, **108** (3), 577–98.
Katz, J.S. (1994), 'Geographical proximity and scientific collaboration', *Scientometrics*, **31**, 31–43.
Katz, J.S., and B.R. Martin (1997), 'What is research collaboration?', *Research Policy*, **26** (1), 1–18.
Klepper, S. (2001), 'Employee start-ups in high-tech industries', *Industrial and Corporate Change*, **10**, 639–74.
Leydesdorff, L., and S.E. Cozzens (1993), 'The delineation of specialities in terms of journals using the dynamic journal set of the SCI', *Scientometrics*, **26** (1), 135–56.
Liang, L.M., and L. Zhu (2002), 'Major factors affecting China's inter-regional research collaboration: regional scientific productivity and geographical proximity', *Scientometrics*, **55** (2), 287–316.
Rosenberg, N. (1990), 'Why do firms do basic research (with their own money)?', *Research Policy*, **19**, 165–74.

Rosenthal, S.S., and W.C. Strange (2001), 'The determinants of agglomeration', *Journal of Urban Economics*, **59**, 191–229.

Van Oort, F.G. (2002), *Agglomeration, Economic Growth and Innovation*, Rotterdam: Tinbergen Institute Research Series.

Van Oort, F.G. (2003), *Urban Growth and Innovation*, Aldershot: Ashgate.

Verbeek, A., K. Debackere, and M. Luwel (2003), 'Science cited in patents: a geographic "flow" analysis of bibliographic citation patterns in patents', *Scientometrics*, **58** (2), 241–63.

Wagner, C.S. (2002), 'International linkages: is collaboration creating a new dynamic for knowledge creation in science?', manuscript, Amsterdam School of Communications Research, University of Amsterdam, The Netherlands.

Wagner-Doebler, R. (2001), 'Continuity and discontinuity of collaboration behaviour since 1800 – from a bibliometric point of view', *Scientometrics*, **52**, 503–17.

APPENDIX

Source: Web of Science, Institute of Scientific Information, www.isinet.com
Date: 16-01-03 for US data and 24-05-03 for EU data
Category Name: Biotechnology & Applied Microbiology

Category Description: The Biotechnology & Applied Microbiology category includes resources on a number of subjects that relate to the exploitation of living organisms or their components. In CC/AB&ES, the emphasis is on applied biology, including industrial microbiology. Applications include industrial chemicals and enzymes, biosensors, bioelectronics, pesticide development, food, flavour and fragrance industry applications, waste treatment, and pollution bioremediation.

Journals: Acta Biotechnologica, Applied Microbiology and Biotechnology, Biochemical Engineering Journal, Biodegradation, Biofutur, Biomass & Bioenergy, Bioprocess and Biosystems Engineering, Bioresource Technology, Biosensors & Bioelectronics, Biotechnology Advances, Biotechnology and Applied Biochemistry, Biotechnology and Bioengineering, Biotechnology Letters, Biotechnology Progress, Canadian Journal of Microbiology, Critical Reviews in Biotechnology, Current Opinion in Microbiology, Cytotechnology, Enzyme and Microbial Technology, Extremophiles, Folia Microbiologica, Food Technology and Biotechnology, Journal of Bioscience and Bioengineering, Journal of Biotechnology, Journal of Chemical Technology and Biotechnology, Journal of Industrial Microbiology & Biotechnology, Letters in Applied Microbiology, Metabolic Engineering, Nature Biotechnology, Process Biochemistry, Seibutsu-Kogaku Kaishi, Trends in Biotechnology, World Journal of Microbiology & Biotechnology, Yeast.

4. Knowledge Intensive Business Services and regional development: consultancy in city regions in Norway

Heidi Wiig Aslesen

I. INTRODUCTION

The knowledge economy reflects the tendency for economic competitiveness to be more linked up to new ways of producing, using and combining diverse knowledge, than to certain industries or technologies per se. The term is also related to the acceleration and complexity of technological change, and to the growth of demand for advanced knowledge and skills by firms. Firms' ability to make use of information, to create and to manage knowledge, is a critical factor in the knowledge economy and makes innovation an important driving force. Innovation processes are now regarded as complex and dynamic and a result of cumulative dynamic interaction and learning processes involving many actors; they are also characterized by innovation in non-technological areas, especially in services and new forms of organizations. This widening of the innovation concept puts emphasis on more diverse knowledge requirements by firms, putting firms' learning capacity at the centre. The knowledge economy therefore puts a quantitative and qualitative shift in the demand and need for knowledge and learning.

Knowledge Intensive Business Services (KIBS) are services concerned with the supply and management of knowledge and intangible assets (so-called 'knowledge-about-knowledge'). This group of firms has experienced enormous growth in the last decade[1] (see Miles, 2003 and Wood, 2002), especially among the computer industry and management consultancy. The growth has been confined especially to city areas, suggesting that this is where the demand–supply interaction is best developed (Daniels, 1991; Howells, 1988; Marshall, 1988), contributing to making geographic location (that is, larger cities and urban areas) increasingly important. The growth of KIBS is often used as an indicator of the more general structural changes projected by the knowledge economy. KIBS are often seen as a driving force behind the spread of new knowledge in the innovation system, through information and communication technologies (ICT) and new ways of organizing industrial activity (post-Fordist principles). KIBS are thus supposed to make a distinctive contribution to enhance competitiveness and innovation in other industries. As producers of intermediate inputs they are also perceived to play the role as bridging institutions in innovation systems.

The thesis in this chapter is that KIBS play an increasingly important role in the knowledge based economy by creating, transforming and spreading knowledge. The aim of this chapter is to look more closely into *how and for what kinds of firms* KIBS may contribute to regional development through knowledge generation and diffusion.

Focus

The focus of this chapter is on a particular type of KIBS firm, namely Management Consultants and Technical Consultants[2] (hereafter referred to as Consultants), which is one of the largest sub-groups among the so-called KIBS[3] actors. The sub-group is also among the fastest growing industries in Norway (Braadland, 2000). Firstly, this chapter examines how these actors relate and link up with external actors in their own knowledge creating processes and secondly how they exploit and diffuse knowledge in the innovation system through their clients. Consultants are expected to influence business change and innovation by conveying and adapting technical and managerial experience to their clients. Management consultancy is a knowledge industry founded upon transfer of management models, theories and procedures that are created in universities, large consultancy companies or within client organizations (Bryson, 2000); they are important suppliers of non-technological innovations. The decision to focus on Consultants is made on the basis of the assumption that these intermediate service actors play an important role in innovation in firms and therefore play an important role in regional development.

The main questions of the chapter are:

1. How do KIBS contribute to regional development processes?
2. In what way(s) are they important for the generation of knowledge in client firms?

Method and Data[4]

This chapter is based on three main sources: 1) A telephone survey of knowledge intensive firms in city regions in Norway, with responses from 800 different types of 'knowledge firms', including 200 Consultants and 200 potential Consultancy clients. The respondents are found in three city areas in

Norway, (i) the Oslo region, (ii) the three largest city regions in Norway (after Oslo), and (iii) a group of medium sized cities in Norway. 2) Face-to-face interviews with 13 firm leaders in Consultancy firms in Oslo, including a number of the largest global actors. 3) Data from 'Statistics Norway's Central Register of Establishments and Enterprises' are used to describe the distribution of firms and employment in Consultancy by region.

This chapter is organized as follows: Section II discusses main characteristics of the knowledge economy focusing especially on the role played by KIBS in the innovation system in an 'urban' economy. Section III presents empirical evidence from KIBS firms in city areas of Norway in order to assess if or how such firms contribute to regional development processes. Section IV concludes the chapter by summarizing and discussing theoretical assumptions and empirical evidence.

II. KNOWLEDGE ECONOMY AND REGIONAL DEVELOPMENT

This section describes the role of Knowledge Intensive Business Services in the knowledge economy; further, it focuses on why these knowledge intensive activities seem to cluster in city areas. Lastly this section looks into the specificity of the KIBS–client interaction and asks whether KIBS supply always means learning and knowledge acquisition for the client.

KIBS in the Knowledge Economy

There are different definitions of the concept the 'knowledge economy'; one important feature seems to be the focus on the de-materialization of production. Jones (2002) argues that the economy is becoming 'informationalized', and KIBS are seen as playing a leading role since they are involved in knowledge production and use in a rapidly changing world of increasing complexity and uncertainty. The knowledge economy is therefore an innovation driven economy where innovation is seen as a social, spatially embedded, interactive learning process that cannot be understood independently of its institutional context (cf. Braczyk et al. 1998; Lundvall 1992; Freeman 1998). Important elements in the learning economy remain specific and tacit and rooted in specific organizations, indicating that the knowledge economy is characterized by new forms of knowledge creation and diffusion, which is less dominated by technology (Gibbons et al., 1996). The increasing interdependence of technological and organizational change is a significant feature of systems of innovation in the knowledge economy. Increased interest in non-technological innovations is associated with the connection between the organizational innovation and firms' learning capacity, making organizational learning processes more important for creating and maintaining competitiveness. A further characterization is the increasing innovation in services and new forms of work and firm organizations (Strambach, 2002), suggesting that innovation is not only restricted to research and technology intensive areas.

This changed understanding of the innovation concept and processes is an important element in the knowledge economy and has made quantitative and qualitative shifts in the need and demand for knowledge in business. Vital requirements in the knowledge economy are linked to economic, technological and socio-cultural knowledge and competence, indicating the need for multidisciplinary application and problem oriented knowledge in innovation systems. An indicator of these changes can be linked to the spectacular growth in economic transactions relating to knowledge (Maskell and Malmberg, 1999; Antonelli, 1999), and to the rapid growth of KIBS as referred to earlier. KIBS are therefore looked upon as important elements in a knowledge economy and represent a vital part of a well-functioning innovation system; their main 'input' is knowledge (notably, professionally qualified labour) and their main 'output' is knowledge (however, only weakly measured). Strambach (2002) has linked KIBS to the innovation system in that they:

- Transfer knowledge in the form of expert technological knowledge and management know-how
- Exchange empirical knowledge and best practice from different branch contexts
- Integrate different stocks of knowledge and competencies that exist in innovation systems
- Adapt existing knowledge to the specific needs of the client.

Both formal and informal networks and cooperation are essential for the functioning of KIBS and this is an indication of their integration function.

KIBS in cities

This shift in modes of production, as referred to above, seems to privilege the information-rich environment of cities. In addition there is the trend towards vertical disintegration and increased specialization of firms which also favour the return of cities as production sites where agglomeration is helping to reduce the transaction cost and increase the information flow (MacLeod et al., 2003). This increased demand for services in all industries is a key aspect of the growing importance of cities (Sassen, 2000). In the 'new' economy cities stand out as centres for service-based activities and emerging knowledge-intensive industries (Cooke 2002; Cooke et al., 2002). The concentration of KIBS in core metropolitan regions seems to be independent of the innovation systems that prevail in the cities. KIBS are said to have much in common with organizations within the public knowledge infrastructure (Gadrey and Gallouj, 2002). It is argued that KIBS develop into an informal (private) 'second knowledge infrastructure', according to Cooke et al. (2002), a 'private system of innovation' (PSI) is emerging on the basis of this 'new' economy. 'In and near the great cities are found a rich private infrastructure of innovation support whose presence has become particularly visible during the period of emergence and consolidation of the "new economy"'.

Cities have long been described as centres for transactions; changes that are reflected in theories of agglomeration. These theories now put less weight on physical transport and communication costs but increasingly emphasize the significance of *immaterial transactions* when explaining the innovation advantages of cities, such as 'face to face' contact with business partners. Other important locational factors are highly qualified labour, which to a lesser degree want to work outside city areas; the same holds for more qualitative resources such as an active and dynamic business environment. Another factor that can explain city location is the more strategic motivation linked to competition in particular markets, leading to co-location in the same geographical area as the market leader ('follow the leader'). The status linked to being located in a certain area can also be seen as an explanatory factor for city location, suggesting that location is not just a matter of pure economic considerations, in the first instance, but also more symbolic capital. Such immobile resources, the phenomena of density, agglomeration and proximity are features that may explain why KIBS tend to concentrate in larger cities.

KIBS–client interaction and innovation

KIBS are defined as private sector firms providing knowledge based services to other business and non-business organizations,[5] and the knowledge they provide is strategic, technical and professional advice mainly employing the skills of information gathering, processing, and in particular interpretation of information. KIBS are significant because they offer specialist knowledge to other organizations in a rapidly changing, increasingly uncertain, and internationally oriented economic environment (Wood, 2002). KIBS are highly innovative in their own right but perhaps more important is the function of facilitating learning and innovation among their clients in other economic sectors. Consultants' knowledge comes from experience gained from a large, empirically validated and highly varied knowledge base (Creplet et al., 2001), and from codified sources. This knowledge is used to meet clients' needs, and KIBS can be seen as immaterial firms working out problem solving activities and organizational change, much reliant on the cognitive ability of their employees (or knowledge workers). Consultants can solve clients' problems either by providing them with *a set of solutions* that have to be matched to firms' problems or when clients cannot identify their own problems, conceptualizing the specific pattern of the problem before trying to solve is. These services are intensively tailored to the specific needs of the clients, and client participation is a fundamental characteristic of knowledge intensive services.

Terms used to denote the link between the service provider and client are numerous (interface, interaction, co-production, 'servuction' (Gallouj, 2002, p. 39), socially regulated service relationship, service relationship). The service providers acquire both explicit and tacit knowledge about the customer firms that enables them to adapt innovative problem solutions to the specific requirements of the organization and to integrate them into the clients' firm structure and culture. Two types of competencies are operative in the KIBS–client process; those of the service provider and those of the client. Gallouj (2002) indicates three reasons for looking more closely at the client–provider interface:

1. It may be the subject of innovations (organizational changes, interface management methods and so on)
2. It is the 'laboratory' where a form of innovation often neglected in economic analysis (ad hoc innovation) is initiated
3. The quality of the client firm's competencies is one criterion for the success of innovation and technology transfer

The purchase of business services, therefore, may affect the functioning of both service and manufacturing firms. However, there are few detailed case studies that actually have looked into the dynamics of the interaction between KIBS and their clients, and have explored how knowledge is managed and transferred across the KIBS–client boundary. However, Webb (2002) has carried out an explorative study focusing exactly on these processes, and he concludes that if KIBS are to influence their clients' technological trajectory, the clients must learn how to manage the knowledge and the innovation process associated with the 'service package'. His case studies show that if KIBS are to play a role, the client is much dependent on appropriate knowledge management practices to maintain new knowledge in the organization. These findings draw attention to the fact that the ability of KIBS to influence their clients' knowledge generating processes might vary enormously. The prerequisites of a successful learning process between KIBS and the client challenge the view of these service providers as *always being* 'innovation agents' (Metcalfe and Miles, 2000) for their clients.

The dynamics and quality of interaction between KIBS and their clients are also important if KIBS are to play a role towards learning and innovation. KIBS' impact on the innovation performance and productivity of an economic system will also depend on the relative share of knowledge intensive industries in the national economy, and the type of inter-sectoral linkages that exist between KIBS and manufacturing/services (Windrum and Tomlinson, 1999).

III. KIBS AS KNOWLEDGE GENERATORS IN THE REGIONAL ECONOMY

This section first gives an overview of the location pattern of KIBS activity in city areas in Norway, followed by a short characterization of consultancy actors in the Oslo region. Thereafter it examines the role and activities of Consultants, based on in-depth interviews with consultancy firms and on survey results.[6] It focuses on how Consultants act as economic agents, and how they receive and spread knowledge in the regional economy. Finally, it presents empirical evidence to highlight whether and how they are important for the generation of knowledge in client firms.

Consultancy Activity in Norwegian City Regions

This chapter focuses on Consultants as a sub-category of KIBS and particularly in city regions. The location pattern of 'Other business activities' in Norway is clearly skewed towards city regions. The Oslo region is clearly overrepresented both with regard to number of firms and number of employees within 'Other business activities' (see Tables 4.1 and 4.2). As much as 39.6 per cent of the firms are located within the Oslo region; the figures are significantly higher than for other city regions in Norway. Hordaland (with the city of Bergen) is in second place and third is Sør-Trøndelag (with the city of Trondheim) with 8 per cent and 6.6 per cent respectively. Oslo is in a class of its own with regard to these industries, and it is far ahead of the other large cities in Norway. The growth of firms has also been slightly stronger in the Oslo region than in rest of the country.

Consultancy activity in the Oslo region can roughly be divided into two main categories: 1) Global Management Consultants (MCs) and 2) Regional Management Consultants.

Global MCs have extended their presence throughout Europe over the last 20 years through branches and subsidiaries. Many of the largest MC firms are present in Norway, normally established through mergers and acquisitions of regional consultancy activity. These are firms that are specialized in certain main MC activities (Boston Consulting group, McKinsey, A.T. Kearney, Booz Allen & Hamilton), and multifunctional firms (like KPMG, Cap Gemini and Ernst and Young). These major players have expanded their core skills in recent years from accountancy and computing into more general, and often

Table 4.1 Regional distribution of firms in 'Other business services' (NACE 74) (2001)

Industries	**NACE**	**Total**	**Relative share of firms (%)**				
		Norway	**Oslo region**	**Hordaland**	**Rogaland**	**Sør-Trøndelag**	**Rest of the country**
Other business activities	**74**	35914	39.6	8.0	6.6	4.9	40.8
Sum Business Services*	**All**	70053	35.2	8.7	7.2	5.1	43.9

Note: * Sum Business Services include NACE 70 + 71 + 72 + 73 + 74.

Source: Statistics Norway's Central Register of Establishments and Enterprises

Table 4.2 Regional distribution of employment in 'Other business services' (NACE 74) (2001)

Industries	**NACE**	**Sum Norway employment**	**Relative share of employees (%)**				
			Oslo region	**Hordaland**	**Rogaland**	**Sør-Trøndelag**	**Rest of the country**
Other business activities	**74**	160765	46.1	8.4	8.1	5.4	32.1
Sum Business Services*	**All**	234685	47.7	8.3	7.5	6.0	30.5

Note: * Sum Business Services include NACE 70 + 71 + 72 + 73 + 74.

Source: Statistics Norway's Central Register of Establishments and Enterprises

more profitable, consultancy work. They address clients that are often themselves MNCs, some of them with headquarters located in the Oslo region.

Regionally based MCs have spun out from existing activity – mainly in the Oslo region. The many small and medium sized consultancies, including sole practitioners, are often found within 'niches', based on their 'local knowledge'. The regionally based consultancy firms also have nationally based MNCs as their clients, providing them with supplementary services. The regional Consultants have experienced positive development in recent years. What they lack in their 'service portfolio' is being compensated for by strategic alliances and networks (often with competitors) which make them able to take on larger projects. Nevertheless, the large global MCs still have the largest turnover, number of assignments and number of employees in the region.

Table 4.3 gives brief characteristics of the Global and Regional MCs in Oslo.

Table 4.3 Two main categories of Management Consultants in the Oslo region

	Global Management Consultants	Regional Management Consultants
Originate	Originates mainly from the USA in the early 1920s	Mainly Oslo based firms developed in the 1970s and later
Expertise	IT and management	Follows up consultancy activities that are induced by global actors, can be seen as supplementary activities to global actors, specialization related to 'niches' and to 'local knowledge'
Analytical level	Often directed towards MNC and CEO and top management, and with focus on 'industry' level. Analytical level depended on core activities	Directed towards large firms, and top and middle manager, dependent on core activities. More focused towards the 'firm' level
Client base	MNC located in Oslo	Large firms in the Oslo region, also some medium sized firms located outside the Oslo region

Consultants in Regional Innovation Systems

Through our survey we found that Consultants serve the whole national market with their services. However, the *local* market is of great importance for Consultants, average sales being 43 per cent. Average sales to international markets are 17 per cent, significantly smaller than local sales, but Consultants perceive the competition experienced in international markets to be quite important for triggering competitiveness. A diversified portfolio of customers located locally, nationally and internationally, gives possibilities of knowledge diffusion, making Consultants important satellites and disseminators of information between clients at different spatial levels, thus emphasizing their integration function in innovation systems (Wood, 2002).

Some of the Consultants in our survey are global consultancy firms operating in city regions in Norway. Many of these actors are important spreaders of new consultancy products, methods and instruments developed through formal R&D functions of mother companies. The transformation process from tacit knowledge to standard products – which is easy to transmit – is said to be hastened by large international firms, fuelling the spread of global knowledge to national and local actors.

Table 4.4 How important are the following actors in developing the Consultants' competitiveness? (N = 199) (1= irrelevant and 6=of major importance)

	Average score
Competence within the firm or enterprise	5.6
Clients, customers	5.1
Suppliers	3.5
Competitors	3.5
Consultancy firms	2.8
Research institutes, universities, Higher education Institutions	2.7

Consultants' ability to exploit 'local' strengths seems to be an important prerequisite for consultancy competitiveness. Competence within the firm (Table 4.4) – mainly recruited locally – is the single most important factor for developing competitiveness. Human capital is the carrier of knowledge in KIBS (such as skills, experience and contacts), and Consultants thereby represent a localized pool of specialized expertise and knowledge in the regional innovation system. Application and context related knowledge and experience play an important role in KIBS' learning processes and in their competitiveness.

The most important *external* factors for developing competitiveness are clients and customers. Further, geographical proximity to customers is the most important factor explaining city location. The importance of proximity to clients emphasizes the tacit and explicit character of the services provided, services that are hard to transfer through distant relationships. Studies emphasize that horizontal flows of knowledge are more important in service industries than in manufacturing industries (König et al., 1996), and that innovation activity to a larger degree is based on external relationships (Kotschatzky, 1999). Further, the survey showed that private sector clients were perceived to be the most stimulating client group, while least important in this sense was public administration as a client group.

Linkages with research institutes, universities and other higher education institutions are perceived to have little impact on the development of Consultants' competitiveness. These findings suggest that targeted research and development activities in R&D departments have little relevance for the generation of these innovations. KIBS knowledge base is often more loosely formulated and codified and more based on cumulated experienced based knowledge through Consultants' customer projects. KIBS firms' innovation activities are in many studies characterized to be incremental, step-by-step processes, where new elements and combinations of services are a part of an overall, continuous process of development guided by the strategy of a firm (Scarborough and Lannon, 1989; Sundbo, 1997). This form of knowledge generation makes formal R&D projects between R&D units and the knowledge infrastructure less relevant.

Survey results also show that Consultants primarily search locally for the competence needed for innovation purposes. Only 22 per cent of the Consultants had to look elsewhere in the country for innovation competence, whereas 13 per cent of the consultancy firms had to look outside the country. The local dimension is therefore highly relevant for these Consultants' innovation activities; their most important knowledge 'input' is regionally based and their most important knowledge 'output' is regionally embedded.

Informal contacts and meetings with people working in the same business sector seem to be of crucial importance in order to sustain competitiveness. The availability of arenas for such informal meetings and the possibility for firms to meet colleagues informally is, in interviews with Consultants, perceived as a very important location factor. It provides the Consultants with the opportunity to keep up-to-date with developments, of being 'close to events' and accessing knowledge about market and technological trends, and for acquiring information about potential partners. These findings underline the fact that informal networks in city areas are important for information transfer between actors, confirming the importance of 'buzz' (Storper and Venables, 2002) being an advantage for industries with a knowledge base built upon tacit knowledge.

Our findings show that Consultants might be viewed as spreaders of global codified knowledge into the regional economy. Those Consultants that are a part of a multinational enterprise are able to spread working methods locally, emphasizing their role as 'diffusers of information' and may therefore be important for knowledge production in the region of location. Through having customers from regional, national and international markets they are able to spread 'best practice' between geographical levels. The local dimension is of greatest importance to Consultants' own generation of knowledge and innovation. This 'localism' indicates that Consultants' ability to receive global knowledge *and at the same time* to be able to adapt it to local circumstances is an important prerequisite for knowledge generation and diffusion in the regional economy.

Consultants and their Services

Consultancy firms' role in regional development is linked to their *ability* to provide services that clients need so that, indirectly, it can increase their clients' competitiveness and innovation activity. This is dependent on the client's ability to use the services provided in their own organizational learning processes. So who then uses consultants, and what for?

Our survey to potential consultancy users[7] showed that more than half the respondents (53 per cent) had, in the period of the last three years, made use of Consultants. However, there are differences between industries and size of firms in this regard. The use of Consultants is most common among R&D intensive firms, such as pharmaceutical firms and firms in telecommunication (67 per cent and 64 per cent respectively), and among firms with more than 20 employees (especially firms with 20–40 employees).[8] Other Norwegian studies (Aslesen and Isaksen, 2004) have looked at the relationship between the satisfaction with consultants as an information source in the innovation process, and enterprise size and R&D intensity, and found that the relationship is positive. This suggests that both use of Consultants and satisfaction with use of Consultants in relation to innovation, are to be found among certain actors in the regional economy; firms of a certain size that engage actively in long term strategic innovation. This implies that KIBS knowledge generating activities are limited to only a part of the innovation system, at first hand.

Interviews with Consultants reveal that the largest consultancy users in the Oslo region are headquarters of mature national firms, which have branches spread out in Norway. This implies that technical and management changes initiated by city headquarters are to be implemented exactly in divisions or departments located outside the city of Oslo. Consultants' work will thus have an effect not only locally, where most of the day-to-day interaction between consultant and clients takes place, but also outside the city. In this way local consultant activity in the city of Oslo will be part of national production systems as well.

Table 4.5 The main reason for clients to buy the Consultants' services (N = 94) (1= irrelevant and 6 = of major importance)

Sectors	Lack of relevant specialized knowledge	Lack internal capacity	Used in a time-limited project	Have good experiences with earlier use of consultants	Needs strategic counselling	Has a strategy towards buying such products/ services externally
All	5.1	4.5	4.5	4.4	3.8	3.6

The most important reason for consultancy use (Table 4.5) is lack of relevant specialized knowledge. We do not know what type of knowledge the clients lack, but through interviews we found that most consultancy use is directed towards more operational knowledge necessary for day-to-day operations, such as logistics, management and maintenance of machinery and equipment. The Consultant, defined as a knowledge worker, is challenged to use her high levels of education and specialist skills and combine these assets with the ability to identify and solve problems. In this way the Consultants deliver an interpretation of reality highly conditioned by the type of demand they face (Creplet et al., 2001); we do not know how successful this interpretation always is. 'Lack of internal capacity' and 'Time limited projects' are also important reasons for Consultancy use. This suggests that some of the services demanded could be linked to transactions that are low frequency (as opposed to high frequency), and that these transactions are to be externalized because internal provision under most circumstances would be too costly (Larsen, 2000). Maintaining an internal capability to perform low-frequency tasks would occupy too many resources. The second lowest score was given to 'Needs strategic counselling'. We understand this to be linked to more critical functions in the firms, and related to activities and functions that in the user firm's perception are core to its business and therefore to be kept internally.

More than two thirds of the consultancy users perceive proximity as a facilitating factor with regard to use of Consultants. The availability of Consultants locally is in this way an important prerequisite for consultancy use. Other studies have also pointed to consultancy clients' 'restricted search process' (Bryson and Daniels, 1998; Rusten, 2000), and relate it to the difficulty in determining the quality of the Consultants' expertise – which is intangible and difficult to measure. Knowledge intensive services cannot be readily demonstrated prior to production and consumption; this is often referred to as 'information asymmetries' that may affect the impact and effectiveness of the service provided by KIBS. Since the parties have very different degrees of information about the product that is traded, the question of trust is a significant one in such relationships (Miles, 2003). To be able to overcome this imperfect market, clients employ individuals and companies that the client already knows directly or indirectly (Rusten et al., 2004).

We were also interested to know whether Consultancy users also acquired core knowledge from KIBS. Core knowledge relates directly to the fundamental activities constituting the basis of the firm (Larsen, 2000) that have a direct impact on process and product development in the firm. When clients demand such services there is a high degree of uncertainty, since they include the necessity for transfer of knowledge and learning in the recipient firm. We therefore controlled for factors that affected firms' ability to receive and absorb core knowledge in consultancy projects. Client firms were asked in what ways the consultant had contributed to innovation related tasks in the firms, controlling for size and innovation cost intensity.[9]

Numerous firms responded that the questions were irrelevant, indicating that a large number of firms internalize activities related to core knowledge. Other studies also emphasize that consultants rarely are dominant forces in promoting innovations, but are catalysts of wider change (Wood, 2002). This is in many ways an obvious point since core knowledge must be mastered internally to be able to stay in business.

Firms that responded positively to whether Consultants had contributed to innovation related tasks in the firms, reported that the most important contribution is their ability to draw 'new professional and technological expertise' into the client firm. In this way Consultants have a role as a source of information and knowledge. This supports the notion that Consultants' extended range of expertise (acquired nationally or internationally) is used in local client firms (see Figure 4.1). Firms that have high shares of innovation costs and firms that are large gave a higher than average score to services such as 'new professional and technological expertise', the Consultant's contribution towards 'crystallizing needs in innovation activity' and towards giving the client 'a deeper understanding of the firm's core areas'. This suggests that the role of Consultants as advisers and co-producers of innovation is to some extent linked to internal capabilities of the client firms. Positive indirect effects of consultancy use can only arise as a result of organizational learning processes (Antonelli, 1998; De Bandt 1995) and characteristics such as size and innovation strategy could be important prerequisites for taking part in learning processes with KIBS.

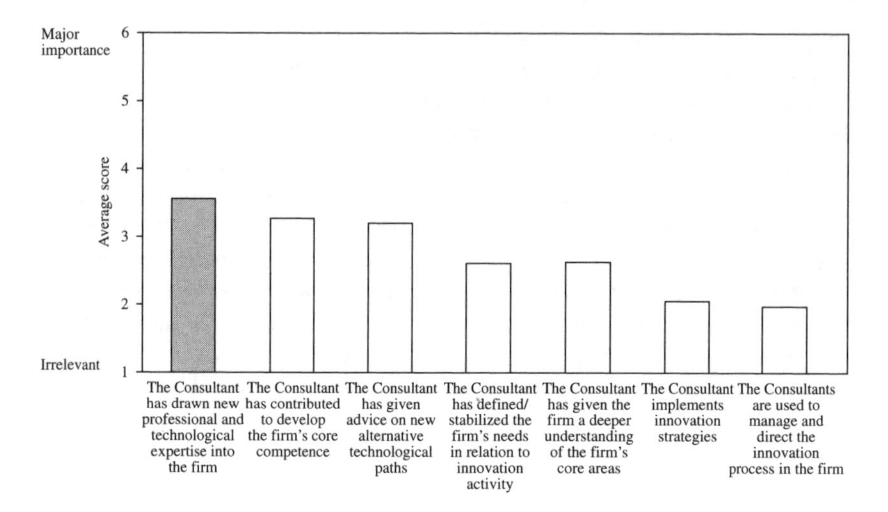

Figure 4.1 To what degree has the consultancy firm contributed to innovation related tasks in the firm? (N = 69)

IV. CONCLUSION

The thesis in this chapter is that KIBS play an increasingly important role in the innovation process in a knowledge based economy. The aim of this chapter was to look closer into how KIBS may contribute to regional development through knowledge generation and diffusion.

Empirical evidence clearly indicates the spatial clustering of KIBS in the larger cities in Norway. One of the most important agglomeration advantages cities represent for Consultants are static externalities like a large and demanding market, a pool of specialized labour and an active and dynamic business environment. However, Consultants have a diversified geographical set of clients in their portfolio, making them bridging institutions between regional and the national/international innovation systems through recycling of information and knowledge between clients. This intensifies dynamic externalities between different spatial levels. Consultants' ability to receive global knowledge and to adapt it to the local context is an important prerequisite for the exploitation of Consultants' knowledge in the regional economy.

The regional innovation system is an important contributor to knowledge creation and exploitation for KIBS which are much dependent on external relations in their own knowledge generating processes. However, the knowledge infrastructure seems to be less important as an agglomeration advantage for Consultants, possibly due to Consultants' knowledge base being founded more on cumulative experienced-based knowledge than structured R&D. Informal networks are of great importance to Consultants, emphasizing the importance of being located in city regions where 'light institutions' are dense and the 'buzz' intense.

Consultants contribute with different kinds of knowledge to client firms. Much of the knowledge contribution is linked to operational knowledge that helps clients overcome operational problems within fields in which the clients lack expertise or resources. Consultants' competitiveness is to a large degree linked to the human capital embedded in the knowledge workers, and therefore is reliant on the ability of their employees to combine skills and their ability to identify and solve problems. Our results show that Consultants can also contribute with knowledge more directed towards the firm's innovation activity, but, that the use of Consultants as co-producers of innovation is linked to certain background characteristics of firms; they are large and have an innovation strategy. Based on the presented empirical evidence it seems reasonable to conclude that Consultants play an important role as knowledge generators and spreaders in the knowledge economy, contributing to regional development. However, our results point to the fact that *a limited set of actors*, mainly firms of a certain size and firms with an innovation strategy, are the main users of consultants, especially for innovation purposes. Even with these background variables it is *never given* that consultancy use triggers learning and innovation. The knowledge generation process in a consultancy–client project is complex and seldom happens 'by accident'. More research into the complexities of project learning is needed.

NOTES

1. In Norway, computers and business consultancy was among the eight fastest growing industries from 1995–1999.
2. NACE 7414,74209,74202
3. Even though the term KIBS is often used, it is hard to find a precise definition, especially in statistical terms. Practical studies are often based on slightly different adaptations of established classification systems. In this chapter the following NACE classification seems relevant as defining KIBS; 642,671,672,721,722,723,724,725,726,741,742,743,744.
4. This chapter builds on an ongoing project about 'Big cities as driving forces behind the growth of "the new economy": A study of knowledge intensive business services' carried out for the Norwegian Research Council.
5. Peter Wood (2002) uses the term KIS (knowledge intensive services) with this definition, but says in his book that the terms are more or less synonymous.
6. The survey gathered information from 199 Consultants, 57 per cent are to be found among technical Consultants and 43 per cent among management Consultants. Most of the Consultants in the survey are to be found in the category of 5–19 employees, the management Consultants have a larger share of firms in this group than the technical Consultants, as much as 85 per cent, leaving few firms in the larger groups. Technical Consultants also have firms among the larger groups, 20 per cent of the firms have more than 20 employees.

7. The telephone survey was directed at four different business sectors, representing both knowledge intensive firms clustered in city areas in Norway (NACE 22,33,64) and not so knowledge intensive but large manufacturing sectors in city areas (especially Oslo, NACE 22). By selecting different business sectors, it might be possible to detect differences in the use and role of knowledge intensive business services in city areas, suggesting that these actors play different roles vis-à-vis different actors. Two hundred firms responded to the survey, of which 65 per cent were in 'Publishing, printing and reproduction of recorded media', and 22 per cent were found in 'Manufacture of medical, precision and optical instruments, watches and clocks'. There were also respondents from the pharmaceutical industry (6 per cent) and from actors within telecommunication (7 per cent).
8. It is important to have in mind that the survey was not a random stratified sample of industries and size of firms.
9. Innovation cost intensity is defined as innovation costs as a percentage of turnover. We approach the problem by constructing categories of firms, depending upon how much they spend on innovation inputs. We have constructed three categories, with innovation intensities 'less than 1 including 0', '1–3.99' and '4 or above'. These categories are somewhat arbitrary, and the choice of demarcation lines will affect the differences between the categories. The categories do, however, apply the same borderlines as used by the OECD to classify low, medium and high tech industries based on R&D expenses.

REFERENCES

Antonelli, C. (1998), 'Localized technological change, new information technology and the knowledge-based economy – the European evidence', *Journal of Evolutionary Economics*, pp. 177–98.

Antonelli, C. (1999), 'Localised knowledge perlocation processes and information networks', *Journal of Evolutionary Economics*, **6**, 281–95.

Aslesen, H., and A. Isaksen (2004), 'Kunnskapsintensive tjenester: Motor i storbyenes næringsliv?', in Vatne, E. (ed.), *Norske storbyers funksjon i norsk økonomi*, (forthcoming).

Braadland, T.E. (2000), *Norske vekstnæringer på 90-tallet*, STEP-report 6/2000.

Braczyk, H.-J., P. Cooke, and M. Heidenreich (eds) (1998), *Regional Innovation Systems*, London: UCL Press.

Bryson, J.R (2000), 'Spreading the message. Management consultants and the shaping of economic geographies in time and space', in J.R. Bryson, P.W. Daniels, N. Henry, and J. Pollard (eds), *Knowledge, Space, Economy*, London: Routledge.

Bryson, J.R., and P.W. Daniels (1998), 'Business link, strong ties and the walls of silence: small and medium-sized firms and external business service expertise', *Environment and Planning C: Government and Policy*, **16**, 265–80.

Cooke, P. (2002), *Knowledge Economies. Clusters, Learning and Cooperative Advantage*, London: Routledge.

Cooke, P., C. Davis, and R. Wilson, (2002), 'Innovation advantages of cities: from knowledge to equity in five basic steps', *European Planning Studies*, **10** (2).

Creplet, F. et al. (2001), 'Consultants and experts in management consulting firms', *Research Policy*, **30** (9).

Daniels, P. (1991), *Services and Metropolitan Development: International Perspectives*, London: Routledge, Chapman and Hall.

De Bandt, J. (1995), 'Indirect productivity of business services, through non-material investments', in G. Felli, F.C., Rosati, and G. Tria (eds), *The Service Sector: Productivity and Growth*, Heidelberg: Physica Verlag, pp. 157–73.

Freeman, C. (1998), 'The economics of technical change', in D. Archibugi and J. Mitchie (eds), *Trade, Growth and Technical Change*, Cambridge: Cambridge University Press, pp. 16–54.
Gadrey, J., and F. Gallouj (2002), *Productivity, Innovation and Knowledge in Services*, Cheltenham, UK and Northampton, MA, USA: Edward Elgar.
Gallouj, F. (2002), 'Knowledge-intensive business services: processing knowledge and producing innovation', in Jean Gadrey and F. Gallouj (eds), *Productivity, Innovation and Knowledge in Services*, Cheltenham, UK and Northampton, MA, USA: Edward Elgar.
Gibbons, M., C. Limoges, H. Nowotny, S. Schwartzman, P. Scott and M. Trow (1994), *The New Production of Knowledge: the Dynamics of Science and Research in Contemporary Societies*, London: Sage
Howells, J. (1988), *Economic, Technological and Locational Trends in European Services*, Aldershot: Gower.
Jones, A. (2002), 'The "global city" misconceived: the myth of "global management" in transnational service firms', *Geoforum*, **33**, 335–50.
König, H., M. Kuku, and G. Licht (1996), 'Kooperationsverhalt von Unternehmen des Dienstleistungssektors', in E. Helmstäder, G. Poser, and H.J. Ramser (eds), *Beiträge zur angewandten Wirtshaftsforschung, Festschrift für Karl Heinrich Oppenländer*, Berlin: Duncker und Hunmblot, pp. 217–43.
Kotschatzky, K. (1999), 'Innovation networks of industry and business-related services-relations between innovation intensity of firms and regional inter-firm cooperation', *European Planning Studies*, **7** (6), 737–57.
Larsen, J.N. (2000), 'Supplier–user interaction in knowledge-intensive business services: types of expertise and modes of organisations', in B Miles and I. Miles (eds), *Services and the Knowledge Based Economy*, London: Continuum.
Lundvall, B.-Å. (1992), *National Systems of Innovations – Towards A Theory of Innovation and Interactive Learning*, London: Pinter Publishers.
MacLeod, G., M. Raco, and K. Ward (2003), 'Negotiating the contemporary city: Introduction', *Urban Studies*, **40** 1655–71.
Marshall, J. N. (1988), *Services and Uneven Development*, Oxford: Oxford University Press.
Maskell, P. and A. Malmberg (1999), 'Localised learning and industrial competitiveness', *Cambridge Journal of Economics*, **23**, 167–85.
Metcalfe, J.S., and I. Miles (eds) (2000), Innovation Systems in the Service Economy: Measurement and Case Study Analysis, Dordrecht: Kluwer.
Miles, I. (2003), 'Knowledge Intensive Services' Suppliers and Clients', Ministry of Trade and Industry, Finland, studies and reports 15/2003.
Rusten, G. (2000), 'Geography of outsourcing: business service provision among firms in Norway', *Tijdschrift voor Economische en Sociale Geografie*, 9 (12), 122–34.
Rusten, G., H. Gammelsæter and J.R. Bryson (2004), 'Combinational and dislocated knowledges and the Norwegian client consultant relationship', Service Industries Journal 2004 no. 1, 155–70.
Sassen, S. (2000), 'Cities in the global economy', in Paddison, R. (ed.), *Handbook of Urban Studies*, London: Sage Publication, pp. 256–72.
Scarborough, H., and R. Lannon (1989), 'The management of innovation in the financial service sector: a case study', *Journal of Marketing Management*, **5** (1), 51–62.

Storper, M., and A.J. Venables (2002), 'Buzz: the economic force of the city', paper presented at the DRUID Summer Conference, 6–8 June Copenhagen.
Strambach, S. (2002), 'Change in the innovation process: new knowledge production and competitive cities – the case of Stuttgart', *European Planning Studies*, **10** (2).
Sundbo, J. (1997), 'Management of innovation in services', *The Service Industries Journal*, **17** (3), 432–55.
Webb, I. (2002), 'Knowledge management in the KIBS–client environment: a case study approach', PREST discussion paper series, September.
Windrum, P., and M. Tomlinson (1999), 'Knowledge-intensive services and international competitiveness: a four country comparison', *Technology Analysis and Strategic Management*, **11** (3), 391–408.
Wood, P. (2002), *Consultancy and Innovation: The Business Service Revolution in Europe*, London and New York: Routledge.

5. The cluster as a nexus of knowledge creation

Mark Lorenzen and Peter Maskell

1. INTRODUCTION

Current wisdom has it that many industrial clusters around the world mainly exist because they facilitate *localized knowledge creation* across incumbent firms. While frequently illustrated by case studies and other anecdotal documentation, most will probably agree that the jury is still sitting and that it will probably take a while before we have sufficiently solid empirical evidence to prove or discharge this widespread assertion.

The main aim of the present chapter is to contribute to the refinement of a few selected conceptual categories deemed crucial for subsequent empirical testing of knowledge-based cluster hypotheses. We confine ourselves to situations where knowledge creation in a cluster is *not* university-driven but takes place in an interactive way across firms engaged in traditional manufacturing or service industries – in particular consumer goods and services – even if sometimes heavily supported by local research and educational institutions. The essence of such clusters is thus the localized knowledge creation processes taking place in inter-firm relations and transactions on local markets.

A theoretical focus on the transaction costs of market relations (Coase, 1937; Dahlman, 1979; Storper, 1995) may help explain a general propensity for vertically disintegrated industries to cluster, but still leave us unable to understand if there are aspects of *knowledge creation* activities in market relations that are more sensitive to distance than other activities taking place on the market (such as, for example, outsourcing in order to take advantage of comparative advantages). In other words, before we can understand clustered knowledge creation as a result of market relations, we need to be clear on what knowledge creation is, and how market relations may help in the process while taking into account both aspects of cost and uncertainty.

The chapter is structured as follows. The next section focuses on two categories of knowledge creation that are both based on market relations and often found in clusters: incremental knowledge creation through spillovers, and experimental knowledge creation through projects. Section 3 then explains why clustering propagates both these knowledge creation activities. Section 4 illustrates our argument by presenting case study evidence of clustered knowledge creation in the pop music and furniture industries, and section 5 concludes the chapter.

2. INCREMENTAL AND EXPERIMENTAL KNOWLEDGE CREATION

In this section, we discuss knowledge creation as it happens in two particular and significant forms of market relations among firms: incremental knowledge creation through vertical and horizontal spillovers, and experimental knowledge creation through project relations.

Incremental Knowledge Creation

Since Bengt-Åke Lundvall's (1985) seminal contribution, much of the literature on inter-firm learning has focused on vertical relations where interaction among specialized users and producers helps them to solve problems beyond the ability of each individual firm, 'pushing' and 'pulling' knowledge – and incentives for change – along the value chain (Rosenberg, 1972; Freeman, 1982; 1991).

Håkansson (1987) investigates the *long-term* aspect of such relations, arguing that knowledge spillovers may over time facilitate in-depth changes in the firms involved. Many vertical market relations are, however, of only short duration and serve to make firms *flexible*, rather than facilitate dedicated investments and in-depth learning (Piore and Sabel, 1984). Nevertheless, they have potential for facilitating knowledge spillovers as shifting market relations among firms serve to spread around an abundance of broad information on different issues. Hence, flexible vertical relations serve as inspiration for smaller and less focused incremental knowledge creation, such as additions to or minor changes of product designs.

Firms do not only learn from interacting with partners that possess complementary but different competencies along the vertical dimension of the value chain (Richardson, 1972). Many important knowledge spillovers take place along the horizontal dimension where firms with similar competencies monitor the efforts and performance of their closest competitors (Maskell, 2001a), or informally trade their knowledge (von Hippel, 1998). As the knowledge exchanged in such market relations is, again, in-breadth rather than in-depth, horizontal knowledge spillovers mostly facilitate incremental learning and technological changes.

Experimental Knowledge Creation

In some industries, knowledge creation has to be more radical because of *uncertainty* (Knight, 1921) in terms of unforeseeable changes in technology, supply and demand. In particular, high demand uncertainty raises a range of problems related to knowledge creation (such as how to identify and advance product and process innovations and improvements that can match unforeseeable market demands), as well as problems related to cost and time efficiency (such as how to efficiently respond to unforeseeable demand volumes, through varying production volumes and product varieties).

In such industries, firms need regularly to redefine vital aspects of their product, through targeted *experimentation* (Nelson and Winter, 1982; Rosenberg, 1992; Foss and Foss, 2002). Experimentation can be seen as open-ended invention and testing of new products and marketing methods, on uncertain markets, over limited (if often flexible) test periods. Industries where knowledge creation takes place through experimentation encompass those dominated by non-continuous production (such as construction), highly ambiguous consumer tastes (for example fashion, film, music) or customization (advertisement, consultancy, and so on), where unique and highly customized products have to be created within a definite timeframe. In these industries, firms with highly complementary capabilities constantly and concurrently form new *temporary* vertical market relations because this enables them to find solutions to a specific customer's demand within a definitive period (Goodman and Goodman, 1976; Ekstedt et al., 1999; Hobday, 2000; Grabher, 2002). Such *project relations* are particularly suited for 'not keeping losers for too long' and for 'not losing winners' (Carlsson and Eliasson, 2001, 6).

3. CLUSTERING AND KNOWLEDGE CREATION

In this section, we outline some reasons why firms, when engaged in experimental and incremental knowledge creation, have a propensity to cluster geographically.

Networks vs. Clusters

Networks and clusters are different ways of *organizing the market* in order to accomplish particular tasks and reap particular benefits.[1]

Firms build long-term, stable network relations to lower transaction costs and facilitate knowledge exchange (Demsetz, 1968; Wilson, 1975) and by doing so they create a certain structuring of the market. Many networks begin with 'dyadic' (that is, bilateral) relations between two firms and may expand to encompass a growing number of partners, by utilizing investments in already existing relationships as channels to new partners (your-friend-is-my-friend). Organizing the market through network building is basically a process of intensifying relations over time. Network parties contribute in strengthening their links and dilate their scope to involve several or all layers of the firms (Sabel, 1992; Ford, 2002). Each new link created, each new experience with the partners' peculiar ways, and each new routine and convention facilitates future exchange and makes the interaction function without too much fuss (Egidi, 1995). With continuous interaction and information sharing, former misunderstandings and suspicions are gradually eliminated and the interaction can encompass a still wider range of plan alignment and joint knowledge creation. Step by step, the cognitive distance is diminished as emerging *codebooks* – shared languages and ways of communicating and understanding information (Cowan et al., 2000; Lissoni, 2001) – increase firms' cognitive abilities to coordinate activities and plans or share knowledge even if (partly) tacit. Over time, the repeated interactions can also give rise to in-depth incremental knowledge creation, of considerable significance for the overall competitiveness of the firms involved.

Once the element of relation-specific sunk cost is large enough, a qualitative change takes place, as the scope for opportunistic behaviour (Williamson, 1975) becomes negligible. In networks, the accumulated sunk cost makes the partners behave as if they *trust* each other (Glaeser et al., 1999). Trust will thus characterize a relation between business firms when each is confident that the other's present value of all foreseeable future exchanges exceeds the possible benefits of breaking the relations. The larger the sunk costs, the greater the confidence and the trust.

One important consequence of high levels of relation-specific sunk costs is that the flow of knowledge between the firms in a network does not have to be strictly reciprocal or take place at precisely the same time. The overall exchange of knowledge is intensified and deepened when business partners believe that some piece of knowledge offered free of charge today will be repaid at some later moment in some way or another (von Hippel, 1987).

Building networks is, however, not always the most efficient way of organizing market relations to bring down transaction costs and facilitate knowledge creation. In particular the building of stable network relations will be less suited to enhance the competitiveness of firms in industries characterized by high levels of uncertainty on many dimensions. It simply makes little sense for firms to engage in network building with what will soon become yesterday's partners. Firms finding themselves in such circumstances tend instead to opt for a strategy of being a stakeholder in a *cluster.* In a cluster, the organization of markets takes place with the participation of more firms and on a broader level than networks, but this also allows for lowering of transaction costs and for knowledge creation.

Firms opting for co-localization strategies participate in building communities of firms that share institutions, just like in networks, but the cluster institutions are often confined in scope (usually applicable to firms in one or a few related industries only) and always restricted in space (usually to be found on a local or regional level only).

Market relations among clustered firms rely on *collective institutions* helpful in reducing transaction costs without imposing high switching costs precisely because they are based on social traits rather than on the idiosyncratic, partner-specific investments and dyadic sharing of information that characterize networks. Let us deal with how clustering facilitates knowledge creation in market relations, dealing with experimental and incremental knowledge creation in turn.

Clusters and Experimental Knowledge Creation

Because the participants in the market relation firms which create knowledge through experimentation, that is, project relations, originate from different firms and only work together temporarily, they have few incentives and little time to develop the kind of coordination mechanisms that emerge in stable business networks.

However, clustering of projects often helps to diminish this problem. The sheer clustering of firms and people boosts the incidence of 'weak ties' (Granovetter, 1973) that keep transaction costs at bay through mechanisms of reputation and *social trust*. Weak ties in the guise of personal networks of friends and 'friends' friends' are much more sensitive to geographical distance than other relation types, because they depend on face-to-face meetings and are nurtured by incidental meetings on the street and in civic life (Granovetter, 1982; Becattini, 1990; Lorenzen 2002). Another effect of interaction among people in weak ties is a gradual cognitive alignment, that is, *social codebooks* of a communal social culture including collective beliefs, values, conventions and language, that significantly assist firms in obtaining and understanding information (Lorenzen and Foss, 2003). This also facilitates knowledge creation in projects, where participants have no time to develop codebooks anew every time they initiate a new project.

Clusters and Incremental Knowledge Creation

Much exchange and creation of knowledge in a cluster will follow market relations along the vertical dimension of the cluster or with partners accessed through external 'pipelines' (Bathelt et al., 2002), but more knowledge is, perhaps, created along the horizontal dimension of clusters, consisting of firms with similar capabilities and performing like tasks in parallel (Maskell, 2001b). Weak ties help reduce information costs for the 'insiders' of the cluster by spreading information and knowledge through meetings, gossip and direct observation. Hence, weak ties are a source of information and knowledge spillovers that are usually much richer, broader and more varied (and, sometimes, also redundant) than the investment-driven and thus more targeted information sharing taking place within networks.

Even when conducting the same activities, most firms (that is, owners, managers and employees) hold different perceptive powers, divergent insights and dissimilar attitudes, just as they will deviate in their valuation of the information at hand and will entertain differing beliefs about their chances of success if using one of several possible approaches to similar problems (Maskell, 2001c). Consequently, firms develop a variety of solutions as an intricate part of their daily operations, and clustered firms undertaking similar activities find themselves in a situation where every difference in the solutions chosen, however small, can be observed and the outcomes compared.

While it might be easy for firms to blame inadequacies in local or national factor markets when confronted with the superior performance of competitors located far away, it is impossible when the premium producer lives down the street.

As long as the firms share a common language and social codebooks ease their interpretation of local events, little partner-specific trust is required as a prerequisite for learning. The sequence of variation, monitoring, comparison, selection and imitation can take place without any direct relations among firms. The variation between and among firms doing similar things in a cluster simply promotes the generation of ideas and guides interpretations without imposing uniformity. Hence, perhaps the most important effect of clustering is how it propagates incremental knowledge creation along the horizontal axis of local market relations.

4. EMPIRICAL ILLUSTRATION

In order to illustrate the categories introduced above, this section presents empirical evidence from two clustered industries that are different in terms of uncertainty, especially regarding knowledge creation: the EU pop music and furniture industries. The two industries are both quite important in terms of employment and value-added. In spite of the current alleged 'crisis', the global pop music industry has grown by 35 per cent during the last decade, with turnovers rising from USD 27 billion to USD 37 billion (IFPI, 2001), primarily due to technological and stylistic innovations and globalizing markets.[2] The EU furniture industry, accounting for just about half global furniture sales, is one of the largest manufacturing industries in the EU, and continues to enjoy high employment, output and exports (Lorenzen, 1998; Maskell et al., 1998). In 2000, the EU furniture industry had a turnover of USD 96.6 billion, and the industry's almost 90 000 firms employed almost 900 000 persons in 1998 (UEA, 2003). In the following sections we will take a closer look at the clustering taking place in the two industries while focusing on the process of knowledge creation.

The Pop Music Industry

The activities within pop music[3] are very diverse with high degrees of specialization and disintegration as well as important differences in terms of competencies. Most important is, perhaps, the difference between 'artistic' and 'humdrum' competencies (highlighted by Caves, 2000), the first being populated with freelance artists and small 'artistic' firms, the second by firms sourcing, marketing, and selling pop music consumer products like CDs, but also scores (sheet music) and tunes or jingles for mobile phones, and so on (Andersen and Miles, 1999). It is the activities of the latter 'humdrum' pop music firms that concern us here.

Even within the 'humdrum' segment there are competence divides. In fact, the segment is broken down into a number of specialized firms with dense and complex vertical market relations, because sourcing, marketing and selling music requires competencies that are not easily integrated. These activities usually involve (at least) event and concert firms; media firms; AD (Art Direction) firms; distributors; retailers; publishing agencies; financial and legal services; as well as record companies.

The market organization of the industry reflects the high degree of uncertainty in the global demand for the main product: the pop music CD (Huygens et al., 2002; Lopes, 1992; Negus, 1992). First, the product cycles for CD albums are usually very short (and even briefer for CD singles). Second, as consumer tastes are highly unpredictable, the strategy applied by end producers of music (that is, record companies) is to ensure a steady stream of novel products. Any release of music CDs is in a sense an open-ended search process, where new products need to be tested on uncertain consumer markets, over limited test periods. The same goes, albeit to a lesser extent, for new national penetration efforts or marketing methods.

Product innovation in the pop music industry is a process of knowledge creation under uncertainty, through experimentation (Lorenzen and Frederiksen, 2003), and to facilitate such knowledge creation, pop music firms use inter-firm projects. Each new act of knowledge creation, that is, each new experiment of producing, marketing and selling a new CD is thus built on a new market relation, combining a bundle of partners, including at the very least a record company, one or more artists (some of whom are signed for only one CD), a publisher, an AD provider, and often, in addition, media firms and event firms (some of which are also often used only once or twice). The market relation is designed as a temporary project, with some partners (for example AD, media and event firms) participating only in parts of the process and others remaining at the heart of the relation for the project's entire lifespan. The artist remains in the project throughout, as (s)he is needed not only for creating the musical content of the CD, but also for marketing it through live and video performances. The publisher takes care of payments (royalties) to the artist and record company after the project is over, but may also sometimes be actively involved in signing artists and finding music content. The most important agent, however, establishing and coordinating the project and usually involved in all aspects of it, is the record company. The record company first signs artists – the source of musical content in CDs – and then 'pushes' the music through the other parts of the value-adding process by signing on firms with supplementary competencies and visions.

Over time, project relations in pop music organize the market into relatively stable clusters of projects, where record companies, publishers, AD, media and event firms keep most relations local when producing new CDs (Power and Lundequist, 2002). Whereas independent record companies, AD and event firms participate in the creation and marketing of a new CD and keep their relations within clusters, major record companies, while participating in clusters, also deal with global distribution and sales and hence often function as gatekeepers to relations outside the clusters (Power and Hallencreutz, 2002; STEP, 2003).

Let us as an example look at the pop music clusters in Stockholm and Copenhagen (Power and Hallencreutz, 2002; Lorenzen and Frederiksen, 2003). Within these European pop music clusters, new project partners can easily be found, because many have worked together in earlier projects. Such experienced people, with know-how and know-who specialized to pop music projects, are central to coordination (and sometimes also initiation) of CD projects, and are always in high demand. As is the case for Stockholm and Copenhagen, pop music clusters are typically found in the major cities of the world (Scott, 1999; 2000). Here, we find national branches of major international record companies and publishers, the bulk of AD, media and event firms plus related legal and financial services, as well as many independent record companies and artists. The record companies alone are often found within a few hundred metres, in the city cores or in other high-prestige areas of the urban cluster (STEP, 2003).

One effect of the clustering of projects within the pop music industry is of course that it lowers time costs when running projects. However, the major positive effect of the clustering of people with accumulated experience with project coordination is their many weak ties, making information about people's and firms' skills and availability accessible to all local firms. Hence, clustering is crucial for the experimental knowledge creation that goes on in the many project relations in the industry.

The Furniture Industry

As in the music industry, it is furniture firms carrying out the end activities in the value chain[4] that have the highest tendency to cluster, but their reasons for clustering are very dissimilar from pop music firms. In spite of increased global competition, the size structure of the European producers of finished wooden or upholstered furniture and specialized components – henceforth referred to merely as 'furniture' firms – seems relatively unaffected by the wave of vertical integration that has swept through other industries. In the furniture firms, internal scale and scope economies are still rather limited, even if a slowly growing number of European producers have managed to target export markets on a large scale with mass-produced (typically pine wood) furniture. The furniture segment continues to consist of small and medium sized producers, with market relations along the value chain, as well as horizontally interwoven (Lorenzen, 1998; Maskell, 1998). To a very high degree, these market relations rest on an organization of the market in clusters. To understand why, we shall look at the demand for furniture.

The export markets for EU furniture firms have a medium-level demand uncertainty as unpredictable volume fluctuations intermix with a constantly increasing demand for product varieties. Furniture producers need to offer increasingly wide ranges of varieties of their models (in some cases, customize them to one or very few customers), and, furthermore, to be able to deliver securely and quickly. For the bulk of furniture producers, this is done through keeping a modest size while maintaining a portfolio of flexible relations to specialized suppliers. By being able to call on different suppliers at very short notice, such small and medium sized end producers can combine different inputs, allowing them to deliver furniture with quite different characteristics, at delivery times that are often considerably shorter than their large, integrated and automated competitors. Vertical flexible relations are supplemented by less frequent horizontal flexible relations, where firms pass on excess orders to each other.

Knowledge creation is another important competitiveness factor in the furniture industry. Consumer markets (particularly, the medium- and high-end segments) demand ever more frequent product innovations (in many cases, a new model design annually or bi-annually). Most product innovation is incremental, with a genuinely novel model introduced only every few years and subsequent ongoing adjustments and add-ons to the model design (Lorenzen, forthcoming 2004). Such product innovation is facilitated by knowledge creation through vertical market relations. First, for the ongoing incremental changes to the designs, relations to suppliers of specialized components play a central role. Second, for the infrequent design of genuinely novel models, producers often draw on relations to external designers.

The EU furniture industry is organized in clusters. Producers/assemblers of finished furniture and components are often found in non-urban industrial districts, where a high rate of spin-offs from existing firms has created a significant co-location of producers, often in geographical areas spanning only tens of kilometres and a handful of villages. Some of these clusters are found in regions with long craft traditions, as in Italy (Bambi, 1998; Lojacono and Lorenzen, 1998) some in rather recently industrializing but still predominantly rural areas like West Denmark (Lorenzen, 1998). Within furniture districts, being of small geographical size, weak ties (in professional associations as in civic life) are frequent among managers and workers.

This organization of the industry in clusters of furniture firms facilitates both flexibility and variety in deliveries and knowledge creation. Weak ties create transaction cost reducing collective institutions, allowing firms to shift their relations quickly and cheaply. Hence, furniture firms within clusters use each other again and again for both vertical and horizontal flexible relations, sometimes functioning as suppliers, sometimes as customers, sometimes giving favours, sometimes receiving them – exchanging and creating knowledge incrementally in the process. Gossip and direct observation, facilitated by weak ties, also play a role for incremental knowledge creation through small process adjustments and add-ons to existing products.

Discussion

The two cases considered both suggest that clustering facilitates knowledge creation in market relations among firms. But clustering takes different forms in the two industries. In the pop music industry, knowledge creation is experimental, complex, and demands dedicated attention over a specified period of time. Hence, it requires a dedicated market relation, namely inter-firm projects. In the furniture industry, product innovation is an incremental and relatively simple process, and imitation is abundant. In this industry, horizontal knowledge spillovers through weak ties and monitoring suffice to facilitate knowledge creation.

Even if supporting different types of knowledge creation, clustering in the two industries has one crucial aspect in common: low costs of information, sustained by collective institutions that are predominantly found in clusters. In both industries, the community aspect of weak ties serves to bring down transaction costs, as well as propagating social learning. Hence, this collective institution, which depends on clustering, is a prerequisite for the knowledge creation that competitiveness within both industries hinges on.

5. FINAL REMARKS

Theoretical explanation of why industrial clusters exist habitually rests on the assumption that such co-location of related or similar economic activities is economically beneficial in some important respect. Many claims have been made during the last decade regarding the importance and virtues of 'knowledge' and 'learning' – for all aspects of the global economy – and this line of thinking has forcefully influenced the cluster discourse. Rather than accepting the claim at face value, this chapter has been aimed at developing theoretical dimensions that enable us to decompose sweeping statements of cluster learning into concepts that more easily lend themselves to testing. The chapter has defined categories of knowledge creation, and discussed how these may relate to particular aspects of industrial clusters. Whereas earlier conceptualization of the economic efficiency of clustering has tended to focus *either* on (transaction) cost efficiency aspects *or* knowledge aspects, the present chapter has attempted to combine these aspects into a more encompassing view.

The chapter has revolved around a conceptualization of different types of market relations among clustered firms. We have argued that a key virtue of industrial clusters is that they are able to support several forms of market relations along both vertical and horizontal dimensions of value chains, because clusters host weak ties and collective institutions connected to these. This reduces transaction and communication costs, supporting not only flexible relations and project relations, but also stable network relations. The chapter's focus on different types of market relations allows us to suggest an answer to a difficult question: *Can we say that industrial clusters, under certain conditions, are efficient with respect to knowledge creation, compared not only to non-clustered firms, but also to solitary, larger, integrated firms?* Or, in other words, why would a cluster consisting of N firms of size S be a more efficient nexus of knowledge creation than one integrated firm of size N∗S?

If some clusters are comparatively efficient with respect to knowledge creation, it is because they, through simultaneously nursing different forms of market relations (flexible relations, projects and networks), facilitate different types of knowledge creation, allowing these to spill over into each other. This is radically different from what integrated firms can do. While most single firms – large or small – need to be narrow in their knowledge creation processes, some clusters are able to embrace both technologically focused knowledge creation processes (demanding large investments and much time), and broader and less economically risky knowledge creation processes.

Hence, a cluster may be an efficient nexus of knowledge creation compared to an integrated firm, because local combinations of different market relations allow for simultaneous *exploration* and *exploitation* of knowledge. Exploration of radically new knowledge is prominent in young clusters in emergent (for example, high-tech) industries. Here, we find an abundance of project relations and flexible relations, facilitating experimentation and in-breadth knowledge creation. However, early phases of exploration are often followed by phases of consolidation of knowledge creation – and this does not necessarily mean consolidation in terms of integration of firms. When experimentation and in-breadth knowledge creation needs to be supplemented with exploitation, projects and flexible relations are likely to be supplemented with more stable networks, allowing for incremental in-depth knowledge creation, cashing in on earlier exploration. Even the high-tech Silicon Valleys of the world are not characterized by only radical innovation, but rather by intricate mixes of different types of market relations, facilitating different types of knowledge creation.

Of course, in mature clusters – for example, in many skill-based manufacturing clusters in the consumer goods industries – knowledge creation has long been consolidated. Here, incremental in-depth knowledge creation in stable networks serves to exploit the outcomes of the in-breadth knowledge creation, taking place in flexible relations and through horizontal monitoring. The famous Italian or German industrial districts are well known for their abundance of vertically and horizontally interwoven market relations, allowing for a patchwork of knowledge creation processes.

Evidence tells us that while some industrial clusters are able to successfully supplement knowledge exploration with exploitation, and to transcend one type of knowledge creation to another when external (for example demand) conditions shift, other clusters lose ground after periods of rapid growth, their ability to create knowledge along new lines seemingly limited. We may say that such clusters are 'locked in' to a particular type of knowledge creation that is not efficient under all conditions. We still know very little about what distinguishes the winning clusters from those that become locked in. It is evident that we need to learn more about the dynamics – and limitations – of non-planned, non-university-driven knowledge creation in clusters. This chapter has suggested a specific line of research in order to gain such knowledge. Contemplating the organization of the market as constituted by a mix of different types of market relations is taken as the micro-foundation for addressing cluster development at the more aggregated level.

In the present chapter, we apply this approach to understand the cluster as a nexus of knowledge creation and build the foundation for a range of testable hypotheses. For example, we would expect clusters that are locked in with respect to knowledge creation to have an insufficient institutional ability to nurse particular forms of market relations when needed, or be characterized by an inefficient dominance of particular market relation types over others. However, our focus on market organization can be used as a foundation for understanding a variety of further aspects of industrial clusters.

NOTES

1. A more elaborate version of the argument presented in this section can be found in Maskell and Lorenzen (forthcoming).
2. EU labour market statistics on the pop music industry are only sparsely available, but in 1997, EUROSTAT had registered 22 400 persons employed in the EU (minus B; D, EL; IRL; and L) in the NACE codes 22140 (publishers of sound recordings) and 22130 (reproduction of sound recordings) alone. A 1999 statistical mapping of the Scandinavian pop music industry which also included the NACE codes 92311 (performing artists); 22150 (other publishers); 24650 (prepared unrecorded media); 51433 (wholesale CDs, tapes, records, videotapes); 52453 (stores for records and videotapes); 52454 (stores for music instruments and scores); 92320 (theaters and concert halls); and 36300 (music instruments), listed 24 530 persons working in 9184 firms (STEP, 2003) in Denmark, Finland, Iceland, Norway and Sweden alone.
3. Represented (albeit not perfectly) by the NACE codes 22140 (publishers of sound recordings); 22150 (other publishers); and 22310 (reproduction of sound recordings).
4. Represented by NACE codes 361110 (producers of chairs etc.); 361120 (upholsterers); 361200 (producers of office furniture); 361300 (producers of kitchens); 351410 (producers of wooden home furniture), plus (with some error) 203010 (producers of lists); 203020 (producers of construction wood); and 205110 (turners).

BIBLIOGRAPHY

Andersen, B., and I. Miles (1999), 'Orchestrating intangibles in the music sector: the royalties collecting societies in the knowledge based economy', paper prepared for the CISTEMA Conference, October.

Bambi, G. (1998), 'The evolution of a furniture industrial district: the case of Poggibonsi in Tuscany', in M. Lorenzen (ed.), *Specialization and Localized Learning: Six Studies on the European Furniture Industry*, Copenhagen: CBS Press.

Bathelt, H., A. Malmberg, and P. Maskell (2002), 'Clusters and knowledge: local buzz, global pipelines and the process of knowledge creation', DRUID working paper, accessed at www.druid.dk.

Becattini, G. (1979), 'Dal "settore" industriale al "distretto" industriale. Alcune considerationi sull'unit... di indagine dell'economia industriale', *Rivista de Economia e Political Industriale*, **V** (1), January–April.

Becattini, G. (1990), 'The Marshallian district as a socioeconomic notion', in F. Pyke and W. Sengenberger (eds) *Industrial Districts and Inter-firm Cooperation in Italy*, Geneva: ILO.

Carlsson, B., and G. Eliasson (2001), 'Industrial dynamics and endogenous growth', paper presented to the DRUID Nelson and Winter Summer Conference, Aalborg, accessed at www.druid.dk.

Caves, R. (2000), *Creative Industries: Contracts Between Art and Commerce*, London: Harvard University Press.

Coase, R.H. (1937), 'The nature of the firm', *Economica*, **4** (16): 386–405.

Cohen, M.D., R. Buckhart, G. Dosi, M. Egidi, L. Marengo, M. Warglien, and S.G. Winter (1995), *Routine and Other Recurring Action Patterns of Organizations: Contemporary Research Issues*, Santa Fe: Santa Fe Institute.

Cowan, R., P. David, and D. Foray (2000), 'The explicit economics of knowledge codification and tacitness', *Industrial and Corporate Change*, **9** (2), 211–54.

Dahlman, C.J. (1979), 'The problem of externality', *Journal of Law and Economics*, **22** (1), 141–62.

Demsetz (1968), 'Why regulate utilities?', *Journal of Law and Economics*, XI (April), 55–66.

Egidi, M. (1995), 'Routines, hierarchies of problems, procedural behavior. Some evidence from experiments', CEEL working paper 2–95, University of Trento.

Ekstedt, E., R.A. Lundin, A. Soderholm, and H. Wirdenius (1999), *Neo-industrial organizing: renewal by action and knowledge formation in a project-intensive economy*, London: Routledge.

Ford, D. (ed.) (2002), *Understanding Business Marketing and Purchasing*, London: Thomson Learning.

Foss, K., and N.J. Foss (2002), 'Organizing economic experiments: property rights and firm organization', *Review of Austrian Economics*, **15** (4), 297–312.

Freeman, C. (1982), *The Economics of Industrial Innovation*, London: Pinter Publishers.

Freeman, C. (1991), 'Networks of innovators: a synthesis of research issues', *Research Policy*, **20** (5), 5–24.

Glaeser, E.L., D. Laibson, S.J.A. Scheinkman, and C.L. Soutter (1999), *What is social capital? The determinants of trust and trustworthiness*, NBER working paper no. 7216, Cambridge MA.

Goodman, R.A., and P.L. Goodman (1976), 'Some management issues in temporary systems: a study of professional development and manpower – the theater cases', *Administrative Science Quarterly*, **21**, 494–501.

Grabher, G. (ed.) (2002), 'Production in projects: economic geographies of temporary collaboration', special issue of *Regional Studies*, **36** (3).

Granovetter, M. (1973), 'The strength of weak ties', *American Journal of Sociology*, **78** (6), 1360–80.

Granovetter, M. (1982), 'The strength of weak ties: a network theory revisited', in P.V. Marsden and N. Lin (eds), *Social structure and network analysis*, Beverly Hills: Sage.

Håkansson, H. (ed.) (1987), *Industrial Technology Development: a Network Approach*, London: Croom Helm.

von Hippel, E. (1987), 'Cooperation between rivals: informal know-how trading', *Research Policy*, **16**, 291–302.

von Hippel, E. (1998), 'Economics of product development by users: the impact of "sticky" local information', *Management Science*, **44** (5), 629–44.

Hobday, M. (2000), 'The project-based organization: an ideal form for managing complex products and systems?', *Research Policy*, **29**, 871–93.

Huygens, M., C. Baden-Fuller, F.A.J. Van Den Bosch, and H.V. Volberda (2002), 'Co-evolution of firm capabilities and industrial competition: investigating the music industry, 1877–1997', *Organization Studies*, **22** (1), 971–1012.

The International Federation of Phonographic Industries (IFPI) (2001), *The Recording Industry in Numbers*, London: IFPI.

Knight, F.H. (1921), *Risk, Uncertainty, and Profit*, New York: Harper and Row.

Lissoni, F. (2001), 'Knowledge codification and the geography of innovation: the case of Brescia mechanical cluster', *Research Policy*, **30** (9), 1479–500.

Lojacono, G., and M. Lorenzen (1998), 'External economies and value net strategies in Italian furniture districts', in M. Lorenzen (ed.), *Specialization and Localized Learning: Six Studies on the European Furniture Industry*, Copenhagen: CBS Press.

Lopes, Paul D. (1992), 'Innovation and diversity in the popular music industry 1969 to 1990', *American Sociology Review*, **57** (1), 56–71.

Lorenzen, M. (ed.) (1998), *Specialisation and Localised Learning. Six Studies on the European Furniture Industry*, Copenhagen: Copenhagen Business School Press.

Lorenzen, M. (2002), 'Ties, trust, and trade: elements of a theory of coordination in industrial clusters', *International Studies in Management & Organization*, **31** (4), 14–34.

Lorenzen, M. (forthcoming), *Localized Learning and Cluster Capabilities*, Cheltenham, UK and Northampton, MA, USA: Edward Elgar.

Lorenzen, M., and N.J. Foss (2003), 'Cognitive coordination, institutions, and clusters: an exploratory discussion', in D. Brenner and T. Brenner (eds), *Co-operation, Networks and Institutions on Regional Innovation Systems*, Cheltenham, UK and Northampton, MA, USA: Edward Elgar.

Lorenzen, M., and L. Frederiksen (2003), 'Experimental music: product innovation, project networks, and dynamic capabilities in the pop music industry', IVS/DYNAMO working paper, Copenhagen.

Lundvall, B.-Å. (1985), *Product Innovation and User–Producer Interaction*, Aalborg Universitetsforlag industrial development research series no.31, Aalborg.

Maskell, P. (1998), 'Successful low-tech industries in high-cost environments: the case of the Danish furniture industry', *European Urban and Regional Studies*, **5** (2), 99–118.

Maskell, P. (2001a), 'The theory of the firm in economic geography: or why all theories of the firm are not equally well suited for application within the conversation on space', *Economic Geography*, **77** (4), 329–44.

Maskell, P. (2001b), 'Towards a knowledge-based theory of the geographical cluster', *Industry and Corporate Change*, **10** (4), 921–44.

Maskell, P. (2001c), 'Knowledge creation and diffusion in geographic clusters', *International Journal of Innovation Management*, **5** (2), 213–37.

Maskell, P., and M. Lorenzen (forthcoming), 'The cluster as market organization', *Urban Studies*.

Maskell, P., and A. Malmberg (1999), 'Localised learning and industrial competitiveness', *Cambridge Journal of Economics*, **23** (2), 167–86.

Maskell, P., H. Eskelinen, I. Hannibalsson, A. Malmberg, and E. Vatne (1998), *Competitiveness, Localised Learning and Regional Development. Specialisation and Prosperity in Small Open Economies*, London: Routledge.

Negus, K. (1992), *Producing Pop: Culture and Conflict in the Popular Music Industry*, London: Edward Arnold.

Nelson, R.R., and S.G Winter (1982), *An Evolutionary Theory of Economic Change*, Cambridge, MA: Belknap Press.

Piore, M.J., and C.F. Sabel (1984), *The Second Industrial Divide: Possibilities for Prosperity*, New York: Basic Books.

Power, D., and D. Hallencreutz (2002), 'Profiting from creativity? The music industry in Stockholm, Sweden and Kingston, Jamaica', *Environment and Planning A*, **34**.

Power, D. and P. Lundequist (2002), 'Putting Porter into practice? Practices of regional cluster building: evidence from Sweden', *European Planning Studies*, **10** (6), 685–704.

Richardson, G.B. (1972), 'The organisation of industry', *Economic Journal*, **82**, 883–96.

Rosenberg, N. (1972), *Technology and American Economic Growth*, White Plains, NY: Sharpe.

Rosenberg, N. (1992), 'Economic experiments', *Industrial and Corporate Change*, **1**, 181–203.

Sabel, C.F. (1992), 'Studied trust. Building new forms of cooperation in a volatile economy', in F. Pyke and W. Sengenberger (eds), *Industrial Districts and Local Economic Regeneration*, Geneva: ILO, pp. 215–50.

Scott, A.J. (1999), 'The US recorded music industry: on the relations between organization, location, and creativity in the cultural economy', *Environment and Planning A*, **31** (11), 1965–84.

Scott, A.J. (2000), *The Cultural Economy of Cities*, London: Sage.

Shuker, Roy (2001), *Understanding Popular Music*, 2nd edn, London: Taylor & Francis.

STEP (Center for Innovation Research) (2003), *Behind the Music: Profiting From Sound: A Systems Approach to the Dynamics of Nordic Music Industry*, Oslo: STEP.

Storper, M. (1995), 'The resurgence of regional economies, ten years later: the region as a nexus of untraded interdependencies', *European Urban and Regional Studies*, **2**, 191–221.

UEA (Association of European Furniture Producers) (2003), 'The EU Furniture Industry, Outlook 2003', http://www.ueanet.com/outlook.htm

Williamson, O.E. (1975): *Market and Hierarchies – Analysis and Antitrust Implications. A Study in the Economics of Internal Organization*, New York: The Free Press.

Wilson, D.T. (1975), 'Dyadic interaction: an exchange process', in B. Anderson (ed.), *Advances in Consumer Research, vol. 2*, Cincinnati: ACR pp. 394–97.

6. Knowledge life cycles inside local economic systems*

Lucio Poma and Silvia Sacchetti

1. PRODUCTION SYSTEMS AND KNOWLEDGE

Within production systems, knowledge is important for a number of reasons: it confers value to products, it generates innovative dynamics, it simulates technological development, it creates competitive advantages, it favours the creation of relations amongst economic actors, and attracts activities. As a consequence, nowadays knowledge can be seen as one of the most significant elements for the competitiveness of advanced economies and, in particular, of local production systems.

We keep our focus on those aspects of the relationship between knowledge and the economy that are related to production. We approach a particularly vast concept, which can refer to the knowledge incorporated inside technologies, human capital, firms, networks of firms, or within linkages amongst firms and other actors on the territory. Knowledge can be the outcome of past experiences, the fruit of intuition and research, the result of the imitation of secrets of production. Knowledge can be contextual, or the tacit capacity which derives from specialization and successful experiences. In parallel, knowledge is subject to diffusion: amongst individuals, organizations, within a locality or between different territorial systems.

When talking about knowledge in production, the core dimension is the relationship between tacit knowledge, which involves human resources on the one hand, and the knowledge codified inside production machineries and technical manuals on the other. If in Smith's (1776 [1994]) analysis the main focus is on *manufacture*, for which human skills and the tacit knowledge of the craftsman are fundamental, subsequently, in the work of Marx (1867) the machine becomes the core of production and the sphere of action of individuals shifts from that of physical production to the organization, the coordination and control of machineries.[1] Increasingly, production becomes related to the design, organization and control of machines: it shifts from physical production to the production of knowledge (Pollock, 1957; Kern and Schumann, 1984).

If Smith centred his analysis on manufacturing and Marx and Taylor on the factory, today the complexity which characterizes production activities pushes an enquiry about knowledge beyond a strict focus on machines and human resources. Linkages amongst firms and between firms and institutional actors become important knowledge repositories as well. Past and future receive a different meaning with respect to common connotations. We link past to the knowledge settled inside the firm; on the other side we see future as the capacity of a firm to generate new knowledge. This capacity develops along two directions. We call the first the *adaptive function* of firms, meaning that the capacity to create new knowledge is functional to an understanding of the evolving socioeconomic phenomena with which the firm must interact. The firm adapts its internal organization and knowledge to exogenous changes. We name the second connotation the *innovative function.* In this case, the capacity to generate knowledge is functional to the ability to plan and design new production and organizational opportunities as well as to increase competitiveness. In this case, the firm is not a follower but a proactive actor of change.

2. TACIT AND CODIFIED KNOWLEDGE

Most of our actions depend, for their achievement, on our knowledge. We can see this knowledge as composed of a sub-group of knowledge, of which the individual is aware when acting, and of a vast sub-group of knowledge of which individuals are not conscious. This second set is tacit knowledge (Polanyi, 1958). By doing things, the individual acquires practical knowledge and through a process of trials, errors and adjustments he/she memorizes the sequence of actions that steered him/her successfully to his/her objective. This sedimentation of 'memory' forms tacit knowledge. Codified knowledge represents an extrapolation of tacit knowledge which occurs when the latter is 'translated' and fixed inside manuals or incorporated by machineries. Codified knowledge is the language through which knowledge transfer occurs. Craft enterprises and more generally small firms are principally built on tacit knowledge, whilst as size increases firms transfer to mainly codified and standardized knowledge. Codified knowledge can be transmitted more rapidly. Its main limitation is that it does not allow the transfer of all the capital that is included inside tacit knowledge. Large firms, by virtue of their scale and standardization of production need to rapidly instruct labour and therefore they will mainly transfer codified knowledge. Conversely, small firms and craft firms rely essentially on tacit knowledge. Although with different intensity, we can find both the components of knowledge, tacit and codified, in the large as well in the small firm.

2.1 Some Empirical Evidence

The results of a recent research undertaken in the Italian province of Reggio Emilia (Emilia-Romagna) seem to support some of the above-mentioned hypotheses. Firms have been classified according to the R&D intensity that characterizes sectors. In particular, Pavitt (1984) provides criteria to classify firms on the basis of the attitude of a sector to produce innovation. Inside certain industries firms ask for the technology produced by other sectors. Others, conversely, mainly rely on their internal R&D. According to this criterion, following Pavitt (1984), we classify firms using the four categories: 'supplier dominated' (SD), 'scale intensive' (SI), 'specialized suppliers' (SS) and 'science based' (SB).[2]

We found that firms belonging to SS sectors are particularly oriented towards hiring managers with a university degree. Therefore, sectors such as those producing control equipment or specific high-tech components for other firms favour the introduction of individuals with a strong codified knowledge base, provided in this case by education. In parallel, a corresponding amount of firms hire managers without a university degree. This result suggests the existence of industrial realities for which the degree of complexity that characterizes a sector does not require high levels of codified knowledge (as represented by a university degree), but encourages individual learning inside the firm, in some cases with the help of training programmes.

The learning process which brings managers to knowledge maturity takes, on average, three years for SD and SI sectors, whilst it takes more time for SS and SB sectors (four and five years, respectively, see Figure 6.1). These results suggest that in sectors where knowledge and complexity evolve more rapidly, managers need to improve their individual knowledge through a learning process which is based also on experience and on the skills acquired inside the firm.

The presence of people with university degrees is important for the industrial development of a territory because it increases the possibility for firms to catch new technological or market opportunities. However, the Italian production system is not entirely able to capitalize on this fundamental resource. The percentage of firms that, during the last five years, have hired executives and white-collar workers with a university degree is 43 per cent. Until 20 years ago these tasks were undertaken by workers with secondary education. In parallel, 79 per cent of firms have experienced difficulties in finding specialized workers and technicians.

On the face of these results, firms seem to be confronted by a bottleneck which is not caused by the impossibility of accessing workers with the highest education, but by the lack of individuals with specific technical competences or, in other words, people who are able to use technologies.

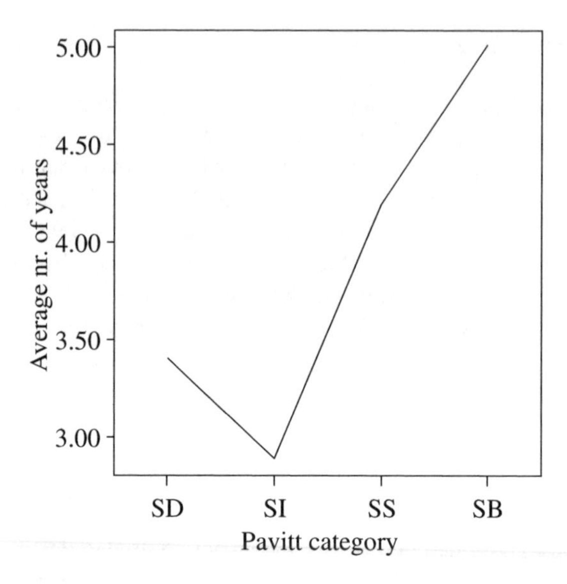

Figure 6.1 Average number of years that are necessary for the training of a manager by Pavitt categories

The length of the training period of workers with specific technical competences, in particular, varies according to the size of firms. We observe that firms invest in the training of skilled blue-collar workers over a period which goes, on average, from a bit less than two years to two and a half years (see Figure 6.2).

In particular, if we consider firms of up to 500 workers (Figure 6.2), we observe a strong inverse correlation (–0.88) between the learning period and the size of the firm. The difference between small firms (<29 employees) and larger firms (100–500) is remarkable: the learning period for a specialized blue-collar worker in firms with less than 29 employees lasts 50 per cent more than the learning period required inside firms with 100–500 employees.

We read these results in line with the Smithian principle of the division of labour: as the size of the firm increases, individuals adapt to an increasingly focused functional specialization, which requires, as the division of labour augments, shorter learning periods. This result is consistent with what we have noticed before with respect to tacit and codified knowledge: as larger firms rely more than smaller firms on the specificity of tasks and on codified knowledge, individual knowledge is more focused and can be 'transferred' more rapidly than tacit knowledge.

At the same time, what we have observed so far has to be linked to the different degrees of complexity and to the different levels of ability and skills

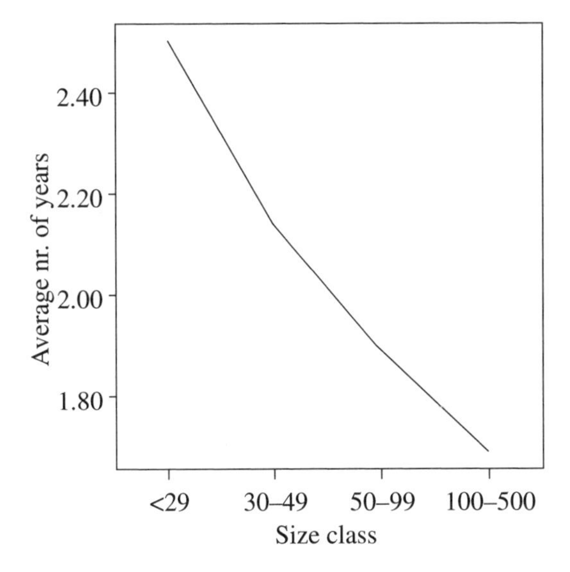

Figure 6.2 Relation between firm's size class and the average number of years to reach knowledge maturity for a skilled blue-collar worker

that characterize various sectors and functions. In Table 6.1 we relate the length of the learning period of a skilled worker with the nature of the sector. Results support the hypothesis that we have advanced: firms operating in SI sectors require shorter learning periods. In parallel, in labour intensive sectors (those defined as SD) the maturation of a skilled blue-collar worker takes longer. The greatest number of years is needed, on average, for specialized suppliers (SS) where we find firms producing technologies and products which require internal competences in design and development.

Table 6.1 Average number of years to reach knowledge maturity for a skilled blue-collar worker by Pavitt category

Pavitt category	Number of years
SD	2.4
SI	1.6
SS	3.0
SB	2.3
Average	**2.3**

These results emphasize the importance of the tacit and codified nature of knowledge that belongs to a skilled worker for all dimensional classes; learning lasts for over two years on average. The incidence of longer learning periods inside smaller firms, which are mainly labour intensive firms belonging to SD sectors, may be linked to what we were arguing before; tacit knowledge characterizes small firms especially. Indeed, consistent levels of tacit knowledge may be acquired only by accumulating experience and specific learning. This process requires time. The time needed to transfer knowledge, here meant as transmission of *skills*, *dexterity* and *judgement*, is linked to the degree of division of labour and to the innovative characterization of the sector.

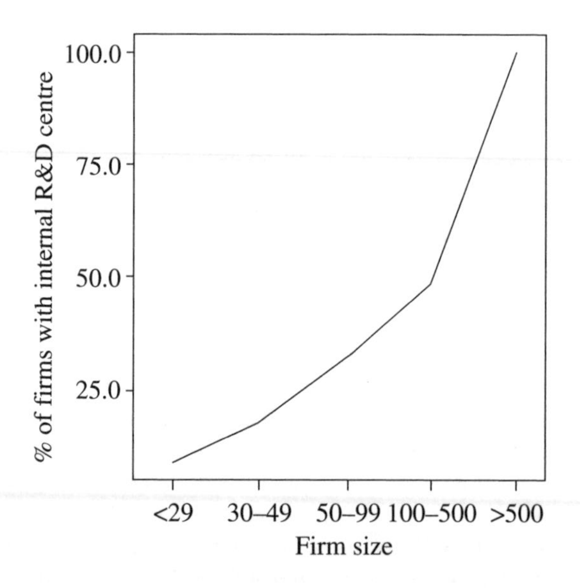

Figure 6.3 Relationship between internal R&D and firm size – frequencies within size class (%)

Evidence of the relationship between codification of knowledge and the size of the firm comes also from data on R&D centres (Figure 6.3). Our empirical work has shown a strong correlation (0.94) between the size of the firm and R&D centres inside firms. The frequency of firms with an internal R&D centre increases as size augments. From 8.5 per cent of firms with less than 30 employees, frequencies shift to 48 per cent for firms with 100–500 employees and to 100 per cent for firms with more than 500 employees.

3. KNOWLEDGE PRODUCTION

Inside a closed economy the 'institutional spaces' of production and exchange tend to overlap. As markets open, these two institutional spaces are increasingly diverging. Competition does not occur only amongst firms through techniques and technologies, but also amongst territories, juxtaposing and comparing different institutional contexts in different countries. This wider competitive environment is one of the factors which has contributed to the design of a new international division of labour. Advanced economies are experiencing difficulty in competing on costs against economic and institutional contexts where salaries are kept at the level of subsistence. Therefore, firms in advanced economies are obliged to improve the quality of their production, augmenting value-added and emphasizing the 'knowledge value' incorporated by goods or services. Physical production is the outcome of the institutional context where knowledge circulates. The tacit element of this knowledge surfaces and flows inside new information and communication technologies.

Knowledge is produced by firms but also by the whole territorial system. The production of knowledge is not a natural and casual event but it is strictly related to the institutional context where knowledge develops and consolidates: knowledge production is part of a 'project' that must be stimulated and governed. The capacity of a country, of its regions and local systems to interpret and stimulate knowledge production determines the conditions and the modalities of competition, as well as the position of these territorial systems inside new production dynamics.[3]

A new role for knowledge appears. Knowledge is not a complementary element incorporated by skills, it is not reduced to learning by doing or learning by using, but it is the engine of development. It is the creation of knowledge which provides the tools to interpret economic complexity and uncertainty. This has induced advanced economies to a transition from physical production, which implicitly wells up from knowledge, typical of Fordism and partly of post-Fordism, to the explicit production of knowledge.

Table 6.2 shows the evolution of entrepreneurs' investment expectations in the province of Reggio Emilia.[4] In particular, the first three typologies of investments (research and product innovation, computer and software systems for business, computer and software systems for production activities) identify investments in intangibles, whilst the remaining typologies refer to physical capital.

Data indicates the ratio between investments at time *t* (actual investments) and investments planned by firms the year before, at time *t*–1. The ratio shows which typologies have been overestimated (percentage is below 100) and which, on the other hand, have required a larger commitment with

Table 6.2 *Percentage of actual investments on expected investments, Province of Reggio Emilia 1994–2000*

Type of Investment	1994	1995	1996	1997	1998	1999	2000
Research and product innovation	103	49	203	117	59	139	89
Computer and software systems for business	117	103	235	169	105	206	125
Computer and software systems for production	100	63	179	161	88	182	93
Enlargement of sites	107	82	205	205	116	169	
Enlargement of production lines	151	76	195	138	107	175	88
Restructuring/conversion of production lines	91	80	134	126	106	3	95
New production lines	89	45	131	163	90	0	83
Total investments	98	65	180	129	84	131	102

Source: Authors' elaboration on data from Assindustria Reggio Emilia (Industrial Association of Reggio Emilia)

respect to expectations (percentage is over 100). As far as intangibles are concerned, we observe important underestimations since 1996. Investment in research and product innovation, in particular, is the most rising and falling typology. This stresses the delicate equilibriums of research outputs: planned investments for the realization of specific projects could be interrupted before and when, for instance, unexpected difficulties arise during the research process. We also observe that investments in ICTs (computer and software systems for business and production) are constantly underestimated.

3.1 Information and Communication Technologies (ICTs) and Knowledge Production

The recognition of ICTs' relevance, recognized also by Agenda 2000, assumes a special meaning if we think about the massive presence of SMEs in European industry. SMEs can be seen as the nodes of a thick network of relationships. The production of knowledge implies collective interaction amongst territorial actors. Production and its environment are not separated, they are two indissoluble dimensions; one is visible and includes physical production, the other is invisible and relates to the production of knowledge. The space of these interactions may be local, or it may go beyond regional and national borders. ICTs, with respect to the speed and flexibility of exchange, may facilitate cooperation. This increases information flows and improves the possibility to share information with remote actors through the creation of long-distance networks, for example to manage just-in-time systems or to co-design products remotely.

3.2 Some Empirical Evidence

Results from our empirical research in Reggio-Emilia show that 52 per cent of firms use ICTs to interact with other firms: 42 per cent of users utilize EDI, whilst 16 per cent rely on ERP. A crucial point that emerges from our analysis is that ICTs are perceived and used as accelerators of old production and organizational modalities rather than as radical technological changes that redefine production and the organizational context. In particular we have observed that firms in Reggio-Emilia do not exploit the communication potential (knowledge circulation) of ICTs, nor their project making potential (knowledge production). Indeed, 95 per cent of users rely on ICTs to communicate, and 80 per cent to transfer files. Both these two functions could be substituted by traditional technologies, such as the telephone or mail. Only one quarter of ICT users apply ICTs to co-design products in partnership with other firms. ICTs are therefore a useful instrument to enhance the circulation of codified knowledge amongst firms, whilst

Table 6.3 Objectives that are pursued with the use of ICTs

Motivation	% of user firms
Communication	95.1
File transfer	80.3
To manage integrated process information	36.1
Co-design products	26.2
To accelerate post-sale servies	23.0
To delegate customer services	13.1
To create new products in partnership	8.2
Other	4.0

the creation and design of products are undertaken according to traditional methods.

ICTs break with previous technological paradigms and imply a new codification of competences and knowledge. In terms of industrial organization, the small firm owner generally has a deep knowledge of its machineries; he/she is able to adapt them to the productive process introducing incremental innovation as a distinctive action of SMEs. Moreover, he/she is also able to estimate the productivity of the machinery and assess the convenience of a new purchase. Technology dissemination policies focus, in this case, on information. The introduction of ICTs breaks down this mechanism. Knowledge must be codified anew. This can be done more easily by large enterprises where most of the knowledge is codified, rather than by small firms which are more used to tacit forms of knowledge. In the latter case, the entrepreneur may not have the capability to adapt his knowledge to the new paradigm.

We considered entrepreneurs' perceptions of the magnitude of change introduced by ICTs. Thirty-two per cent of user firms believe ICTs to be essential (see Figure 6.4).

The declared essentiality of ICTs for inter-firm production relations suggests that for one third of firms these technologies are not juxtaposed with traditional communication technologies as an alternative, but they are conceived as opening new opportunities. When the technological change induced by ICTs is followed by organizational change we can assume that firms will increase their productivity. Sixty-four per cent of user firms have indeed declared to have modified their structure as a consequence of ICTs (see Figure 6.5).

Amongst these, we observe a neat predominance of firms that have enlarged their structure. This suggests some considerations about the implications of technological change on labour. Knowledge is a form of capital (Sacchetti, 2003) which deteriorates over years. Lately, the cycle that includes learning,

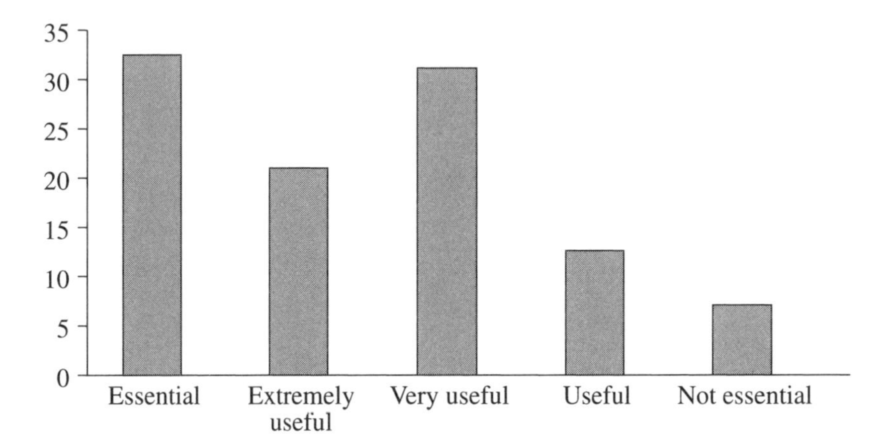

Figure 6.4 Entrepreneurs' judgement on ICTs

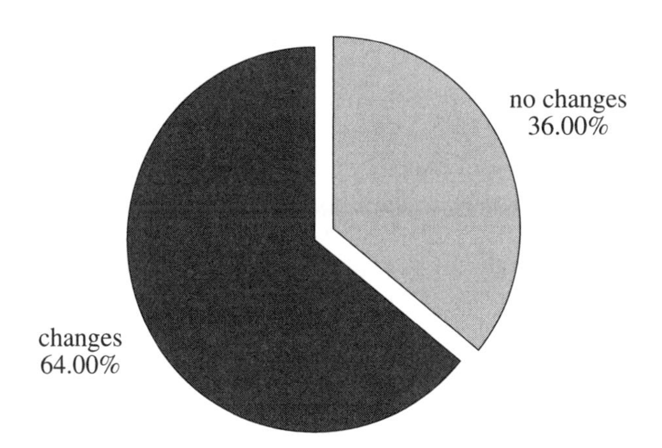

Figure 6.5 Organizational changes within ICT users

the creation and use of knowledge has become shorter (the 'lead time of knowledge'). The life cycle of technologies, where technologies represent the application of scientific knowledge, has become shorter and this is particularly evident when thinking about the frequency with which ICTs renew themselves. Rapid changes may create a demand for specific competences. In this case, it seems that the technological change introduced by ICTs has not induced the substitution of labour for technologies. Rather, ICTs have created the space for new competences. Amongst the firms which have restructured their organization by virtue of ICTs, 84 per cent have enlarged their structure by hiring new personnel.

4. THE KNOWLEDGE LIFE CYCLE INSIDE THE FIRM

Our analysis of the production of knowledge introduces a concern about the relationship between knowledge dynamics and local economic systems, and knowledge dynamics inside firms. The answers to our questions – what are the mechanisms and factors that make knowledge capital either grow, consolidate or decay – require the introduction of a new concept, that of *knowledge life cycles*, which aims at capturing declining and ascending flows of knowledge within firms and local economic systems.

Resources continuously combine and in so doing they create new value which is a cause of the wealth of nations. Knowledge is one of these resources. Better still, it is knowledge that enables the process of bringing resources together.

More generally we can say that all resources are subject to a process of obsolescence which, over time, diminishes their value. Technologies are changing as well: their equipment, their power engines, and their technique. On technological trajectories (Dosi, 1982) we can count a number of contributions. Economists have been flanked by labour sociologists and psychologists who have enriched literature with contributions on the obsolescence of specific capabilities and of human resources. Less relevance has instead been given to the obsolescence of knowledge per se and to its production context, where by context we refer to the firm or to the territory. Our perspective builds on the idea of knowledge production.[5] Shifting from physical to knowledge production, we radically change the subject of the analysis.

The knowledge capital of a firm needs to be constantly renewed. Therefore, it requires continuous inward flows of new knowledge. Knowledge flows allow a firm to renew its competences when otherwise competences would reach, at first, the stage of maturity and then they would start a declining phase that would weaken the value-added produced by the firm. This would therefore decrease the firm's contribution to the knowledge capital and wealth of its local system.

We build on two main hypotheses. The first is that although knowledge represents a form of capital which accumulates over time, such capital could not be economically relevant or, in some cases, it could produce distorting effects. The second hypothesis is that, inside the firm or the territory, the accumulation of knowledge does not proceed along a straight trajectory and indistinctively, but it is articulated along different phases, which allow us to advance the hypothesis of a knowledge life cycle.

Figure 6.6 graphically shows our hypothesis with respect to the knowledge life cycle of firms. It develops along four stages: 1) knowledge acquisition, 2) knowledge sedimentation and adaptation, 3) routine usage of knowledge, 4) knowledge decay.

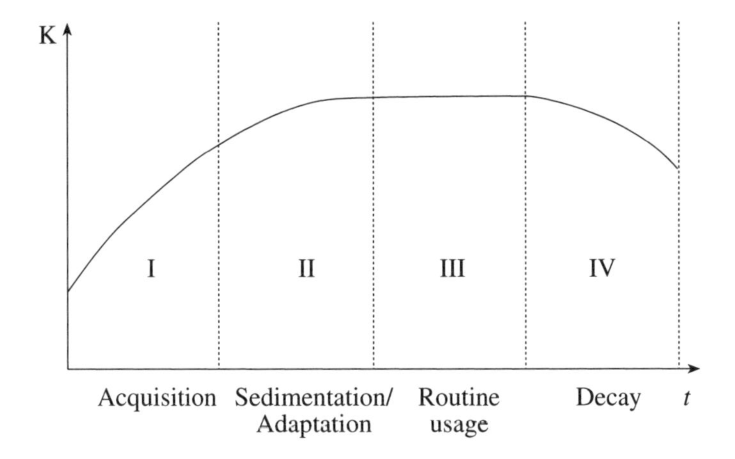

Figure 6.6 *Knowledge life cycles inside firms and territories*

In the first stage, *knowledge acquisition*, the firm acquires the knowledge which is then incorporated inside physical production in an innovative or differentiated manner. Knowledge acquisition may occur from the outside or the inside. In the first case knowledge can be obtained from three main channels: technology and machineries, human resources, and linkages with other firms.

When a firm buys a new machine it appropriates the knowledge incorporated by the machine itself. The firm can then implicitly use this knowledge through physical production. The firm can interact with the knowledge incorporated inside the machinery, causing continuous incremental adjustments which reveal new productive potential. This, for instance, is typical inside industrial districts.

External knowledge can be obtained also from labour, especially when hiring skilled personnel. In this case the firm appropriates both codified and/or tacit knowledge. An employee without any previous working experience will bring to the firm the codified knowledge that he/she has learned during his/her education. When the educational level of the worker is not very high but the worker has accumulated experience, skills and specific competences, the firm will acquire mainly tacit knowledge. Finally, if an individual has a high educational level and working experience, the firm obtains both forms of knowledge.

Linkages with other firms may represent a third source of external knowledge. One of the objectives that can motivate networking is the circulation or creation of knowledge. Literature has explored equilibriums and risks associated with cooperation and competition when firms transfer knowledge and information (Bettis et al., 1992).

Besides external sources, a firm can get new knowledge by creating it internally. As we have mentioned, a characteristic of firms inside industrial districts is the ability to introduce incremental innovations and to continuously adjust their machineries to the needs of production activities.

Furthermore, a firm can internally increase knowledge with respect to human resources. This is the case when the firm organizes internal training courses or groupware for managers, or when the tacit transfer of knowledge from the master to the apprentice leads to innovative adjustments.

To end with, firms can rely on internal R&D centres. Small firms that cannot support a specific internal structure dedicated to research can, nonetheless, assign part of their resources to the development of a new product or process.

After acquisition, the firm moves to the second stage (*sedimentation and adaptation*) during which knowledge is laid down and adapts. At this stage the firm starts to select the knowledge previously acquired on the basis of its strategy and of its expected market positioning. Cognitive layers of knowledge overlap and consolidate to form the intangible capital of the firm. That part of tacit knowledge which is considered strategic is codified. Knowledge is socialized[6] inside the firm. Moreover, the firm increases the intensity with which it moulds external knowledge according to its specific activities, through machineries, capital and linkages with other firms. This adaptive function is the most interesting leverage of innovative dynamics. The combination of internal and external knowledge, tacit and codified, may generate new knowledge that is injected in the physical production of goods. At this second stage, knowledge still follows a rising trend which increases the firm's knowledge capital.

At the third stage, *routine usage*, the firm concentrates on the production process of goods rather than on the production process of knowledge. Knowledge is completely transformed into the physical production of goods. The knowledge that was previously acquired, accumulated and adapted by the firm is now totally consolidated. Tacit knowledge, which has been arranged in the form of codified knowledge, is now part of routines and, consequently, a number of knowledge dimensions are taken for granted. Knowledge routines are then transformed into production routines. The firm exploits the knowledge that has been accumulated during the previous two phases by transferring that knowledge to goods. Usually, during this third stage firms concentrate on process innovation or on frenetic activity aimed at the reduction of production costs. Knowledge production ceases and the knowledge capital of the firm is temporarily stable. In Figure 6.6 the curve representing the cycle becomes flatter, as physical production prevails over the production of knowledge.

As we mentioned at the beginning of this section, one of the premises of our theoretical model was that the function of the knowledge accumulated inside the firm could not be an increasing function. In the fourth stage, *decay*, the knowledge that was accumulated during the first two phases and that was not nourished all through the third stage, becomes obsolete and loses part of its validity. The value-added incorporated by the good diminishes and sometimes disappears. In this case the *application* of the knowledge capital accumulated over the years does not represent a convincing barrier and a distinguishing competitive characteristic with respect to potential entrants. The past does not matter any more. In this situation, changes in competitive dynamics are reflected in the inadequacy of the application of the firm's knowledge capital. Firms facing this phase have two possibilities. They can disregard their knowledge capital to focus on cost reduction or they can start producing new knowledge. This means that during the third stage the firm should launch its process of knowledge production either by accessing external knowledge or by increasing the resources dedicated to internal production of knowledge.

These four stages describe a hypothetical sequence of situations. Evidence shows that there are firms that, given their age, are still travelling along the first or the second stage at most. There are firms that have been on the declining phase for years but still can keep their market share intact. There are firms that have a long history behind them and that continually launch the first and the second stage: some amongst these succeed in translating knowledge in physical production, other firms fail, or do not meet consumers' demand with their products. Growing firms suit the first situation in which physical production successfully incorporates the firm's knowledge, whilst the last two situations include firms which are experiencing some difficulties, and some of them are closing down.

4.1 Some Empirical Evidence

In our empirical work we have related the age of firms to the presence of an internal R&D centre. We have then observed that whilst young firms do not include a structure specific for R&D, one quarter of firms founded before 1990 undertake R&D in an internal centre (see Table 6.4).

Within these two groups of firms, whose distinguishing feature is the year of foundation, firms started in 1900–1939, 1960–1969 and 1980–1989 have the highest frequencies of R&D centres (see Figure 6.7).

We observe a sort of cycle that describes the presence of firms for which, today, the actual knowledge capital is also enriched by internal R&D activities. Inside the first class (1900–1939), firms are mainly identifiable with SS and, in particular, with mechanical industry. Amongst firms founded between 1960–1969 there are SI and SS sectors with chemical and mechanical firms sized (today) between 100 and 500 employees. The same sectoral character-

Table 6.4 Firms' age and internal R&D

Age		Firms with R&D centre	Firms without R&D centre	Total
Firms started before 1990	Nr. of cases	33	99	132
	%	25.0	75.0	100.0
Firms started after 1990	Nr. of cases	1	20	21
	%	4.8	95.2	100.0
Total	Nr. of cases	34	119	153
	%	22.2	77.8	100.0

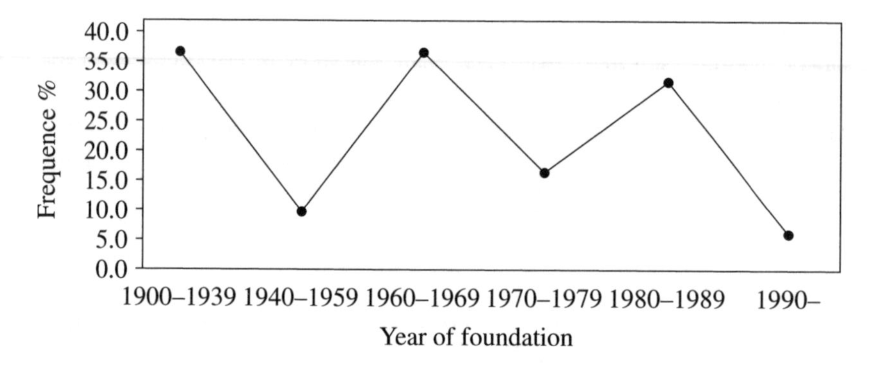

Figure 6.7 Relationship between firms' age and R&D

istics illustrate the type of firms founded between 1970–1979, which at present are not so oriented towards organizing R&D within a proper internal structure. Between 1980 and 1989 we principally find firms belonging to SI sectors but also firms from SD sectors, which are market leaders in textiles and clothing. More recent firms (from 1990) can be associated with SD sectors (mainly textiles and clothing without leadership roles) or with traditional sectors. In concurrence with Pavitt's assumptions, these firms do not rely on internal R&D.

Our observations suggest that local specific competences which rely today on R&D began with producers of specific mechanical components. In parallel, with a more strict focus on products and marketing, sectors such as textiles and clothing that are usually defined as SD but which in this territory are characterized by the presence of leader firms, confer high value-added to their production by means of R&D. Internal R&D, undertaken inside specific centres, seems to be linked to the industrial sector of the firm and, within the sector, to the firm's age. This data suggests that firms (mainly leaders) that have consolidated their structure and their knowledge capital tend to renew and enlarge this capital also through intentionally planned R&D.

Further evidence comes from a different research undertaken in another province (Forlì-Cesena)[7] where the results of direct interviews suggest that for a number of very old firms the past is not very important[8] (see Table 6.5).

Table 6.5 The importance of past experience (percentage of firms for which the past is important by size class)

Size class	Frequency within size class (%)
20–49	25
50–199	50
200–499	71
Average amongst classes	**49**

Sixty-seven per cent of firms in the sample assign an important role to past experience. Medium–large firms are remarkably above the average frequency (71 per cent of cases). This is probably an indicator that larger firms have more remote origins with respect to smaller firms. The same research results emphasize that experience is perceived as an advantage mainly by firms that are at least 30 years old (see Figure 6.8). In parallel, the crucial role of the past seems to diminish when the past becomes particularly distant, that is for firms created before the 1940s.[9] Data seems to suggest that knowledge within firms is cyclical and goes through ascending and descending phases. As a consequence, like other forms of capital, knowledge needs to be nourished and renewed.

5. THE KNOWLEDGE LIFE CYCLE INSIDE LOCAL SYSTEMS

In section 4 we hypothesized the existence of ascending and descending flows of knowledge inside firms. We have also considered the firm as an open system that interacts with its territory: the firm both appropriates local knowledge and releases knowledge to the territory. Beside knowledge life cycles inside firms, we can design the knowledge life cycle of a territorial system. Of course, production does not take place in a vacuum. The knowledge

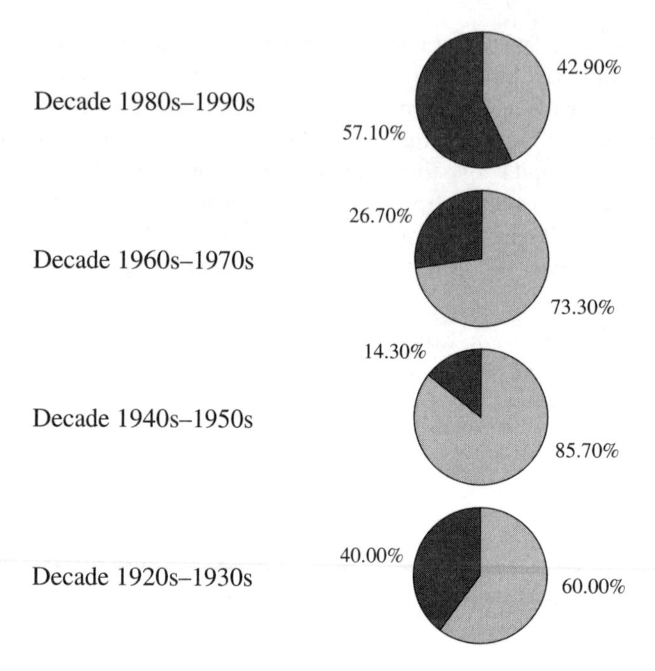

Figure 6.8 The importance of past experience and knowledge by firms' age[10]

retained by firms may (or may not) have an impact on the knowledge capital of localities and, vice versa, local economic systems influence the extent to which local knowledge can be accumulated over time.

The nature of the knowledge accumulated and rooted inside a locality identifies the peculiar competences of a local production system. The relationship between the knowledge retained by firms and local systems can be, for instance, illustrated by the image of a large firm that, at different points in time, absorbs knowledge from a territory (for example, in terms of labour) and then releases it outside when increasing, for instance, the knowledge capital of a territory in the form of spin-off firms and new competences. In this case, the firm works as a 'territorial lung': when the firm first settles down it destroys knowledge by absorbing competences when hiring labour, which is a scarce factor for industry especially when it is enriched by highly qualified skills and competences. After that, when the firm starts to interact with the outside system, it can stimulate the establishment of new firms and competences. For instance, it can encourage education and learning, cooperate with other firms for the introduction of innovation, and stimulate knowledge diffusion together with other territorial actors such as universities.

This exchange between the firm and its territory is one of the factors that helps the firm to renew its knowledge and the local system to follow the evolution of techniques and production modalities. Scientific and technological knowledge continuously develops following cyclical patterns. This process causes the obsolescence of the knowledge capital of firms, including the knowledge incorporated inside technologies, the tacit knowledge that is embodied by individual competences and skills, as well as the knowledge included into organizational routines.

Figure 6.9 presents, besides the knowledge life cycle of the firm, the knowledge cycle inside the territorial system. We hypothesize, considering a large firm, the existence of an interaction between a firm's dynamics and the local system.[11]

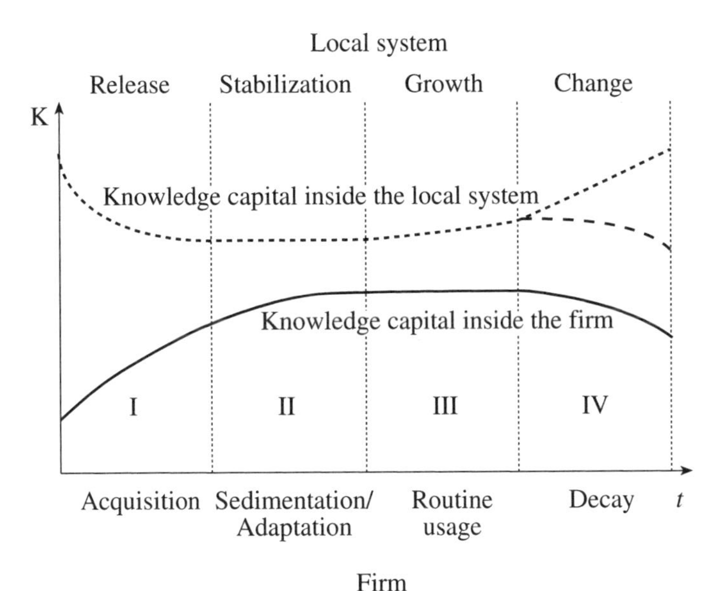

Figure 6.9 The 'territorial lung'

Suppose a situation in which a large firm settles within a territory characterized by a rich knowledge capital. For the large firm a territory may represent a potential of knowledge for three main reasons essentially. A territory is a *potential of tacit knowledge* if a network of small or craft firms already exists, as this network can represent an input of contextual knowledge and of specific learning capacity within a particular industrial sector. Furthermore, a territory is a *potential of codified knowledge* if it includes vocational schools, faculties or university degrees that have contributed over time to diffuse knowledge amongst local people. Finally, a territory is a *potential of tacit and codified knowledge* which is diffused amongst local institutional actors, within their routines, policies and development programmes, their governance capacity to promote the social and economic development of the community. These three factors, which may vary extremely between territories, represent the *whole knowledge potential* that is directly or indirectly appropriable by a large firm when it settles down.

When a large firm is established, we are in the first stage of the cycle, which corresponds to *knowledge acquisition* for the firm and to a *reduction of knowledge* for the territory. The firm will need specialized competences. It is possible that craftsmen will leave their own activities and become employees, a position that would guarantee a fixed salary to them. Some small firms could orient their production towards the needs of the large firm and become subcontractors producing for a single main prime contractor. Their incremental innovative capacity will serve the adjustments required by the large firm. People coming from vocational schools and universities will be absorbed by the large firm, thus jeopardizing entrepreneurship forces inside the local system. To sum up, this first stage is characterized by a sort of internalization of territorial knowledge inside the firm.

In the second stage, the large firm starts to deposit knowledge and to transform the tacit knowledge it has acquired into codified knowledge and production routines. Gradually, the appropriation of territorial knowledge slows down.

The third stage is characterized by the application of knowledge to physical production. The firm consolidates and grows, whilst the absorption of local knowledge stops. The firm starts to release and diffuse knowledge inside the local system. Knowledge diffusion continues more pevasively and intensely in the fourth phase. This is the stage in which the firm externalizes its knowledge. This happens, for instance, when spin-off processes (not necessarily encouraged by the large firm) are activated within the territory, when the firm financially support schools or universities and promotes training courses. Finally, an extreme situation that has, however, been quite frequent for industrial districts, is when the firm goes bankrupt and releases knowledge onto the territory. Specialized workers lose their jobs and – having access to a sufficient financial capital – may become entrepreneurs and start their own activity, generating a small industrial district. At this stage, the firm releases and therefore loses knowledge, whilst the territory increases its knowledge capital.

These two knowledge cycles last over time, waving in opposite directions with different intensity. The intensity of the osmotic function of knowledge between the firm and the territory is linked to the nature of the firm (whether transnational or multinational), to its industrial sector, and to the capacity of territorial actors to manage such a process.

6. CONCLUSIONS

In this chapter we have provided some theoretical insights into the production of knowledge and into the role of knowledge in physical production. Our main finding is that knowledge does not always grow following a cumulative process, but it can evolve or stagnate and, if not renewed, it can be subject to a process of decay. This evolutionary perspective relates both to the firm and to its local system, where the two continuously interact by providing or absorbing knowledge the one from the other. Firms' production decisions, in particular, crucially influence ascending and descending flows of knowledge within their organization and the territory. The territory, in parallel, can accelerate the dynamics of knowledge by proactively favouring interactions and cooperation with outside systems and by supporting a context where knowledge can be transmitted and diffused amongst economic actors.

When economic systems go through phases of structural uncertainty, firms must be able to adapt promptly to new situations at such a speed that the distinction between present and future becomes blurred. On the face of it, according to the way knowledge is organized, created, transferred and diffused inside and amongst firms and between firms and other institutional actors, local economic systems can provide more or less convincing answers to structural uncertainty. Moreover when local actors cooperate and communicate, knowledge is also proactively created and diffused outside firms, thus providing to the local industry the tools to interpret structural uncertainty and, sometimes, to anticipate continuously changing events.

When a new large firm begins a process of interaction with the territory in which knowledge is exchanged, territorial knowledge could, over time, either grow or fall down. As we have mentioned, interaction could, for instance, focus on education and training programmes, or diffused processes of technological change. There are, however, other situations that can lead to radically different results. A firm can be opened to knowledge inputs coming from the territory but may be closed with respect to outgoing flows of knowledge. In this situation the local system does not receive knowledge inputs from the firm and thus cannot increase its capital stock. The firm has accumulated new knowledge, whilst at the same time destroying pieces of local knowledge.

NOTES

* This chapter builds on previous works of the authors, in particular: Poma (2003) and Sacchetti (2003). The empirical work relies on original data that belongs to Antares (Research Centre for Industrial and Territorial Policy) where Lucio Poma is president and Silvia Sacchetti researcher. We would like to thank the participants to the Pisa Regional Studies Association Annual Conference for comments and suggestions. We would also

thank Assindustria Reggio-Emilia. We are especially grateful to Lorenzo Ciapetti and Antares research fellows who have actively contributed to the empirical research projects to which we refer in this work.

1. For a Marxist perspective on the impoverishment of workers' capacity caused by the division of labour, see Braverman (1974).
2. We interviewed 168 firms, mostly manufacturing, and with a size above the Italian average size measured by the number of employees. (See Appendix A.)
3. For an analysis of the impact of different forms of linkages amongst firms, see Sacchetti and Sugden (2003).
4. Data collected during a seven-year survey on a sample of 120 firms.
5. The four phases in the product life cycle theorized by Vernon are linked to consumers' demand for goods. Differently from our perspective, this idea is heavily based on physical production. See Vernon (1966).
6. On the process of knowledge socialization, see Nonaka and Takeuchi (1995).
7. See Appendix B.
8. The frequencies reported below are based on few cases. However, these interviews were planned to obtain an overall feeling of the attitude of representative firms on the issue of past knowledge and experience. We present them not as the evidence of a tendency within data, but as a first result that suggests some hypotheses and further research.
9. The percentage of very old firms who believe that the past is not important is higher than for firms that were born between the 1940s and 1950s.
10. This figure is based on direct interviews with 34 firms.
11. Our analysis, as it is, is not applicable to the entrance of small firms or systems of small firms. Nor is it appropriate with respect to the entrance of a large firm inside a system with a poor knowledge capital.

BIBLIOGRAPHY

Babbage C. (1832), *On the Economy of Machinery and Manufactures*, London: Charles Knight.

Bettis, R.A., S.P. Bradley, and G. Hamel (1992), 'Outsourcing and industrial decline', *Academy of Management Executive*, **6** (1), 7–22.

Braverman, H. (1974), *Labour and Monopoly Capital. The Degradation of Work in the Twentieth Century*, New York: Monthly Review Press.

Dosi, G. (1982) 'Technological paradigms and technological trajectories: a suggested interpretation of the determinants and directions of technical change', *Research Policy*, **2** (3), 147–62.

European Commission, *Agenda 2000*, Brussels: European Community.

Ferguson A. (1767 [1966]), *An Essay on the History of Civil Society*, D. Forbes (ed.), Edinburgh: University Press.

Kern, H., and M. Schumann (1984), *Des Ende der Arbeitsteilung?*, Munich: Werlag Bech'sche; Italian translation (1991), *La fine della divisione del lavoro?*, Turin: Einaudi.

Marx, K. (1867), *Das Kapital. Kritik der Politischen Ökonomie.*

Nonaka I., and H. Takeuchi (1995), *The Knowledge-Creating Company*, Oxford: Oxford University Press.

Pavitt, K. (1984), 'Patterns of technological change: towards a taxonomy and a theory', *Research Policy*, **13** (6), 343–74.

Polanyi, M. (1958), *Personal Knowledge. Toward a Post-Critical Philosophy*, London: Routledge & Kegan Paul.

Pollock, F. (1957), *The Economic and Social Consequences of Automation*, Oxford: Basil Blackwell.
Poma L. (2003), *Oltre il distretto. Imprese e istituzioni nella nuova competizione territoriale*, Milan: Franco Angeli.
Sacchetti, S. (2003), 'Knowledge as capital. How the organisation of production impacts on local development', University of Ferrara Department of Economics, Institutions and Territory working paper no. 4 (April).
Sacchetti, S., and R. Sugden (2003), 'The governance of networks and economic power: the nature and impact of subcontracting relationships', *Journal of Economic Surveys*, **17** (5), 669–92.
Schumpeter, J.A. (1912), *Theorie der wirtschaftlichen Entwicklung*, Leipzig: Duncker & Humblot; English translation (1934), *The Theory of Economic Development*, Cambridge, MA: Harvard University Press; reprinted (1996) by Transaction Publisher, New Brunswick, NJ.
Smith A. (1776 [1994]), *An Inquiry into the Nature and Causes of the Wealth of Nations*, New York: The Modern Library.
Stiglitz, J. (1987), 'Learning to learn, localised learning and technological progress', in P. Dasgupta and P. Stoneman (eds) *Economic Policy and Technological Performance*, Cambridge: Cambridge University Press.
Vernon, R. (1966), 'International investment and international trade in the product cycle', *Quarterly Journal of Economics*, **80** (2), 190–207.

APPENDIX

A) Reggio Emilia Empirical Data: Sample and Methodology

Our universe of firms was formed by manufacturing firms with more than 10 employees. Thirty-four per cent of firms in the sample have over 50 employees and include 87 per cent of employees in the sample. We have collected data in 2001 using a structured questionnaire that was sent to 1900 firms. Questionnaires were submitted to the entrepreneurs/owners or to chief directors; 168 questionnaires were returned, mainly from manufacturing sectors. The average dimension of firms in the sample is 108 employees. When using Pavitt's categories, we have used, with minor adaptations, the classification from OECD STAN database for industrial analysis.

B) Forlì-Cesena Empirical Data: Sample and Methodology

The sample includes 80 firms, of which 47 have more than 50 employees. Data have been collected in the year 2000 through postal questionnaires and direct structured interviews with entrepreneurs. In particular, we refer to a subset of 34 respondents who addressed issues related to the importance of the past during the interview.

7. High-tech industry clustering rationales: the case of German biotechnology

Kerstin Wolter

1. INTRODUCTION

Biotechnology is often heralded as a key sector that will shape future technological development in areas as important as food and healthcare. Although there is good reason to doubt some of the more ambitious predictions regarding the industry's impact in times to come, there have been important changes set off by the emergence of biotechnology in the sectors mentioned above, especially regarding healthcare. Consequently, many regions worldwide strive to position themselves as the next biotechnology centre by building regional agglomerations of companies. What is however not fully understood – both in the case of biotechnology as well as other high-tech industries – are the rationales underlying a specific industry's spatial concentration. Instead, much has been written about the positive effects resulting from agglomeration, starting as early as the 19th century with the formulation of Marshallian externalities (Marshall, 1972). According to Marshall, companies profit from co-location due to the emergence of pooled labour markets, the availability of specialized inputs as well as knowledge spillovers. Additional agglomeration economies lie with public support for the industry, better infrastructural endowments (Brenner, 2000) or the emergence of commonly accepted business behaviour standards (Maskell, 2001). Taken together, these factors are argued to enhance the competitiveness of firms located within an agglomeration relative to those outside of it.

The goal of this chapter is to take a step forward in the analysis. While the existence of agglomeration economies is not doubted, the aim is to investigate in more detail what factors are responsible for creating them in the first place. For an industry to concentrate spatially, there has to be an advantage for firms to locate near others. In the existing literature, agglomeration economies are often mentioned as this advantage. For such economies to emerge, however, a certain number of companies already have to be established locally. Consequently, the important issue is to find a rationale for an industry to agglomerate prior to the emergence of agglomeration economies. If such a 'clustering rationale' exists, it will lead to identical location choices by a number of companies, implying a tendency towards spatial concentration. In later stages of the development of an agglomeration, the spatial concentration is then reinforced by the emergence of agglomeration economies (once a critical mass of companies is located in an area) and constrained by the emergence of congestion costs (resulting from greater numbers of firms competing for industry inputs and local infrastructure raising the local cost structure).[1]

To examine the concept of a 'clustering rationale',[2] it is argued that the spatial concentration of independent firms offers several proximity benefits. It helps reduce transaction costs associated with any type of firm's external relations: search and information, negotiation and decision as well as control and enforcement costs. In addition, it facilitates repeated contact between parties, which is especially important for the transmission of knowledge bound to a specific context or difficult to codify (tacit knowledge). Therefore, the geographic 'cluster' will be understood as a specific way of organizing external firm relations. With regard to the degree of integration among interacting parties, it ranges between the extremes of pure market exchange and inter-firm hierarchy (Martin and Rogers, 1995; Maskell and Lorenzen, 2003). This type of organization can be very efficient for organizing a range of economic activities, especially when the latter involve tacit ('contextual') knowledge.

An industry will thus be found to cluster if sufficient parts of its operations are dependent on relations with external parties and if the benefits offered by proximity in these relations (transaction cost and/or knowledge transmission) are significant. Following this line of thought, two main areas of company activity might be subject to proximity benefits: resource access or inter-company interaction. These are further explained in section 2. Section 3 then presents an example of an industry where tacit knowledge and transaction cost are important for access to key resources: biotechnology. From this, hypotheses are derived regarding the spatial distribution of biotechnology firms which will be tested using the German case in the fourth section. Section 5 concludes.

2. WHY DO INDUSTRIES CLUSTER? RESOURCE-ACCESS VERSUS INTER-COMPANY INTERACTION

It has been argued that geographic proximity can be considered a specific form of 'market organization' of economic activities offering significant savings on transaction and transport costs as well as advantages in the transmission of contextual, tacit knowledge. If these proximity benefits are sufficiently important for industry activity, companies would have an incentive for co-locating, and agglomerations could emerge. Consequently, proximity would have to matter in key industry activities involving external parties and/or a sufficient amount of them. Basically, two areas of industry operations could be subject to this type of proximity benefits: access to scarce, critical resources or interaction with other firms.[3]

2.1 Resource-based Agglomerations

Agglomerations can result from proximity benefits in accessing scarce, critical, partly immobile resources which cannot be sufficiently or efficiently developed within the firm itself. Examples would be skilled personnel, risk capital or knowledge-generating institutions. Two reasons could be held responsible for proximity benefits: transaction cost and tacit knowledge.

- In the case of *skilled personnel*, transaction costs are high if companies hire non-local people: search costs increase and salaries have to be very attractive for personnel to change their place of residence.[4] Consequently, firms depending on key, scarce personnel would have an incentive to locate in areas offering a greater supply of qualified people.
- The provision of capital, especially *risk capital* requires detailed (tacit) knowledge by the investor about the investment company's operations and potential. In order to obtain this knowledge easily, risk capital providers locate near their investments.[5]
- The transfer of *knowledge* (for example, new scientific knowledge) out of research institutions into the private sector often occurs in proximity due to its newness and thereby tacit nature (lack of standards). Firms depending on this type of knowledge as one of their key inputs would be induced to locate near its source to minimize transaction cost involved with knowledge transfer.

Industries relying heavily on one or several of these resources would therefore tend to agglomerate near their source. Such *resource-based agglomerations* differ from their interaction-based counterparts in so far as they require proximity for interaction between companies and resources (which is not to exclude the possibility of local and distant interaction among firms), whereas in interaction-based agglomerations the need for proximity stems from its benefits regarding interaction with other firms.

2.2 Interaction-based Agglomerations

Agglomerations, alongside being a potential location for productive resources offer several benefits in the coordination of economic activity between independent companies. These again relate to transaction costs, which is not to imply that transactions cannot be organized efficiently over large distances. However, in industries with a large amount and frequency of inter-firm transactions, agglomerations offer significant advantages due to these savings. At the same time, proximity facilitates repeated contact between parties which assists the transfer of tacit knowledge. Regarding inter-company interaction, such knowledge can not only relate to commercially relevant issues (for example technology) but also to insight in partner trustworthiness (Granovetter, 1985, 506). Consequently, proximity benefits exist, if inter-company interaction is frequent, and/or if it involves complex or strategically important assets requiring significant trust between partners (Granovetter, 1973, 1364–65). One or both of these features are found in industries with a strong division of labour, that is the development and production of the final product is not conducted within integrated enterprises but takes a 'disintegrated' form involving several, independent parties. Factors favouring such a division of labour stem from: innovation, production or (indirectly) consumption (Figure 7.1).

- A division of labour in *innovative activity*, 'network innovation' (Steinle and Schiele, 2002), would suggest proximity between the necessary actors due to significant transaction cost savings and better opportuni-

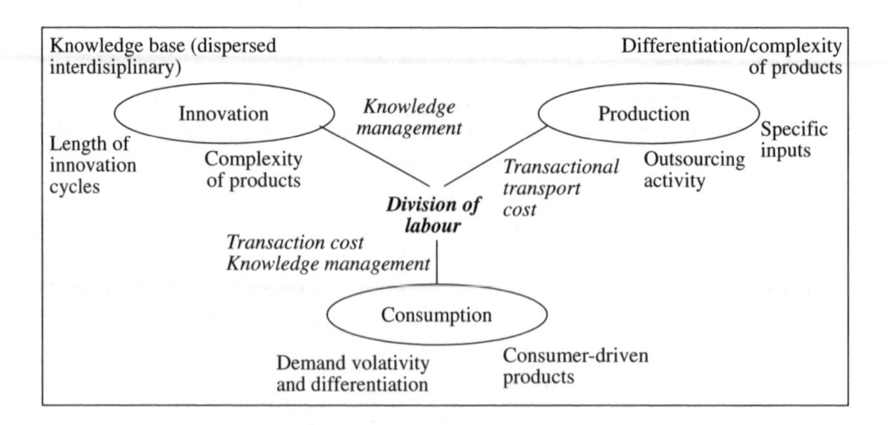

Source: Own illustration

Figure 7.1 Factors favouring 'disintegrated' production/ development

ties for transferring new technological knowledge (which is often tacit, as it still lacks standards for its codification). Networked innovation becomes necessary if industry conditions make it difficult for firms to stay on the forefront of technology through internal effort alone. This can be due to a dispersed and/or interdisciplinary knowledge base, short innovation cycles and complexity of products. Dispersed and/or interdisciplinary knowledge raises the number of actors critical to achieving innovation, whereas short innovation cycles increase the risk of innovating and the need for speed, which can be addressed by pooling resources and capabilities of different parties. Greater complexity of products imply strong benefits from specialization, meaning that advances in the final product will be driven by component manufacturers and product assemblers (Nelson and Rosenberg, 1993).

- A strong division of labour in *production* can demand proximity between parties due to the savings on transaction and transport cost. This division of labour stems from two sources: production conditions or the nature of demand. The former can consist in specific outsourcing strategies (just-in-time logistics) or the differentiation/complexity of the product (where a division of labour means greater variety and specialization benefits). Furthermore, a need for specialized inputs (Storper, 1997) would tend to encourage a vertical division of labour in production.
- Finally, *consumption* can indirectly favour a division of labour in production implying proximity benefits regarding transaction and transport cost. Differentiated demand means a need for product differentiation and thus benefits from a division of labour in production, as described above. Demand volatility raises uncertainty about which and how many products will have to be provided. Together, this brings a need for flexibility which can be achieved by temporary networks of independent producers.[6] Finally, consumers might also be major drivers of product innovation. In this case, network innovation between consumers and producers would imply a need for their geographic proximity (see first section).

In order to derive ideas regarding the spatial distribution of biotechnology firms, it is therefore important to determine now, what part of this industry's activity is subject to proximity benefits: do they mainly apply in resource access or rather in inter-company interactions?

3. BIOTECHNOLOGY'S CLUSTERING RATIONALE: RESOURCES OR INTERACTION?

Biological processes as tools for the fulfilment of human needs have a long history going back to about 6000 BC when the Sumerians and Babylonians engaged in beer fermentation (Kenney, 1986, 1–2). However, the application of biological processes reached a new dimension in the 20th century, when the founding discoveries for modern biotechnology were made in university labs: of these, the discovery of the double-helix structure of the DNA by Watson and Crick (1953) is commonly accepted as the date of birth of modern biotechnology. Combined with the subsequently developed basic biotechnologies including recombinant DNA (Boyer and Cohen, 1973), monoclonal antibodies (Kohler and Milstein, 1975) and protein engineering (developed in the 1980s), completely new avenues were opened for the development of processes and products in areas as important as human health, agriculture, food production and waste management (Porter Liebeskind et al., 1995).

3.1 Biotechnology – an Industry Overview

Biotechnology can therefore be divided into subsectors according to the field of application of its products, including three main areas:

- pharmaceutical, 'red' biotechnology: development of novel tools and products to cure (therapeutics) and identify (diagnostics) diseases;
- agricultural, 'green' biotechnology: application of biotechnological processes in agriculture and food production;
- environmental, 'grey' biotechnology: use of biotechnology processes for environmental protection and industrial production.[7]

These subsectors differ in important aspects such as the pace of knowledge creation and destruction of old capabilities, development times for products or the number and function of established players. For instance, the impact of biotechnology has been greatest in the pharmaceutical segment where a paradigm shift has moved drug development from combinatory chemistry to biotechnology. The segment is characterized by a high pace of knowledge creation combined with long and expensive product development (due to regulatory requirements and distribution cost, Pisano et al., 1988, 208). The resulting distinctiveness of capabilities necessary to create, develop, manufacture and market products has led to a strong segmentation of the value chain with strong complementarities between universities, new biotechnology firms and established pharmaceutical or chemical companies (see Figure 7.2). In agricultural or environmental biotechnology, on the other hand, es-

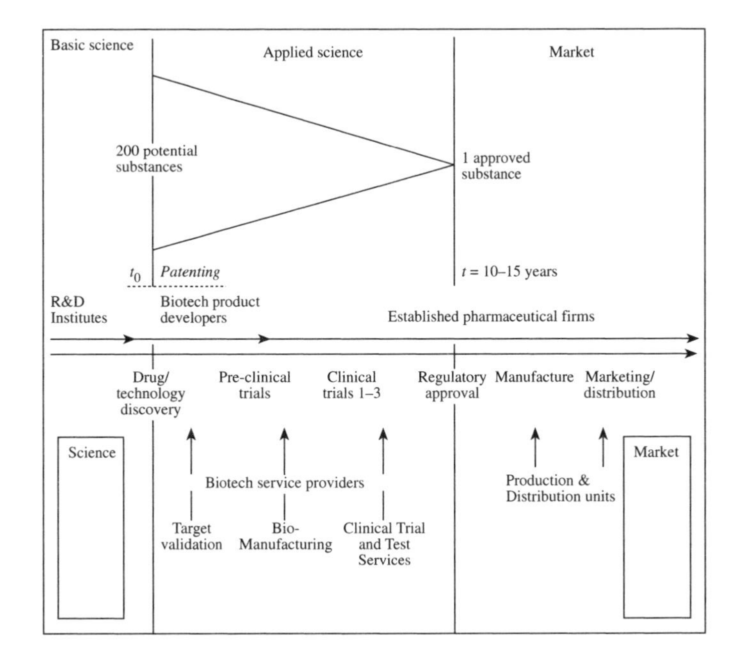

Source: Own illustration.

Figure 7.2 Turning knowledge into products: the pharmaceutical biotechnology value chain

tablished players have been able to maintain their dominance both in terms of research as well as marketing, resulting in less cooperation between new biotechnology firms and established companies.

The focus of the analysis here will be on pharmaceutical biotechnology. This industry sector is chosen for several reasons: firstly, it constitutes the most important biotechnology subsector worldwide, both in numbers of firms as well as market potential. Secondly, it is argued to be the sector with the most important future impact (healthcare) attracting a significant deal of policy attention. Thirdly, red biotechnology has sustained the relatively strongest impact by new biotechnology firms, although existing pharmaceuticals and chemicals firms have been able to retain an important role in the sector due to their capabilities in obtaining product approval and distribution (see Figure 7.2). Finally, pharmaceutical biotechnology is also the most important market segment – in terms of numbers of firms and research institutions – in Germany's industry.

As the industry was 'born' in university research labs (Kenney, 1986) and its knowledge base is continually expanding (Porter Liebeskind et al., 1995, 3), neither the small dedicated biotechnology firms nor the large established pharmaceutical corporations are able to pursue all promising research avenues themselves. Therefore, the basic substances or technologies commercialized by small biotechnology firms tend to be developed in R&D institutes such as universities or other types of research laboratories. These discoveries are then licensed out to biotechnology start-up firms or the responsible scientists leave their institution to commercialize the knowledge themselves.[8] Small biotechnology product developers then further test and develop the product, with assistance from service providers positioned at different steps of the value chain. These service providers are specialized in supporting activities: target validation, bio-manufacturing of tissues to be used in pre-clinical trials, bulk production of complementary products, such as enzymes and reagents and so on. While service providers do have to meet standards regarding their facilities and production processes, their development times and cost tend to be a lot shorter than those of biotechnology product developers.[9]

Due to extensive regulatory requirements, human health products then have to pass through different stages of pre-clinical (not involving human test subjects) and clinical testing (on humans) before obtaining regulatory approval. This testing tends to be expensive and time-consuming implying that the average small biotechnology firm lacks the resources to conduct these steps itself. Usually, this is therefore when an established pharmaceutical company takes up the product's development and marketing/distribution because of their access to hospitals for clinical testing and international production and distribution networks. Pharmaceutical companies' involvement can however also take place at a later point in the product's development, that is after the testing has been conducted. In this case, the testing phase is sub-contracted to specialized Clinical Research Organizations (CROs). The linkage between pharmaceutical firms/CRO and biotechnology ventures usually takes the form of contractual arrangements where the biotechnology venture licenses its technology or its product to the pharmaceutical company in exchange for development funding and royalty payments. A positive outcome of this entire development process in the form of a marketable product is however far from certain since only about one out of 200 newly discovered substances makes it through all testing phases. Developing a new drug from its discovery to its market introduction is therefore both long (it can easily take 10 to 15 years) and expensive (it is estimated to cost $802 million in the United States; Tufts University, 2003, 2).

What can be seen from this brief introduction to pharmaceutical biotechnology is that the small biotechnology firms are usually active in two main areas: they either develop their own products/ technologies for licence to established players ('product developers') or they specialize in providing services to product developers and/or established players ('service providers'). Furthermore, two main industry features bearing on spatial distribution can be identified:

- First, biotechnology is a strongly science reliant industry with a high pace of knowledge creation. This implies three things: on the one hand, small biotechnology firms will depend on external sources of knowledge to discover and develop new technologies. These are especially important in firm start-up, where in most cases biotechnology product developers and service providers both begin working with knowledge developed by research institutions. On the other hand, the high scientific content of these firms' day-to-day operations means a strong dependence on skilled personnel (often with extensive academic training) which is not ubiquitously available. Finally, combined with long development times, the high science reliance makes proprietary knowledge a key asset to firm activity, implying a strong incentive to protect this knowledge by patenting as soon as possible.[10]
- Second, long development times prior to obtaining marketable results bring about a need for external sources of finance (for example venture capital) to sustain biotechnology firms. This need will be more pronounced for product developers due to their longer development times but does to a lesser extent also apply to service providers.

What are the implications of these industry characteristics for the spatial distribution of biotechnology firms (product developers and service providers)? This issue will be addressed in the following section.

3.2 Biotechnology's Spatial Distribution

Empirical evidence shows that biotechnology firms tend to agglomerate spatially.[11] The question then regards the rationale for this agglomeration: do proximity benefits (tacit knowledge, transaction cost) apply more significantly in resource access or inter-company interaction?

3.2.1 Tacit knowledge

It has been argued that, due to the patenting activity mentioned in the previous section, most technological knowledge in biotechnology is not tacit (Johnson and Mareva, 2002), since patenting requires significant disclosure and codification of information. The nature of knowledge is, however, different in the stages prior to patenting. New scientific knowledge might not yet have commonly accepted standards for its communication and would require repeated contact with its creators in order to be transferred. This type of knowledge would first and foremost be expected in interactions between research institutes and biotechnology companies (product developers and service providers) either during firm start-up or in later scientific collaborations dedicated to the creation of new knowledge. Another channel for the transfer of tacit scientific knowledge and thus a driving force for the localization of biotechnology firms could be the interaction among firms. However, due to the specificity of biotechnology applications, finding a partner with complementary assets nearby is often a matter of chance. Consequently, empirical studies of formal knowledge collaborations among companies don't find a dominant role for proximity (McKelvey et al., 2002; Osegowitsch and Anoop, 2001).

Tacit knowledge could also be involved in resource access regarding external finance. Due to long, costly product development, biotechnology firms rely on substantial, high risk financial resources (often in the form of venture capital). Providers of this type of finance, however, require detailed (tacit) knowledge about their investments regarding management capabilities, market potential and so on which can be more easily obtained if investors are located near their investments (Powell et al., 2002). As mentioned before, this aspect would be argued to apply more strongly to product-developing firms than to service providers due to their longer development times.

3.2.2 Transaction costs

The research intensity and science reliance of biotechnology implies a need for specialized, skilled personnel who have often followed extensive academic education. Such personnel are created in research institutions and due to their specialization do not constitute a ubiquitous resource. Proximity to research institutions would therefore lower transaction costs (search and information as well as negotiation and decision cost) in accessing this key resource since costs are high when hiring non-local people: search costs increase and salaries have to be very attractive for personnel to change their place of residence. This again applies to both product developers and service providers.

Proximity between product developers and service providers could offer another area for transaction cost savings in inter-firm arrangements. These again affect search and information, negotiation and decision as well as control and enforcement costs. As has been argued by other studies (Oßenbrügge and Zeller, 2001), service suppliers can additionally benefit from proximity to their 'clients' (product developers) due to greater speed in handling of specialized orders. However, most biological services can be very well specified (for example firms requiring a specifically structured protein) and are therefore also easily conducted through longer-distance market transactions.[12]

Transaction costs in accessing key resources are especially important in the firm formation process (Lemarie et al., 2001; Stuart and Sorensen, 2003):

new firms rely extensively on external resources to develop their scientific, business and financial capabilities (that is they require contact with scientists, skilled employees, consultants and venture capitalists) as they initially lack the financial resources to cater for both their resource and their infrastructural requirements themselves (for example laboratory space). It would therefore be argued that founders of biotechnology firms tend to locate their ventures near their previous place of residence/work (Garnsey, 1998, 372), in order to use their local networks to access external resources. Consequently, transaction costs could also imply that biotechnology firms agglomerate where an above-average number of potential biotechnology founders is available (for example coming from a local research institution).

3.3 Biotechnology – a Resource-based Agglomeration

The previous sections have highlighted that biotechnology firms find significant proximity benefits when accessing resources such as scientific knowledge, skilled personnel, finance and infrastructure. These proximity benefits are found to be specifically important in the start-up phase, when companies have a strong need for external expertise and resources, since they lack the funds and capabilities to develop them internally. Furthermore, proximity benefits apply differently to biotechnology firms depending on the nature of their operations: it is argued that product-developing firms show a greater reliance on external resources due to their longer lead times before obtaining a marketable product than service providers. Nonetheless, the benefits mentioned above apply to both types of firms, albeit to differing extents. Biotechnology therefore constitutes an example of a resource-based agglomeration (scientific knowledge, skilled personnel, finance) despite its aforementioned strong vertical division of labour. Consequently, biotechnology companies are expected to locate near the source of these resources (see Figure 7.3).

The main locational attractor for biotechnology firms (product developers and service providers) is the presence of a local science base, that is, a local research institution. The latter can provide two key resources to firms: scientific knowledge and skilled personnel, and also acts as a source of biotechnology founders which in most cases have followed an academic career before starting their own company (Audretsch and Cooke, 2001, 17). Therefore, the first proposition reads:

> *Proposition 1*: Biotechnology firms (product developers and service providers) will tend to locate near research institutions.

Secondly, the importance of external resources for new biotechnology ventures would imply that firm creation and growth will be more pronounced

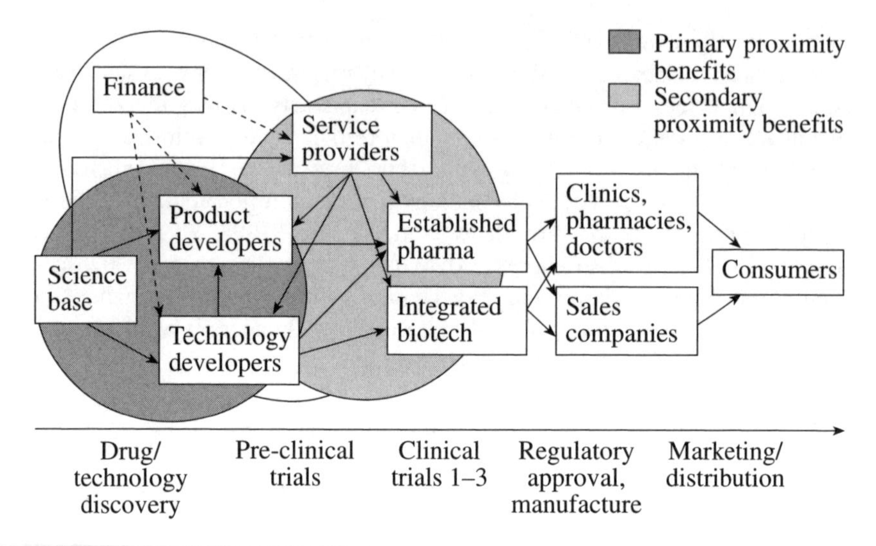

Source: Own illustration.

Figure 7.3 Primary and secondary proximity benefits for small biotechnology firms

in areas with a strong endowment in these resources, especially regarding venture capital.[13] This is specifically true for product-developing firms, due to their longer lead times before obtaining a marketable product. Therefore proposition two reads:

> *Proposition 2*: Biotechnology firms will be more numerous (larger) where finance/venture capital is available. This especially holds for product-developing firms.

These propositions will now be examined using empirical evidence from the German pharmaceutical biotechnology industry.

4. THE GERMAN CASE

Despite the industry's late emergence in Germany, recent sector development has been very dynamic, bringing firm numbers from 185 before 1995 to a total of 598 in 2002. Depending on the definition of biotechnology firms employed in empirical studies, however, the year 2002 can also be found to have brought first signs of consolidation in the industry: according to Ernst & Young data, the number of new firms in 2002 was exceeded for the first time by the amount of bankruptcies and mergers. Consequently, the total firm

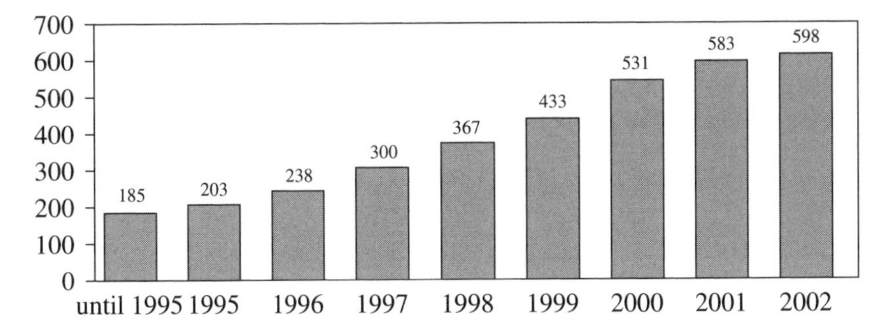

Source: Own illustration based on BIOCOM (2003) data.

Figure 7.4 Development of Category I firm numbers in Germany[14]

numbers in Germany are found to have decreased that year (Ernst & Young, 2003). In contrast, the Association of German Biotechnology Companies finds a slight positive development for 2002 (Figure 7.4).

The BioRegio initiative undertaken by the Bundesministerium für Bildung und Forschung (German Ministry of Education and Research) in 1995 is often given as an explanation for the aforementioned development. Under the programme, regions were invited to compete for federal funding based on concepts of cooperative effort to foster the local biotechnology industry. The

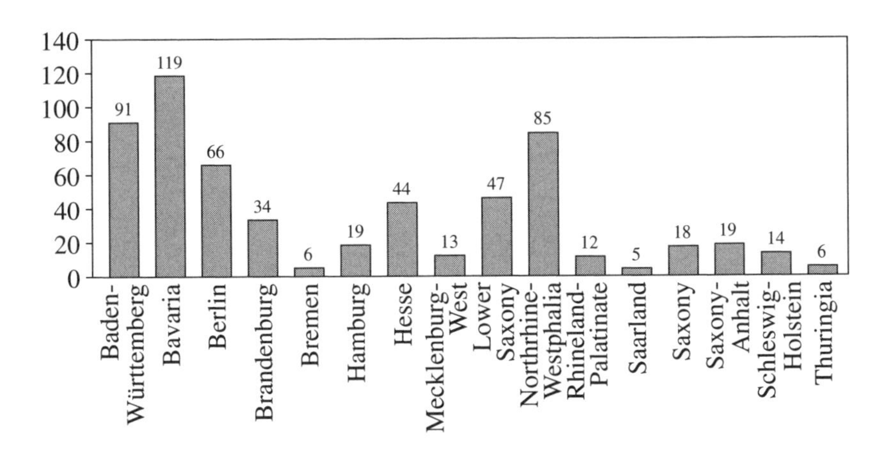

Source: Own illustration based on BIOCOM (2003) data.

Figure 7.5 Distribution of biotechnology firms across German federal states, 2002

grants provided to the three winning regions Munich (city), Rhineland (Cologne, Aachen, Düsseldorf and Wuppertal) as well as the Rhine-Neckar Triangle (Heidelberg, Mannheim, Ludwigshafen) could then be used to fund local biotechnology support institutions as well as a source of risk capital to biotechnology firms themselves. Finance availability was therefore greater in BioRegio winning areas than in other parts of the country.

The industry in Germany is centred in a few regions (see Figure 7.5), with main centres in Munich, the upper Rhine, and Berlin.

4.1 The Data

The map of German biotechnology companies was created using a comprehensive database published annually by the Association of German Biotechnology Companies and BIOCOM AG[15] (BIOCOM, 2003). The database classifies biotechnology organizations according to their role in the sector, distinguishing between research institutions (public), biotechnology companies grouped into different categories (see Table 7.1), finance organizations and support institutions.

Due to time and resource constraints, the initial analysis was restricted to the key actors in biotechnology: research institutions and dedicated biotechnology firms (category I).[16] However, before the data could be used to generate the German biotechnology map, further consolidation had to take place. It has been argued that proximity benefits in biotechnology differ depending on whether companies are product developers or service providers. Consequently, companies in the sample were categorized as product developers if they were actively developing novel therapeutic, diagnostic or medical products. Firms dedicating themselves to the provision of services (contract research, contract manufacturing and the like) were classified as service providers. Since the company nature (product developer or service provider) was not readily visible from company operations listed in the database (in the sense that both product developers and service providers perform R&D for instance), and many companies in Germany follow a dual business model (service provision in order to finance product development),[17] company websites had to be examined prior to any classification in order to gather information as to where the main focus of company activity lay.

Another category that emerged during the research was stand-alone production and distribution facilities, often owned by foreign pharmaceutical companies. The rationale for such facilities lies with the different national legislation that pharmaceutical products have to meet before being allowed on the market. This results in a sort of 'national embeddedness' of downstream activities (Bartholomew, 1997). However, it cannot be expected that production or distribution facilities will have the same tendency to agglomer-

Table 7.1 Categories of biotechnology organizations in the BIOCOM, 2003 database

Research	Public research institutions involved with biotechnology research. Data for research institutions was collected at the institute level for two reasons: first, a university with many institutes involved in biotechnology research yields greater numbers of possible interaction partners. Second, coordination between chairs in one institute tends to be good, allowing their summary under the institution's roof.
Category I firms	Companies involved in research, production or other work employing modern biotechnological processes as well as companies heavily involved in biotechnological research and which, because of their size, type of work or importance to the market, are viewed as a significant component of the biotechnology sector. Category I companies were distinguished into product developers, service providers, distribution and production facilities as the nature of their business would impact on their role for the biotechnology system as well as the extent and nature of linkages they were likely to form.
Category II firms	Companies not belonging to Category I, that provide an appreciable amount of technical products and services to companies in Category I and research institutions
Capital	Public and private organizations investing in biotechnology companies.
Support	Different support organizations such as consultants, science park management organizations, legal advisors and so on)

Source: Own illustration (definitions taken from BIOCOM, 2002).

ate regionally as do service providers and product developers, because their knowledge and products come from the mother corporation rather than a specific locale. The data obtained from this consolidation was then fed into RegioGraph 6.0, a computer programme able to position biotechnology companies on the German map based on their postal code (see Figure 7.6).

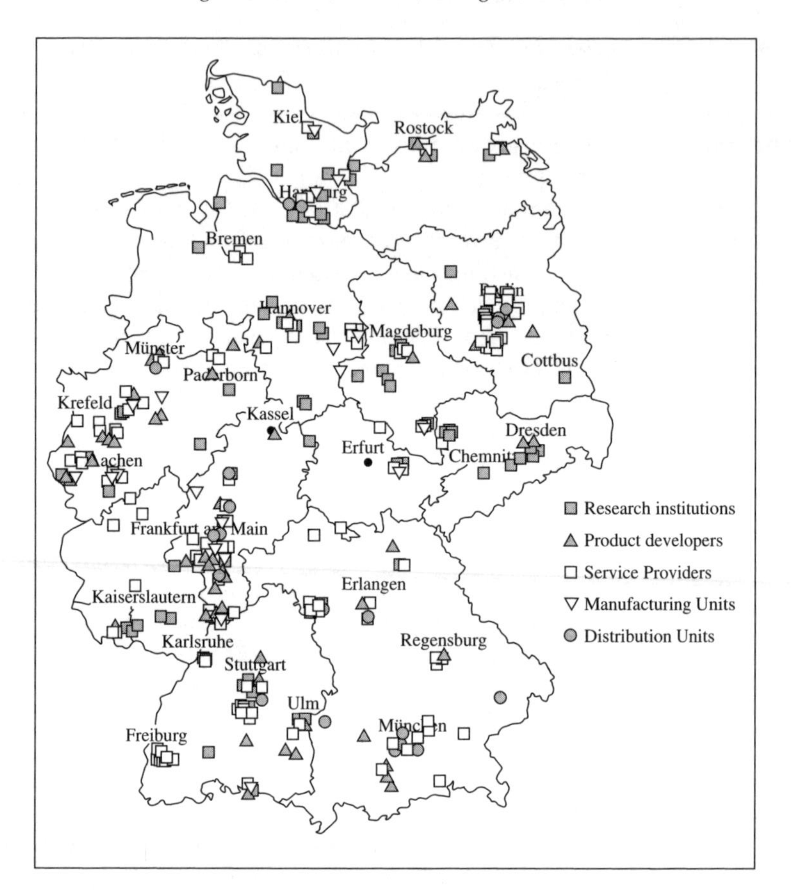

Source: Own illustration (realized with RegioGraph 6.0).

Figure 7.6 The German biotechnology map[18]

4.2 Results and Discussion

The first proposition constituted that biotechnology firms would tend to locate near research institutions. In addition, it was argued that this agglomeration tendency would be stronger for product developing firms due to their longer development times. As can be readily observed from Figures 7.7 and 7.8, both product developers and service providers exhibit a propensity to agglomerate in areas with a strong presence of research institutions. To gain further insight into the causalities behind this observation, another examination regarding the impact of the presence of a research institution in a city on the total number of biotechnology firms located there was carried out. It was

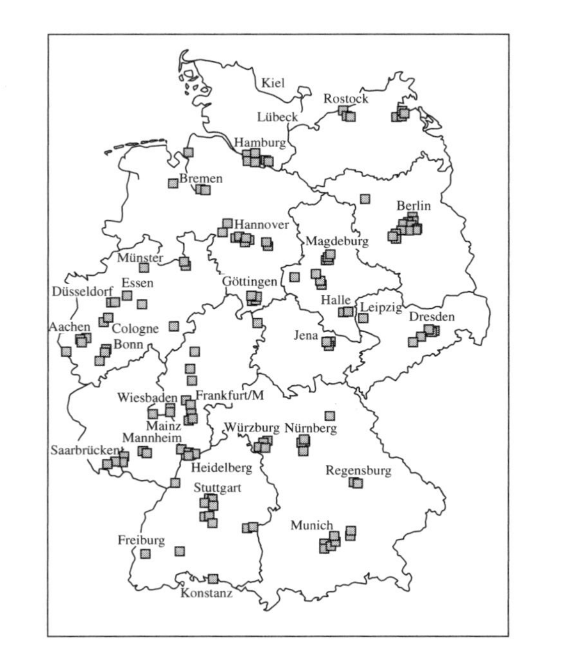

Source: Own illustration (realized with RegioGraph 6.0).

Figure 7.7 Co-location patterns of research centres (left) and research centres + biotechnology product developers (right)

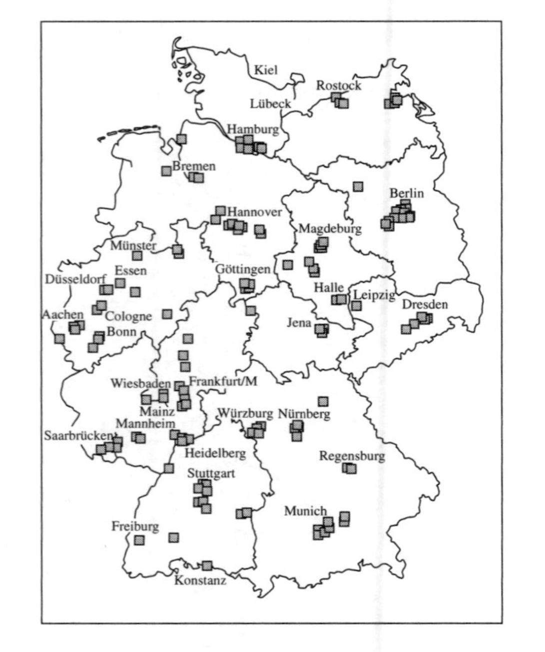

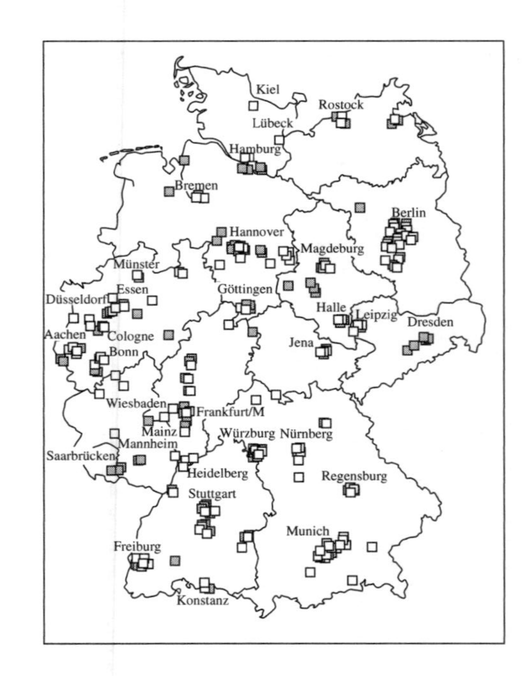

Source: Own illustration (realized with RegioGraph 6.0).

Figure 7.8 Co-location patterns of research centres (left) and research centres + biotechnology service providers (right)

also examined whether this picture changed when examining the co-location of research institutions and product developers/service providers. It emerged that 72.5 per cent (368 out of 509) of all German biotechnology firms were located in the same city as a research institution. The number of local research institutions was also found to have a positive impact on the number of firms in a city ($\rho_{xy} = 0.82689$). This correlation was somewhat weaker when distinguishing between product-developing firms ($\rho_{xy} = 0.79546$) and service providers ($\rho_{xy} = 0.78340$). However, the overall weaker correlation found for service providers acts as a preliminary support for the first proposition.

Of course the empirical evidence provided cannot yet lead to the establishing of a causal relationship between the location of research centres and that of biotechnology firms. Correlation between the two variables only expresses that a greater number of research institutions in a city also sees a greater number of biotechnology firms. This correlation is slightly stronger in the case of biotechnology product developers than with service providers, which might be attributable to the longer development times of product developers and thus their stronger reliance on proprietary knowledge. However, a simple correlation cannot indicate how statistically relevant this relation is, nor does it allow for a straightforward causality as the direction of the latter cannot be determined (that is, is it biotechnology firms driving the location of research centres or the other way round?). To derive such a hypothesis, more extensive statistical testing would be needed. However, this preliminary evidence does support proposition one, implying that apparently in Germany there are significant proximity benefits in accessing key resources. This seems to lead to a clustering of biotechnology firms near research institutions, although a word of caution regarding the current state of statistical relevance of this result has to be provided.

The second proposition stated that biotechnology firms would be more numerous (larger) in areas with a greater availability of venture capital, especially regarding product-developing firms (again due to their longer time to market). Interestingly enough, inequalities in the distribution of finance did not seem to have a specific influence on the number of biotechnology companies. The exclusive provision of funds to selected regions throughout the BioRegio contest could have been expected to create greater numbers of biotechnology companies in these areas than in non-winner regions, especially when considering that venture capital is far from being abundantly available in Germany. Taking the two most successful biotechnology regions (in terms of company numbers), Munich and Berlin, however, it emerges that despite its success in BioRegio, Munich hosts in total fewer pharmaceutical biotechnology companies than Berlin (54 versus 57).[19] Furthermore, the development in terms of total firm numbers has not been any more dynamic in Munich after BioRegio than in Berlin (see Figure 7.9).

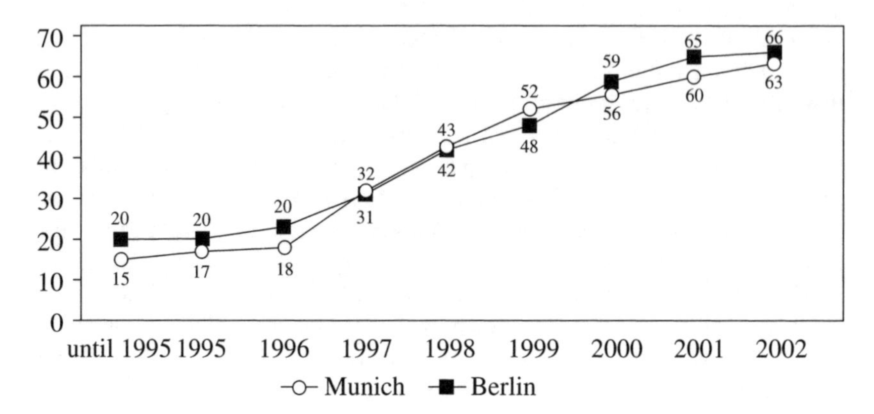

Source: Own illustration (data taken from BIOCOM, 2003).

Figure 7.9 The evolution of biotechnology in Berlin and Munich until 2002

In terms of product developers, Munich hosts a slightly larger number of firms than Berlin (32 to 29) whereas in Berlin, service providers are better represented (28 to 19). In total numbers alone, these differences don't appear striking enough to support proposition 2. Therefore, the average size of product developers and service providers (measured by employment) was determined for both locations. Controlling for firm maturity (which would imply greater numbers of employees), it was found that product developers in Munich employed on average 51.4 employees and were about 6 years old (average founding year: 1997). Regarding service providers, employment averaged 33 employees and firm age amounted to about seven years (average founding year: 1996). In Berlin, both types of biotechnology firms were smaller on average. Product developers employed about 32.2 people[20] being on average five years old, and service providers at the average age of nine years had about 17.5 employees. The larger average size of biotechnology firms in Munich could therefore point towards the second proposition regarding the impact of public finance. However, this greater average size could also stem from greater maturity of Munich biotechnology firms which does apply for biotechnology product developers (average founding year 1997 in Munich and 1998 in Berlin) but not for service providers (average founding year 1996 in Munich and 1994 in Berlin).

Empirically, the evidence on the impact of (public) finance availability is therefore mixed, not allowing for final conclusions regarding the second proposition. It should however be noticed that, for one thing, public finance is accessible for biotechnology firms outside BioRegio areas through other federal programmes (for example, BioChance or BioProfile) and state or regional governments are very active in providing assistance to new biotechnology ventures, including finance. Furthermore, proximity to the Berlin-based pharmaceutical giant Schering (maintaining numerous links with small local companies) could have helped to compensate for the relative shortage of federal funding in the area.

5. CONCLUSIONS AND OUTLOOK

The focus on agglomeration economies as a cause for the emergence of spatial concentrations of economic activity falls short of explaining how the critical number of companies required for the emergence of agglomeration economies came to locate in the area. Therefore, this chapter introduced the concept of industry 'clustering rationales': geographic proximity offers several benefits in coordinating economic activities with external parties (tacit knowledge, transaction and transport costs). If a sufficient extent of firm activity was subject to these proximity benefits in an industry, firms would tend to exhibit identical location choices enabling the emergence of an agglomeration and subsequently agglomeration economies/congestion costs.

Depending on the area of industry activity subject to proximity benefits, a distinction was drawn between industries requiring proximity in order to access scarce, (partly) immobile critical resources (resource-based agglomerations) and those benefiting from proximity in interaction with other independent firms (interaction-based agglomerations). An examination of the pharmaceutical biotechnology sector revealed that the industry, due to its science reliance and long product development times constituted an example of a resource-based agglomeration: proximity benefits were pronounced in accessing new scientific knowledge, skilled personnel and external finance. It was then proposed that German biotechnology firms would be found to locate in areas where biotechnology research institutions (as a source of scientific knowledge, skilled personnel) and/or external finance would be available.

Preliminary empirical evidence supported the first proposition of biotechnology firms agglomerating near research institutions. External finance availability (at least in terms of federal risk capital) had less of an impact on firm numbers than could have been expected. However, firms in an area with federal funding (Munich) were found to be larger on average than in 'self-sufficient' areas (Berlin), although in the case of product developing firms, this size difference could also be attributed to differing average firm maturity between both centres.

A number of interesting research questions emerge from this. First, the link between the localization of biotechnology research centres and firms merits further attention. Can a clear causality be established? Or is the observed joint distribution attributable to other factors (for example, the size of metropolitan areas)? How can resource endowment of areas be captured empirically for statistical testing? While some parts of resource endowments are easily quantified (infrastructural assets such as ICT infrastructure), other more qualitative aspects are difficult to capture (personnel skills[21]). Does the quality of research offered by different institutions have a significant impact on the geographic distribution of biotechnology firms, that is do 'leading' research institutions attract more biotechnology ventures? Secondly, the nature of biotechnology as a resource-based agglomeration could have an important impact on the development of biotechnology centres: if firm reliance on external resources declines with time[22] as companies are increasingly able to cater for their resource and infrastructural needs themselves, what are the consequences for the agglomeration itself?

NOTES

1. It is argued that more firms in the area initially decrease local costs because their presence leads to a greater emergence of providers of infrastructure, business services and so on. After a while, however, congestion costs set in since infrastructure and other local factors cannot grow without limits. Then, the increased competition for these factors by more firms drives up their prices, that is, local costs.
2. Please note that the term 'cluster' is here used in a very generic sense, that is as a synonym for agglomeration. It does not mean the identically denominated concept (Porter, 1998).
3. A significant body of literature argues that tacit knowledge has a self-reinforcing property regarding agglomerations: on the one hand, tacit knowledge demands proximity for its transfer. On the other hand, it is often argued that tacit knowledge evolves in agglomerations due to proximity between parties and active interaction among them (Maskell, 2001). However, this second aspect – while important for the agglomeration's later development – is of less importance in the context proposed here since the focus is on the rationale for agglomeration emergence where only limited numbers of companies in an area can be expected, thereby limiting the potential for creating tacit knowledge among them.
4. If a change of residence can be achieved at all.
5. See among others Powell et al. (2002).
6. Such networks bring together resources when they are needed and adapt according to changes in demand. This type of demand is crucial in Italian industrial districts (Piore and Sabel, 1984) which focus on fashion-driven markets (volatile demand) or customized machinery (differentiated demand).
7. Grey biotechnology focuses on the detection and removal of toxic substances (environment) and the provision of novel production processes for fine chemicals (industrial production). Sector definitions were taken from Ernst & Young (2002). Sometimes, a fourth, newly emerging sector is mentioned: *maritime, 'blue' biotechnology*, dedicated to the search of maritime natural compounds for application in pharmaceutical and food production.
8. An empirical study (Audretsch and Cooke 2001, 17) revealed that in the US, 50 per cent of all biotechnology start-up founders had pursued an academic career beforehand. Twenty-five per cent were found to come from an established pharmaceutical company.
9. Often, biotechnology service providers also make use of processes and/or technologies developed in research institutions. Consequently, they follow a parallel initial development to product developers but are able to market their products/services themselves.

10. Since it can take about 10–15 years before obtaining a marketable product out of a newly discovered substance/technology, firms will for much of the development process depend on their proprietary knowledge of the substance/technology as the key asset. This also holds – albeit to a lesser extent – for service providers who rely on proprietary (patented) knowledge regarding processes/technologies for their operations.
11. For evidence on the US case see among many others Cortright and Mayer (2002).
12. It is argued, therefore, that the proximity benefits regarding resource access would be more essential in driving service provider location choice. For this reason, co-location patterns between product developers and service providers were not examined empirically.
13. Sufficient financial resources are important for continuous product development and might even compensate for shortcomings in other infrastructural aspects.
14. Of these, about 86 per cent are to some extent involved in pharmaceutical biotechnology.
15. An information provider specialized in biotechnology.
16. Established players such as pharmaceutical and chemical firms (for example Bayer, Schering) are included in category I due to their importance for the German biotechnology market.
17. Companies following such a business model were classified as product developers since service provision is usually a supplementary task in their operations.
18. Please note that the programme RegioGraph does not make any graphical account for multiple firms with the same postal code. This might lead to an underestimation of the apparent number of firms within the main agglomerations of Munich and Berlin.
19. Berlin is however more strongly specialized in pharmaceutical biotechnology whereas Munich also hosts a significant number of companies in 'green' biotechnology. Berlin's relatively stronger specialization could, however, also explain the small gap between both regions in terms of firm numbers (as could any difference in research profile between both areas).
20. Berlin-based pharmaceutical firm Schering (founded in 1871, employment 25 056) was left out of the mean value calculation to avoid data bias.
21. Skills which could in biotechnology (due to its science reliance) be approximated by formal (academic) qualification.
22. As is found for the French case by Lemarie et al. (2001) in a study on the geographic scope of biotech firm networks over time.

REFERENCES

Audretsch, D.B., and P. Cooke (2001), 'Die Entwicklung regionaler Biotechnologie Cluster in den USA und Großbritannien (The development of regional biotechnology clusters in the United States and Britain)', Stuttgart Akademie für Technologiefolgenabschätzung working paper no. 107.

Bartholomew, S. (1997), 'National systems of biotechnology innovation: complex iterdependence in the global system', *Journal of International Business Studies* (second quarter), pp. 241–66.

BIOCOM (2002), *VBU Guide of German Biotech R&D Companies 2002*, Berlin: VBU (Association of German Biotechnology Companies).

BIOCOM (2003), 'Biotechnologie – das jahr- und adressbuch (The Biotechnology Sourcebook)', http://www.biocom.de/index1.htm.

Brenner, T. (2000), 'The evolution of localised industrial clusters: identifying the processes of self-organisation', Jena: Max Planck Institute for Research into Economic Systems working paper no. 0011.

Cortright, J., and H. Mayer (2002), 'Signs of life: the growth of biotechnology centers in the US', accessed 6 Aug. 2002 at http://www.brook.edu/dybdocroot/es/urban/publications/biotech.pdf.

Ernst & Young (2002), *Neve Chancen – Deutscher Biotechnologiè Report 2002 (New Opportunities – The Report on German Biotechnology 2002)*, Mannheim: Ernst & Young Germany.

Ernst & Young (2003), *Zeit der Bewährung – Ernst & Young Deutscher Biotechnologie Report 2003 (Times of Probation – The Report on German Biotechnology 2003)*, Mannheim: Ernst & Young Germany.

Garnsey, E. (1998), 'The genesis of the high technology milieu: a study in complexity', *International Journal of Urban and Regional Research*, **22** (3), 361–77.

Granovetter, M. (1973), 'The strength of weak ties', *American Journal of Sociology*, **78**, (May), 1360–80.

Granovetter, M. (1985), 'Economic action and social structure: the problem of embeddedness', *American Journal of Sociology*, **91**, (November), 481–510.

Johnson, D.K.N., and M. Mareva (2002), 'It's a small(er) world: the role of geography and networks in biotechnology innovation', Wellesley College Department of Economics working paper no. 2002-01, Wellesley, MA.

Kenney, M. (1986), *Biotechnology: The University-Industrial Complex*, New Haven and London: Yale University Press.

Lemarie, S., V. Mangematin and A. Torre (2001), 'Is the creation and development of biotech SMEs localised? Conclusions drawn from the French case', *Small Business Economics*, **17**, 61–76.

Marshall, A. (1972), *Principles of Economics*, **8**, London: Macmillan.

Martin, P., and C.A. Rogers (1995), 'Industrial location and public infrastructure', *Journal of International Economics*, **39**, 335–51.

Maskell, P. (2001), 'Towards a knowledge-based theory of the geographical cluster', *Industrial and Corporate Change*, **10** (4), 921–43.

Maskell, P., and M. Lorenzen (2003), 'The cluster – and other current forms of market organization', presented at The 2003 Regional Studies Association International Conference, Reinventing Regions in the Global Economy, 12–15 April, Pisa, Italy.

McKelvey, M., H. Alm, and M. Riccaboni (2002), 'Does co-location matter for formal knowledge collaboration in the Swedish biotechnology–pharmaceutical sector?', *Research Policy*, **1394**, 1–19.

Nelson, R.R., and N. Rosenberg (1993), 'Technical innovation and national systems', in R.R. Nelson (ed.), *National Innovation Systems – A Comparative Analysis*, New York and Oxford: Oxford University Press, pp. 3–28.

Osegowitsch, T., and M. Anoop (2001), 'Technology flows across firms and nations: an assessment of the biotechnology industry', *International Journal of Biotechnology*, **3** (3/4), 217–43.

Oßenbrügge, J., and C. Zeller (2001), 'The biotech region of Munich and the spatial organisation of its innovation networks', in L. Schätzl and J. Revilla Diez (eds), *Technological Change and Regional Development in Europe*, Heidelberg and New York: Physica Verlag, pp. 233–49.

Piore, M.J., and C.F. Sabel (1984), *The Second Industrial Divide*, New York: Basic Books Inc.

Pisano, G.P., W. Shan, and D.J. Teece (1988), 'Joint ventures and collaboration in the biotechnology industry', in D.C.Mowery (ed.), *International Collaborative Ventures in US Manufacturing*, Cambridge, MA: Ballinger, pp. 183–222.

Porter Liebeskind, J., A. Lumerman Oliver, L.G. Zucker, and M.B. Brewer (1995), 'Social networks, learning and flexibility: sourcing scientific knowledge in new

biotechnology firms', National Bureau of Economic Research, working paper no. 5320, Cambridge, MA.
Porter, M.E. (1998), *The Competitive Advantage of Nations*, 2nd edn, Hampshire and New York: Palgrave.
Powell, W.W., K.W.Koput, J.I. Bowie, and L. Smith-Doerr (2002), 'The spatial clustering of science and capital: accounting for biotech firm-venture capital relationships', *Regional Studies*, **36** (3), 291–305.
Steinle, C., and H. Schiele (2002), 'When do industries cluster? A proposal on how to assess an industry's propensity to concentrate at a single region or nation', *Research Policy*, **31**, 849–58.
Storper, M. (1997), *The Regional World: Territorial Development in a Global Economy*, New York: The Guilford Press.
Stuart, T., and O. Sorensen (2003), 'The geography of opportunity: spatial heterogeneity in founding rates and the performance of biotechnology firms', *Research Policy*, **32**, 229–53.
Tufts University (2003), Tufts CSDD Outlook Report, Boston, MA: Tufts University Center for the Study of Drug Development.

8. Industry–science relationships as enhancing regional knowledge economies: a comparative perspective from Japan and the UK

Fumi Kitagawa

INTRODUCTION

There are new trends in industrial strategies in most of the industrialized countries, with universities being recognized as key players in generating the industrial competitiveness of regions as well as nations in the knowledge-based economy. Increasingly, cooperation among industry and universities is encouraged by many national governments to develop cutting edge technology and to promote technology transfer and innovation. It is noted that although some powers and responsibilities related to science and research policy are devolved to regional governments, national (and transnational) governments tend still to retain significant influence.

Most conceptual and empirical studies about 'industry–science relationships' (ISRs) are made at national level (for example OECD, 2002). However, it is important to analyse ISRs at different levels, namely, at local, regional, national and international, with interactions between them, within a framework of 'multi-level governance' (MLG) (Cooke, 2002, 60–61). National or transnational governments are good at setting frameworks for action but less so at detailed strategy in contexts with significant geographical variation, so 'joining up government actions' involving horizontal and vertical governmental relations (Cooke, 2002, 8) will be necessary, at transnational level where appropriate. The chapter highlights the different aspects of national ISR policies between the two countries, namely the UK and Japan, and then examines in each country the extent to which the development of ISRs is embedded in regional economies in relation to government's science and technology policies, and higher education policies in the framework of the multi-level governance.

The Science Park-led 'high-tech fantasy' (Massey et al., 1992) exemplified in successful regions in the US such as Silicon Valley was adopted both in the

UK and in Japan. In recent years, policy instruments forging academia–industry–government links have been rapidly developed in both countries. This chapter attempts to make two contributions: the first is to add a viewpoint on the institutional management of universities in response to the rapidly changing higher education policy reforms in the two countries; the second contribution is to build on the conceptual framework with regard to geographical processes of devolution and globalization within a decentralizing national system of innovation.

The chapter consists of three parts. The first part gives a brief conceptual background on the notion of an ISR, and on the territorial dimensions of university–industry links set within different national systems of science and technology policies, and higher education. In the second part, the chapter outlines the different national contexts of the ISRs in the two countries, as well as referring to that of the US, examining the interactions of the different national models of relationships between science and society in an historical context. Thirdly, institutional mechanisms that encourage ISRs in Japan and the UK are compared with regard to international, national and sub-national (regional and local) policy instruments.

The chapter concludes by arguing that, for universities and policy makers, in order to activate global/national/regional strategic relations in practice, a robust set of institutionally appropriate strategies, policy instruments and indicators is needed. A comparative framework focusing on institutional processes may highlight the complex spatial processes of re-articulation of the 'global economy', not only at national and international level but also at trans-regional level.

1. SETTING THE AGENDA – UNIVERSITIES IN INDUSTRY–SCIENCE RELATIONSHIPS

The importance of innovation as a stimulus to economic growth and wealth creation is now widely accepted. Increasingly, cooperation among industry, universities and national research laboratories is encouraged by many national governments to develop cutting edge technology and to promote technology transfer and innovation. There is growing activity in the realm of commercialization of research results through licensing of intellectual property and spin-off firms. Allegedly, the reduction of R&D capacity in many firms due to downsizing and restructuring has led to more contracting out and externalization of research. It is argued that academic work is becoming increasingly important for industrial activities, and for industry, links to the science base are more important than in the past (OECD, 2002, 16).

Nearly all the OECD countries have spent the last decade transferring publicly funded research away from specialized research institutes towards universities. Consequently, a central component of the public research system is now the university sector. Regarding institutional arrangements, the OECD report views university-based systems of ISRs as enjoying a comparative advantage especially when 'science-based innovation increasingly requires multidisciplinarity and builds on people-based interactions' which universities provide (OECD, 2002, 8). However, only a few studies have rigorously examined the relationships between government policies and science–industry linkages in relation to the strategies and policies of universities, especially in the light of the geographical dimension of their institutional activities (for example, Charles and Conway, 2001). Three schematic types of university-based ISRs are distinguished as useful categories (OECD, 2002):

- Relations involving multinational enterprises and world class universities;
- Relations between universities and high-technology small firms; and
- Relations developing in a regional context between firms and the local university.

Universities fulfil a useful role in blurring the line between these different levels. They can regionalize world class and high technology small firm relationships and make that knowledge available to actors whose innovative locus is much more regional in character. Internationalization of university–industry relations has been developing, for example, through the subsidiaries of multinationals and by intergovernmental cooperation particularly through the European Community (Drilhon, 1993, 97). There is a demand for universities to be both regional and international organizations in globalized knowledge economies, whilst many of the legislative decisions about higher education are made at national level. Universities find themselves now having to pay attention to 'many more political centres' (Paterson, 2001, 150) than before, for example research grants and teaching accreditation from transnational bodies such as the EU, national state and the regional levels.

There is a growing significance of knowledge production attached to the regional level epitomized by the emergence of high-tech regions in the world. Moreover, besides market globalization, the fact that knowledge has gained a key function in advanced production is said to have a particular relevance for understanding the emerging role of sub-national regions in modern economies (Varga, 2000, 139). In light of the 'regional governance' of knowledge production in a multi-level governance structure, a number of context-dependent factors relating to 'the geo-historical characteristics of regions, the knowledge infrastructure and knowledge transfer systems, as well as strategies adopted by individual institutions' (Lawton Smith, 2000, 72) arise. In addition, the power structures in which these institutions are interacting affects how ISRs operate at regional level in the globalizing knowledge-based economy. Universities, seen as the main knowledge institutions in society, are expected to play a principal role in regionalizing ISRs by building relationships with different types of firms.

The degree of decentralization of national university systems affects the nature of university-based ISRs, and seems to determine the development of successful ISRs at local level. Arguably, countries such as the US, with decentralized university systems, where universities have more freedom in their research policies and their relations with industry, have a greater chance of developing successful ISRs than those with centralized ones like Japan.

The extent to which devolved and regional authorities contribute to the funding, management and planning of higher education varies greatly (see OECD/IMHE, 1999, 28; Kitagawa, 2003, 107–8). Devolution processes influence both institutional nature and practices. For example, traditionally highly centralized countries such as France are now taking a more regional approach and one of the main aspects of this policy shift is precisely greater participation by the regions in university development (Drilhon, 1993, 96) creating a unified approach involving local authorities, universities and local bodies. In the UK, some powers and responsibilities related to higher education, science and research policy are devolved to the regional administrations (Scotland, Wales and Northern Ireland).[1]

2. UNIVERSITIES AND ISRS IN THE UK AND IN JAPAN

2.1 Universities and National ISRs in UK and Japan

The histories and cultures of university–industry links in the two countries are profoundly different in general terms. As far as recent industrial and higher education policies are concerned, however, there are some similarities and convergence in a broad sense. Both countries are trying to adapt the models and experiences of US university–industry linkages, aiming at increasing national industrial competitiveness. In the US, academic entrepreneurship and the 'entrepreneurial university' have developed (particularly in certain types of university, for example land-grant schools or technical institutes) since the late 19th century as a 'bottom-up' phenomenon (Etzkowitz, 2003, 109), whilst, in Europe and in Japan, the recent (1990s-onwards) introduction of academic entrepreneurship is seen as a more 'top down' phenomenon in response to the recognition of the 'innovation gap' compared to the US economy.

Both the UK and Japanese governments have increasingly stressed the importance of science policy and knowledge transfer in strengthening the international competitiveness of the national economy (DTI, 1993, 2000; STA, 2002). The roles of universities in enhancing national and regional competitiveness are expressed in several recent government documents and new institutional frameworks (see Boxes 8.1 and 8.2).

BOX 8.1 THE UK GOVERNMENT WHITE PAPERS EMPHASIZING THE ROLE OF HIGHER EDUCATION IN NATIONAL COMPETITIVENESS

1993 Science and Technology White Paper, *Realising our Potential: A Strategy for Science, Engineering and Technology* (DTI)
1998 The Competitiveness White Paper, *Building the Knowledge-driven Economy* (DTI)
2000 The Science and Innovation White Paper, *Excellence and Opportunity* (OST)
2001 The Enterprise, Skills and Innovation White Paper, *Opportunity for All in a World of Change* (DTI/DfEE)
2002 *Investing in Innovation: A strategy for science, engineering and technology.* (DTI, HM Treasury, DfES)
2003 The White Paper, *The Future of Higher Education* (DfES)

BOX 8.2 JAPANESE LEGAL–INSTITUTIONAL FRAMEWORKS PROMOTING SCIENCE–INDUSTRY RELATIONSHIPS

1995 The Science and Technology Basic Law: The Council for Science and Technology Policy (CSTP)
1996 The Science and Technology Basic Plans (1996–2000)
1998 A new legal framework to promote university–industry technology transfer
1998 Abolition of Technopolis Law
1999 The Promotion of New Enterprise Law
2001 The Science and Technology Basic Plans (2001–2005)
General Science and Technology Council attached to Cabinet Office

Both in the UK and in Japan, despite equal legal status being given to all universities, hierarchical financial differences have always existed among institutions of different origins (for example, former polytechnics in UK and 'non-imperial' in Japan). In both countries, the globalization of economic competition further spurred on the tendency of institutions to differentiate, due to special treatments to strengthen leading research universities. In the UK, the 'binary' system differentiating between universities and polytechnics was abolished in 1992. However, in the recent White Paper, *The Future of Higher Education* (DfES, 2003), a new classification and terminology such as 'research-intensive' and 'less research-intensive' universities is expressed, implying stratification and the new explicit and implicit hierarchy emerging in the higher education sector. Since 1949, all universities in Japan have had 'equal' legal status but in terms of financial treatment, there are differences between former 'imperial' universities and other national universities as well as between national, public and private universities. Since the beginning of the 1990s, Japanese university reform seems to have reinforced the differentiation among institutions. For instance, the government is seeking to create 'world class universities' by creating a mechanism for differentiated financial allocation justifiable towards both universities and society (Yonezawa, 2003).[2]

In both countries, collaboration in research between business and the public sector, especially the higher education sector, is becoming more common. In the UK, commercialization of university research started in the mid-1980s and many universities set up private commercializing companies in order to manage their intellectual property rights (IPR). In Japan, following the enactment of a new law in 1998, the new 'formal' system of commercializing university research has just started with the setting up of Technology Licensing Offices (TLOs).

According to a study by HEFCE (Higher Education Funding Council in England) and DTI (Department of Trade and Industry) (1999) the share of UK industry's contribution to total research revenues grew steadily from 5.6 per cent in 1985 to 6 per cent in 1995 and 7.1 per cent in 1999 (Hatakenaka, 2002). It is worth noting that industrial support for research is highly concentrated in a small number of institutions: the top seven universities accounted for over a third of total revenues from industry (Howells et al., 1998). For Japan, the share of business funding of higher education research is less than half the OECD average. The figure was 1.5 per cent in 1985, and has stayed as 2.3 per cent since 1990. Table 8.1 shows the percentage of business funding of the research performed by the government and university sector in the UK, Japan and US against the OECD average as of 1999.

Facing the second decade of Japanese economic downturn, a central focus of national institutional reform efforts is about university–industry links directed at Japan's national innovative capacity. The government has been

Table 8.1 Comparing UK, Japan, US and OECD average in 1999 (%)

		UK	Japan	US	OECD average
Percentage of businesses in the funding of research	Government	21.1	1.8	0.0	4.1
	HE	7.2	2.3	6.3	6.1

Source: OECD, 2001a.

supporting new spin-off company creation from national universities by deregulation and by providing subsidies to R&D activities. In the data provided by METI (Ministry of Economy, Trade and Industry), as of 2001, there were 105 new enterprises spun-off from universities, which compares to 368 in the US in 2000 and approximately 200 in the UK (see below).[3] Pechter (2001, 4) argues that 'the particular direction of reform is perhaps unjustifiably towards the American university–industry policy framework'. He suggests that for Japanese policy makers, rather than making mostly bilateral comparison with the US, multilateral national comparison may be equally important and perhaps even more relevant to Japan's policy formulation (2001, 6).

In the UK context, too, academic entrepreneurial activities are often compared with those in North American institutions (for example Charles and Conway, 2001; UNICO/NUBS, 2001). In 1999/2000, UK universities identified a total of 199 spin-off firms. The UNICO data showed the UK spent £8.9 million on research for each spin-off compared with £24.7 million in Canada and £88.8 million in the US. The compilers cautioned against taking too much stock from these figures since not all spin-offs are created alike. Some attract more investment than others; some are ultimately more profitable than others (Davies, 2002). A longer-term perspective should be taken, following the stages of development of these firms in order to make reasonable sense of the statistics.

In view of these points, this chapter may shed light on some of the underlying problematic assumptions in employing the bilateral benchmarking frameworks primarily in relation to the United States. Mostly the indicators are simple quantitative metrics based on commercializing IPRs such as number of patents, licensing and revenue from royalties. These data, although they are significant on their own, are only a subset of a wide range of university activities within ISRs. It is important to recognize that institutional differences between countries require different generic models (Cooke et al., 2000, 247), and that spin-offs and science parks are only one aspect of academic entrepreneurial activities. IPR commercialization is only one aspect of the wider institutional picture. Sometimes fundamental differences in institutional arrangements are underestimated. For example, the conventional wisdom based on the US/Japan comparison is rather questionable if the informal relationships at the level of faculty members are taken into consideration rather than formal links at the level of an institution.

2.2 Universities, Regions and ISRs in Global Knowledge Economies – a view from Japan and the UK

As already mentioned, in the UK, the governance of science and technology policies is gradually moving to a more 'devolved' structure with recent *regionalization*. Japan seems to be very much centralized in terms of higher education policies and funding as well as governance of science and technology policies.

Limited development of Japanese university-based ISRs

Japanese science policy and the development of ISRs have had three separate phases: 'catch up', Technopolis and cluster development. Japan is known to have developed a broad national technology strategy with long-term scientific and technology goals, including a strong potential direct public dimension such as transport, health and energy as well as in areas such as IT, biotechnology and new materials. In 1980, the MITI (Ministry of Trade and Industry) report highlighted the need to move beyond the 'catch-up' strategy which characterized Japan's post-war development, to the development of fundamental science.

In Japan, close ties between industry and universities have not been reflected in the development of formal university–industry linkages or science park type developments until very recently because in Japan these are generally maintained on an informal and personal level.[4] Starting in 1983, high-technology based local economic development was the key idea of the Technopolis programme. The contribution made by local universities in terms of R&D and developing research infrastructure in these sites in conjunction with the Technopolis Foundation, one of the coordination and support organizations, was noted (Masser, 1990, 50).

However, many problems were found in the ways in which national universities had operated. The critical factors that explain the limited development of industry–science relationships based on the Technopolis programme include both the university system which was not open to society, and the weakening of support organizations lacking personnel equipped with coordination skills. Also, there were rules that prevented researchers at the Japanese national universities from engaging in any formal cooperation with private firms (Schuetze, 2000, 162) but that has been changing in recent years with the introduction of a new legal framework based on the US model, and the transformation of national universities into incorporated status as of April 2004. Another legal change which may affect the geographical dimension of the university-based ISRs is that incorporated status universities can now receive financial support from local authorities, which was prohibited in the past when they were national institutions. This may trigger new relationships between universities and their localities.

The development of UK university-based ISR

The three phases of UK ISRs and science policy can be identified as Wilsonian white heat revolution, Thatcher and Major's privatization and cuts, and New Labour's endogenous growth approach. It has always been a concern of the UK government that its industrial base has decidedly declined in relation to other countries, such as the US and Japan. Harold Wilson's call at the 1963 Party Conference for the modernization of the economy and challenge 'in the *white heat* of the scientific and technological revolution' is well known. The Wilson government of 1964–1970 achieved many initiatives regarding science, technology and industry involving attempts to bridge the strung-out nature of academic–industrial links and of innovation in general. However, after the advocacy of 'white heat' change, the separation of science from technology and of universities from manufacturing production continued (Massey et al., 1992).

The 1980s under the Thatcher government saw a long decade of shrinking government support for universities. This was one of the most important factors that promoted university–industry relationships in the UK, along with other government policy initiatives such as Teaching Company Scheme (TCS), LINK, and Collaborative Awards in Science and Engineering (CASE).[5] In 1985, a report entitled *The Cambridge Phenomenon* was published by a private consulting firm (Segal Quince and Partners, 1985), which concluded that informal networks around the university were critical to the phenomenon of commercialization of science through new firm formation. The 'phenomenon' provided a model of university-based, endogenous innovation-centred growth in UK local economic development. There have been attempts to emulate such a high-tech based local development, but many of them seem to have remained rather aspirational.

Turning to the New Labour government, the most recent spending review (HM Treasury, 2002) states: 'closing the productivity gap with our major international competitors will be achieved more quickly by strengthening the UK's innovation performance, which is underpinned by public investment in the science base'. Throughout this process in the 1990s the purpose of universities' research was consolidated around a heavily instrumentalist economic discourse, with the sole rationale of raising national competitiveness through improving the science base (Henkel and Little, 1999). As part of this endeavour, an effort was made to increase the capacity to convert excellence in basic research conducted in universities to successful product and process innovations.

In the UK, Higher Education Funding Councils are making money available for 'third stream' activities of universities, with notable recent funding opportunities promoting universities' outreach to businesses. Arrangements for this vary in different parts of the UK. In England, HEFCE, in partnership with OST (Office of Science and Technology), grants project-based funding for commercializing university research and has impacts in terms of infrastructure for these activities (Higher Education Innovation Fund, HEIF). In Wales, a Knowledge Exploitation Fund with similar objectives is managed by the Welsh Development Agency. In Scotland, SHEFC created a Knowledge Transfer Grants scheme to help universities invest in infrastructure for knowledge transfer activities. There are also several UK-wide programmes through OST, to promote the knowledge transfer activities of HEIFs, such as the Science Enterprise Challenge Fund and University Challenge Fund.

2.3 Different Multi-Level Governance Structure

There are significant differences between the UK and Japan in the structures of regional/local governance and the implication for higher education and science policies in a regional context. The chapter moves on to consider the implication of regionalizing ISRs for universities' research management.

There are tensions between national and regional science policies. In the UK, the processes of devolution started in Scotland and Wales. It seems that strategic planning at regional level in relation to higher education research expertise is much more advanced in Scotland. In England, the nationally oriented focus of science and technology policies has significant regional implications with over 42 per cent of government R&D expenditure spent in London and the south-east. There is evidently a tension between a science policy oriented around national priorities, and new regional policies aimed at decreasing regional disparities while furthering economic development in the English regions (Charles and Benneworth, 2001). Recently, national science policy has been challenged by demands for a regionalized science and technology policy by the English regions. Yet there is little policy understanding or academic analysis of the consequences of this shift for national science policy or of the significance of an emerging regional science policy.

The development of science parks in the UK is inherently related to the issue of the 'North–South' divide across the country. In the areas which are already prosperous, especially in the south and east, science parks are profitable for the private sector; in the north, the public sector struggles to provide some counter-balance in the form of 'partnerships' with the public sector subsidizing the private, whilst the latter undermines the former's initial objectives (Massey et al., 1992, 12). It is noted that there is also an 'innovation divide' in terms of firms' technological progressiveness and capacity to assimilate new knowledge. London, the south-east and eastern England alone already contain nearly half of all UK high-tech firms and half of its high-tech jobs. Innovation levels are much higher in the area running from East Anglia through to the south coast (Potts, 2002, 988). In 1998, there were some 37 000 high technology jobs or 11 per cent of all jobs in the Cambridgeshire labour market (Cooke, 2002, 145). The Cambridge ICT and biotechnology clusters have been successful and seen as the template for 'clusters' across England.

In England, it seems the advent of the Government Regional Offices (GROs) and Regional Development Agencies (RDAs) have encouraged English regions to strengthen their links with higher educational institutions within their RDA boundaries. These new geographical groupings of universities reflect the emerging regional partnership arrangements in England (The Universities UK/HEFCE, 2001, 24). The White Paper, *The Future of Higher Education* (DfES) published in January 2003 states that the involvement of universities and colleges in regional, social and economic development is critical. Stronger partnerships are encouraged between HEIFs in each region and the RDA and other agencies charged with promoting economic development. (DfES, 2003, 36).[6] The white paper proposed that RDAs be given a greater role in steering the new £90 million Higher Education Innovation Fund (HEIF) money to support outreach from universities to business. In some English regions, regional initiatives such as setting up Regional Science Councils have been implemented, which were then encouraged nationally by DTI.

It is not only the UK central government that decides and influences regional policies. McNay (1994) notes the gradual process of devolution taking place in the UK, with increasing attention being paid to the role of higher education within the regional economy, and attributes this to the influence of the European regions (McNay, 1994, 330). In the European context, the local, regional, national and supranational policy levels are strongly interdependent and interwoven. One of the priorities for the new generation of regional development programmes in the European Union is the promotion of *innovation* whereby the key challenges for policy involve assisting firms and localities to change by enhancing their *learning* capabilities. In the policy environment of the European Union, the prime objective seems to have remained the agenda of the 'competitiveness of Europe versus the rest of the world' (Lawton Smith, 2002, 2). This is because in numerous analyses of the EU's weakness *vis-à-vis* its competitors, namely the US and Japan, innovation has been highlighted as 'a crucial deficit in both business competitiveness and the quest for wider prosperity, cohesion and integration within the Union' (CEC, 1995, cited in Cooke, 2002, 60). In the EU, European regional policy aims at alleviating regional socioeconomic disparities through *innovation* and *learning*. The scale of delivery is now at the regional rather than national scale. In the European Union, various innovation networking programmes at regional level have grown, and more regional authorities seem to have greater competence and confidence to implement the relevant learning processes at regional level (Cooke, 2002, 11). New institutions and networks are being created to deliver these policies, which, in turn, influence the formation and development of UK ISRs.

In Japan, in terms of regional development policies, the extent to which R&D related activities have been heavily concentrated in the area around Tokyo has induced scepticism that technology transfer to peripheral regions is likely to be limited to activities such as simple parts production and assembly rather than basic research. Although it is widely accepted that the links between high technology and regional development have been successfully made through the aforementioned Technopolis programme during the 1980s, it has been pointed out that spin-off effects of new technology on the local economy were limited (Masser, 1990, 51). Moreover, some reservations were made by authors about the role played by universities in peripheral areas given the high concentration of existing R&D efforts in core academic institutions. Problems were foreseen with regard to meeting skill shortages in peripheral regions given the greater job opportunities in the national industrial heartland. In the late 1980s, MITI developed a number of schemes to counter the 'hollowing out' of the Japanese economy and promoted the regionalization of high-tech research and local R&D facilities. However, these endeavours were not implemented to the full extent. This is worth noting in relation to the multi-level governance structure for regional development in Japan.

In Japan, the responsibilities of national and local governments are as follows: the national government is responsible for formulating and implementing comprehensive policies for promoting science and technology; local government is responsible for formulating and implementing policies for promoting science and technology corresponding to national policies and in accordance with local characteristics. There is no institutional mechanism operating at 'regional' level as such in research policy and funding terms (see Abe, 1998, 288–9). Local government operates at the sub-regional level, including prefecture and city levels. However, significant initiatives are currently being undertaken by some prefectural governments, and the central government's policy of developing regional research strengths encompasses this level of government (OECD, 2002, 8). Over 90 per cent of prefecture governments adopted at least one key action programme for science and technology: for example, regional council boards for the promotion of science and technology; and basic plans for the promotion of science technology (OECD, 2002, 18). At the national level, the Council for Science and Technology issued a recommendation entitled *Regional Science and Technology Promotion* in 1995 (Abe, 1998, 316).

More recent new national governmental initiatives since 2001, such as the 'industrial cluster plan' led by METI and the 'intellectual cluster scheme' led by MEXT (Ministry of Education, Culture, Sports, Science and Technology) rest on the cluster model developed by Porter (1990), and are based on models of successful local economic development in other countries, mostly in the US and in Europe. Strengthening university–industry linkages in a local context is emphasized in these initiatives, which, it is hoped, will lead to the creation of high-technology business spin-offs from universities' research. METI has nine Regional Bureaus, which vary in their coordination abilities. MEXT is encouraging the initiatives of local authorities to draw up their own action plans. In Japan, rather than regionalizing HE policies, MEXT and METI are creating networks at regional/local level involving different stakeholders by creating financial incentives. But it is also interesting to note that both ministries are implementing cluster policies of their own, both emphasizing stronger university–industry links at local level. Japan, having no formal regional administrative mechanism as such, without substantially devolving power, paradoxically seems to be achieving 'regionalization' of industry–science relationships. Some local authorities are taking a more 'regional' approach than others by trying strategically to combine the two aforementioned cluster development schemes promoted by central government.[7] Abe (1998) describes the emergence of the concept of a 'regional system' in policy thinking in the Tohoku Region in Japan.

3. COMPARING UNIVERSITIES AS PART OF REGIONAL ISRS – JAPAN AND UK EXPERIENCES

Both in the UK and in Japan, the current environment for universities is demanding and turbulent and, in both countries, to different degrees 'the regions' emerge as a new strategic site for economic and social development where universities are expected to play a critical and challenging role. It was shown that very different spatial–institutional structures of ISRs have been developing in the two countries under comparable national policy orientation.

The key question with regard to Japanese ISRs in light of the regionalization of knowledge economies concerns the extent local authorities can build up skills, institutional capacity and their own knowledge to take initiatives in terms of forging ISRs at local and regional level. In the UK, the central issue seems to be the trade-off between policy priorities aiming at national competitiveness, and new regional policy frameworks aimed at decreasing regional disparities. Whether or not a regional ISR system can be created successfully needs to be examined in relation to the process of devolution from central to local/regional government, which seems to be occurring at various speeds within the two countries.

Both the UK and Japan aim to increase national competitiveness in the global knowledge economy by tapping into local innovative capability leading to new knowledge creation and innovation. The 'region' is increasingly recognized as a strategic site of policy implementation (for example, cluster policies) within the multi-level governance structure. Universities are recognized as the main players at all levels of policies. Networking and partnership formation in the region, bringing together the key stakeholders at the strategic level, are seen to be an effective way of integrating a number of policy instruments coming from different government departments.

From a structural point of view with regard to governance, strategic vertical coordination between RDAs and the national government and the European level is the key for England and the UK, whilst horizontal joined up policy making between different government departments, along with encouraging further processes of devolution, is the key challenge for Japanese regional ISRs. Local policy makers need to strategically integrate the resources made available by different departments of central government and to utilize the expertise of their local universities. Devolution has to be seen as 'a process that requires multi-level partnership and networking' (OECD 2001b, 11) rather than as a simple transfer of power from central to local and regional level.

Formal and informal mechanisms promoting university–industry linkages have been developed in each country within its different historical structure of ISRs. The social background behind the existing relationships should not be underestimated. In Japan, a shift in the university system with more emphasis on 'quality and research at the graduate level' (Kodama and Branscomb, 1999, 13) is seen to be needed whilst current emphasis on university–industry collaboration turns principally on promoting formal IPR commercializing mechanisms. In the UK, the mechanisms of research evaluation have been an added burden to university activities and their ISR development (OECD, 2002, 153). The current discussion in the UK on the metrics regarding third stream activities may provide one of the opportunities to ameliorate the current system of university research evaluation into one that allows more flexibility and strategic positioning of each university's expertise (see Molas-Gallart et al., 2002).

Paradoxically, a 'regioncentric university orientation' (Hagen, 2002, 206) will not assist regional economic development in globalizing knowledge economies. UK universities, for example, have a growing number of research links involving transnational/regional institutional collaboration and public–private partnership formation, many of which are thanks to European research programmes. Some of the successful Japanese regions are creating links with science parks and firms in other Asian countries.[8]

Incentive mechanisms for universities to work with business principally in their region are growing in Japan as well in the UK. However, it is too early to judge the extent to which these policy instruments are developing further ISRs in their regions. There is a tendency to reduce the metrics of these activities towards 'simple' indicators of IPR commercialization. However, there is a realization that what is at issue are the hugely complex processes by which universities achieve social and economic impacts within society, beyond the core business of 'teaching' and 'research' (Molas-Gallart et al., 2002). The impact is being made through the work of 'boundary spanners' or 'animateurs' who enhance 'communicative competency' between organizations, and between universities, industry and government sectors. These functions have had to be fully integrated into the organizational mechanism/culture of universities and/or regional agencies. One of the biggest challenges that the Japanese universities are facing is how to develop the skills of personnel who work as intermediaries in understanding the cultures of the different sectors (that is universities, industry and government). For universities the issue of individual incentives for academic staff to engage in 'third-stream' activities seems to be one of the most difficult tasks to deal with. Strengthening performance-based financial incentives may be an example.

CONCLUDING REMARKS – UNIVERSITIES IN THE GLOBAL–NATIONAL–REGIONAL ISRs

The so-called 'high-tech fantasy' (Massey et al., 1992) permeates worldwide. In particular, it was developed in the UK with its own structure of ISRs, and now the Japanese have embraced the idea in their attempt to revitalize their sluggish economy which was previously driven by high-technology-based innovations. This quick sketch of university–industry links and ISRs in the UK and in Japan may partially illustrate the interactions of policy models with attached value systems.

The interactions between the systems of university research and industry as part of wider systems of ISRs take various institutional forms, and they differ in their nature and intensity (OECD, 2002, 31). The complexity of the whole process of creating regional innovation systems, linked through overarching national industrial, science and technology policies within the globalizing economy, should not be underestimated. The concept of ISRs is useful as it can encompass different geographical scales. There are different models of inter-institutional collaboration of universities–industry–government at a regional level, and it is important to pay close attention to institutional cultural differences, the roles of intermediary organizations and links to external players. Entrepreneurial activities of universities are perceived to need to be an integral part of: a) the core activities and management culture of universities; and b) the regional mechanisms of institutional collaboration and resource allocation.

The aspiration towards being 'world class' abounds in both the higher education sector and in local/regional authorities. All these aspirations and new activities need to address fundamental inequalities in the space-economies of the UK and Japan, and also elsewhere. This would be possible only by recognizing that there are different parthways to being 'world class', through the re-articulation of the global economy, and by recognizing the wide range of resources and of institutional mechanisms required in realizing that aspiration. Individual institutions such as universities and regional agencies are being urged to develop strategies and instruments appropriate to their own context rather than centrally imposed mechanisms. Policy makers, at all levels, in turn, are pressed to create a policy environment in which institutions have the autonomy which enables them to be dynamic, strategic and highly competitive in the international arena.

NOTES

1. In the UK, in order to deal with the devolved higher education funding policy, four Higher Education Funding Councils (England, Scotland, Wales and Northern Ireland) were created in 1992 with the abolition of the University Grants Committee (UGC) and the Polytechnics and Colleges Funding Council (PCFC). On the other hand, there is only a single system of Research Councils in the UK, and the Science Budget is centralized.
2. MEXT (Ministry of Education, Culture, Sports, Science and Technology) is setting up 'Centre of Excellence in the 21st century' (COE 21), which can be regarded as a trial in performance funding.
3. AUTM Licensing Survey FY 2000, http://www.mext.go.jp/a_menu/shinkoku/sangaku/sangakub/sangakub6.htm access date 01/01/03.
4. The dense network of Regional Research and Technology Centres (traditional *Kosetsushi* Centres) is known to have served in translating advanced technological findings at universities and other research institutions into practical applications by SMEs through consultants (see Hassink, 1997).
5. TCS, now renamed as Knowledge Transfer Partnerships, has been in operation since 1975. It supplies funds for academics to provide technology transfer support to companies through student placements. LINK is the government's principal mechanism which started in 1988 for promoting partnerships in pre-commercial research between industry and the university research base. CASE is a programme that provides subsidy support for graduate students undertaking projects in industry.
6. The Lambert Review (2003), commissioned by the Government in November 2002, made a series of recommendations aimed at promoting collaboration between the science base and

business community in the UK. A greater role for RDAs is recommended in facilitating university–business links in their regions. http://www.hm-treasury.gov.uk/newsroom_and_speeches/press/2003/press_129_03.cfm 27/12/03.
7. Structural Reform Special Designated Area (*kozo kaikaku tokku*) is another recent government initiative promoting any comparative advantages in local economic characteristics by reducing legal regulation to the designated area. Some areas are specially designated for the purposes such as promoting university–industry–government links (*san-gaku-kan renkei tokku*), creating new enterprises, and promoting precision techniques.
8. There are notable successful cases growing from the Technopolis programme: for example, Kitakyushu Techno Centre is known for its entrepreneurial activities combining universities, the private sector and local authorities. It is making networks with Korean companies and science parks. See http://www.pref.fukuoka.jp/shoko/fukuokas_potential/incubate.html 03/04/03.

BIBLIOGRAPHY

Abe, S. (1998), 'Regional innovation systems in Japan: the case of Tohoku' in H-J. Braczyk et al. *Regional Innovation Systems: The Role of Governances in a Globalized World*, London: UCL Press.

Charles, D., and P. Benneworth (2001), 'Are we realizing our potential ?: Joining up science and technology policy in the English regions', *Regional Studies*, **35** (1), 73–9.

Charles, D., and C. Conway (2001), *Higher Education–Business Interaction Survey. A Report by CURDS to UK HE Funding Bodies and the Office of Science and Technology*, Bristol: HEFCE.

Cooke, P. (2002), *Knowledge Economies: Clusters, Learning and Cooperative Advantage*, London: Routledge.

Cooke, P., P. Boekholt, and F. Tödtling (2000), *The Governance of Innovation in Europe: Regional Perspectives on Global Competitiveness*, London: Pinter.

Davies, C. (2002), 'UK's spin-offs reap £3 billion reward', *Times Higher Education Supplement*, 25 October.

DfES (2003), *The Future of Higher Education*, accessed 30 January, 2003 at www.dfes.gov.uk/highereducation/hestrategy.

Drilhon, G. (1993), 'University–industry relations, regionalisation, internationalisation', *Higher Education Management*, **5** (3), 95–9.

DTI (1993), *Our Competitive Future: Building the Knowledge Driven Economy*, accessed 6 February, 2003 at www.dti.gov.uk/comp/competitive/main.htm.

DTI (2000), *Excellence and Opportunity – A Science and Innovation Policy for the 21st Century*, London: The Stationery Office Publications Centre.

DTI and DfEE (2001), *Opportunity for All in a World of Change*, London: The Stationery Office Publications Centre.

Etzkowitz, H. (2003) 'Research groups as "quasi-firms": the invention of the entrepreneurial university', *Research Policy*, **32**, 109–21.

Hagen, R. (2002), 'Globalization, university transformation and economic regeneration: A UK case study of public/private sector partnership', *The International Journal of Public Sector Management*, **15** (3), 204–18.

Hassink, R. (1997), 'Technology transfer infrastructures: some lessons from experiences in Europe, the US and Japan', *European Planning Studies*, **5** (3), 351–70.

Hatakenaka, S. (2002) 'Flux and flexibility: a comparative institutional analysis of

evolving university–industry relationships in MIT, Cambridge and Tokyo', PhD thesis, Sloan School of Management, Massachusetts Institute of Technology.
Henkel, M., and B. Little (eds) (1999), *Changing Relationships Between Higher Education and the State*, London: Jessica Kingsley Publishers.
HM Treasury (2002), *Opportunity and Security for All: Investing in an Enterprising Fairer Britain, New Public Spending Plans 2003–2006*, July, accessed 27 May, 2004, at www.hm-treasury.gov-uk/Spending_Review/spend_sr02/spend_sr02_index.cfm.
Howells, J., M. Neveda, and L. Georghiou (1998), *Industry–Academic Links in the UK*, Bristol: HEFCE.
Kitagawa, F. (2003), 'New mechanisms of incentives and accountability for higher education institutions: linking the regional, national and global dimensions', *Higher Education Management and Policy*, **15** (2), 99–116, Paris: OECD.
Kodama, F., and L. Branscomb (1999), 'University research as engine for growth: how realistic is the vision?', in L. Branscomb et al. (eds), *Industrializing Knowledge: University–Industry Linkages in Japan and the United States*, London: The MIT Press.
Lawton Smith, H. (2000), 'Innovation systems and "local difficulties": the Oxfordshire experiences' in Acs, Z. (ed.), *Regional Innovation, Knowledge and Global Change*, London and New York: Pinter.
Lawton Smith, H. (2002), 'Competitiveness and European regional policy: a review and analysis', paper presented at the Regional Studies Association International Conference on Evaluation and EU Regional Policy: New Questions and New Challenges, Aix en Provence, France, 31 May and 1 June.
Masser, I. (1990), 'Technology and regional development policy: a review of Japan's Technopolis Programme', *Regional Studies*, **24** (1), 41–53.
Massey, D., P. Quintas, and D. Wield (1992), *High-tech Fantasies: Science Parks in Society, Science and Space*, London: Routledge.
McNay, I. (1994), 'The regional dimension in the strategic planning of higher education', *Higher Education Quarterly*, **48** (4), 323–36.
Molas-Gallart, J., A. Salter, P. Patel, A. Scott and X. Duran (2002), *Measuring Third Stream Activities: Final Report to the Russell Group of Universities*, SPRU.
OECD/IMHE (1999), *The Response of Higher Education Institutions to Regional Needs*, Paris: OECD.
OECD (2001a), *Science, Technology and Industry Scoreboard: Towards a Knowledge-based Economy*, Paris: OECD.
OECD (2001b), *Devolution and Globalisation*, Paris: OECD.
OECD (2002), *Benchmarking Industry–Science Relationships*, Paris: OECD.
OECD (2003), *Governance of Public Research: Country Case Studies*, country report: Japan, accessed 27 May 2004 at www.oecd.org.dataoecd/24/37/2507926.pdf.
Paterson, L. (2001), 'Higher education and European regionalism', *Pedagogy, Culture and Society*, **9** (2), 133–60.
Pechter, K. (2001), 'Japanese innovation reform in the light of past dialogue: conceptions of convergence as perspectives for comparative system assessment', paper presented at the European Association of Evolutionary Political Economy.
Porter, M. (1990), *The Competitive Advantage of Nations*, London: Macmillan.
Potts, G. (2002), 'Regional policy and the "regionalization" of university–industry links: a view from the English regions', *European Planning Studies*, **10** (8), 987–1012.
Schuetze, H.G. (2000), 'Industrial innovation and the creation and dissemination of

knowledge: implications for university–industry relationships', in *Knowledge Management in the Learning Society*, Paris: OECD.

Science and Technology Agency (STA) (2002), *White Paper on Science and Technology*, accessed 31 May 2004 at www.mext.go.jp/b_menu/houdou/14/06/020615.htm.

Segal Quince and Partners (1985), *The Cambridge Phenomenon*, Cambridge: SQW.

Universities UK/HEFCE (2001), *The Regional Mission: The Regional Contribution of Higher Education*, national report, London: Universities UK; Bristol: HEFCE.

UNICO/Nottingham University Business School (NUBS) (2001), 'Annual survey on university technology transfer activities', conducted by NUBS in association with UNICO and AURIL.

Varga, A. (2000), 'Universities in local innovation systems', in Acs, Z. (ed.), *Regional Innovation, Knowledge and Global Change*, London and New York: Pinter.

Yonezawa, A. (2003), 'Making "world class universities": Japan's experiment', *Higher Education Management and Policy*, **15** (2), 9–24, Paris: OECD.

9. Placing Ireland's transition to a knowledge economy within a global context

Mark C. White and Seamus Grimes

INTRODUCTION

This chapter explores the (Republic of) Ireland's growing capacity for value creation and capture. Once associated with poverty and emigration, a period of rapid growth during the 1990s transformed Ireland, one of Europe's more peripheral regions into one of its relatively more successful regions. Rather than serving as an example for dependent development, Ireland's recent success leads other peripheral places to attempt to emulate its development policies (MacSharry and White, 2000). However the prominence of exogenous factors in the Irish development model stands in stark contrast to the emphasis traditionally assigned to endogenous factors (for example Porter, 1990). Within the regional development literature, the role of local and regional institutions in facilitating innovation and learning receives particular attention (for example Cooke and Morgan, 1998). While not discounting the importance of these issues, several researchers now approach the problem of regional development through more multi-scalar frameworks. As a result, they consider issues such as the roles played by Global Productions Networks (GPNs) or transnational networks of knowledge workers, and thereby account for a wider array of factors that influence a given locale's capacity for value creation, enhancement and capture (Henderson et al., 2002). For peripheral regions with little endogenous capacity for generating knowledge, these latter conceptualizations therefore offer greater scope for understanding ways to exploit external sources of innovation.

This chapter is organized as follows. The next section seeks to contextualize regional development by considering the manner in which different influences at multiple scales affect value creation and capture. The following section then discusses the evolution of Irish industrial policy and the measures taken to extract the maximum benefit from inward investment. Data presented in the subsequent section illustrate the extent to which Ireland's capacity to create and capture value grew over time. The last section explores two embryonic sectors that might contribute to continued economic growth in Ireland. Finally, several conclusions are offered about the successes and shortcomings of Ireland's Foreign Direct Investment led development model and its potential for sustainable regional development in the future.

CONTEXTUALIZING REGIONAL DEVELOPMENT

Throughout the regional development literature knowledge production, particularly at the sub-national or regional scale, assumes a seminal role in generating sustainable economic development (Lagendijk, 2001). Many less favoured regions, however, lack the local capacity for generating knowledge endogenously, and as a result inward investment attraction forms an important component of many regional development strategies (Amin and Tomaney, 1995). These strategies are generally not considered sustainable, so the importance of endogenous development continues to resonate amongst policy makers. Consequently, endogenous growth models focused around the establishment of 'Porterian' clusters represent one of the preferred solutions sold by the regional development industry (Lagendijk and Cornford, 2000). In spite of the prominence given to endogenously-driven development models, more recent conceptualizations are reconsidering the potential for wider influences such as global production networks to foster sustainable economic development (Henderson et al., 2002).

This becomes increasingly evident as the more global nature of R&D networks makes the need to account for non-local sources of innovation even more important (Henderson and Morgan, 2002). Highly localized systems of innovation may inhibit or restrict development if they become too rigid and cut off from outside sources of innovation (Asheim and Dunford, 1997; Scott, 1998). Regional success often depends more on the ability to commercialize technology than actually producing innovative technologies (Grimes and Collins, 2003). For instance, the US biotechnology industry's initial development occurred through the commercial exploitation of knowledge gains made outside of the US. US firms, supported by an active Venture Capital (VC) system, were better equipped than European firms to commercialize the knowledge developed in the mostly public-funded European research system (Cooke, 2001). With the exception of mobile telephony, European firms possess a weak record of commercializing technological innovation. This poor record of commercializing innovative activity explains partly why Europe's market share (ratio of national exports to world exports) in science-based products declined from 48.6 per cent in 1970 to 33.8 per cent in 1995, even though world trade in high-tech industries doubled during the same period (Archibugi and Coco, 2001). As a result, policy makers are more aware of the need to facilitate the commercial exploitation of technology, regardless of its origins.

The growing importance of global sources of innovation therefore influences the formation of regional development policies. Development models focusing heavily on endogenous factors, in order to replicate successful technology regions like Silicon Valley, may be misguided given the changing international environment. In a survey of emerging technology regions, Bresnahan et al. (2001) note that connections to places like Silicon Valley represent one of the 'deep regularities' among these regions. Consequently, emphasis should not be placed on replicating successful regions, but rather on finding ways to integrate with these regions. This interconnectivity occurs most prominently through FDI, but also through transnational networks of skilled knowledge workers. Saxenian (2002) for instance, demonstrates the important roles returning migrants from Silicon Valley play in the development of the Indian, Chinese and Taiwanese technology sectors.

While not dismissing the importance of local factors, analysing processes of regional development must clearly occur within a framework that considers multi-scalar influences. This chapter therefore follows the lead of Henderson et al. (2002) by seeking to contextualize local economic development within the broader reality of global markets. This involves examination, not just of the methods through which places connect to global production networks, but also the manner in which these connections contribute to processes of value creation and capture. As a result, emphasis is placed on understanding how the process of 'strategic coupling' occurs between regional assets and the demands of focal firms in global production networks (Henderson et al., 2002; Dicken and Malmberg, 2001). Institutional influences at multiple scales play key roles in mediating this process (Cooke and Morgan, 1998; Morgan, 1997). Local institutions may act as information brokers relaying the needs of focal firms to local firms or universities or encouraging networking amongst regional stakeholders. Despite the importance assigned to local institutions or 'institutional thickness', the empirical evidence testing their efficacy for embedding MNCs shows that institutional factors may represent a necessary, but not sufficient, condition for embedding MNCs and exploiting the regional development benefits associated with inward investment (Phelps et al., 2003).

In addition to understanding processes of value creation, examinations of regional development must also consider the extent to which particular locales capture value (Henderson et al., 2002). Since the demands of global firms and markets change constantly, this involves tracking the development of the local skills pool or the extent to which locally-based affiliates possess an evolutionary capacity. The capacity for multinational affiliates to upgrade and expand their operations through successful intra-corporate competition creates new opportunities for regions to capture greater value from inward investment (Phelps and Fuller, 2000). Locally based institutions may support affiliate development, but the possibility exists that these efforts merely reduce the exit costs of multinationals (Phelps et al., 1998). The diversity of firm organizational practices and regional capabilities and attributes, makes the regional development outcomes produced by the interaction of firms and territories highly variable in nature (Dicken and Malmberg, 2001). In light of Ireland's small size and history of economic peripherality, these issues are particularly resonant. Since it heretofore lacked the capacity for endogenously led development, Ireland instead accesses global sources of knowledge and global demand to spur regional development. The rest of this chapter describes the manner in which Ireland successfully managed to enhance its internal capacity for value creation and capture.

INDUSTRIAL POLICY IN AN ERA OF FULL EMPLOYMENT

In the late 1950s, the Irish government replaced ineffectual policies of import-substitution industrialization with a programme of export-oriented industrialization in an effort to import development. The new economic policies encouraged inward investment and led to an annual average growth of 4.4 per cent between 1960 and 1973 (Sweeney, 1998). Admission to the European Community in 1973 essentially locked in the new policy regime, and perhaps more importantly broke Ireland's dependence on the UK (FitzGerald, 2000). Nevertheless, Ireland's economic peripherality remained unchanged and a dual economy emerged between under-performing and uncompetitive Irish firms and more productive, but highly dependent foreign-owned branch plants. Ireland appeared to grow, but the dual economy created jobless growth. By way of illustration, multinationals created 20 000 jobs between 1973 and 1988, but indigenous industry declined by 30 000 jobs during the same period (Ruane and McGibney, 1991). Therefore foreign industry acted as a substitute for indigenous industry, rather than a complement (Grimes, 1993).

The 1982 Telesis report made clear the shortcomings of Ireland's FDI-led industrial policy. Telesis questioned the benefits accrued from FDI as the branch plants that typified inward investment used little skilled labour and created few opportunities for local sourcing. Moreover, MNCs were highly unlikely to locate any strategic functions (R&D, marketing, and so on) because doing so adds costs and reduces the level of declared profits, thereby undermining their primary reason for locating in Ireland – the tax regime.

The Telesis Report (1982) further argued that Ireland must strengthen indigenous industry and use investment incentives only for those firms possessing strategic corporate functions. The Culliton Report (1992) reached similar conclusions ten years later when it reiterated, among other things, the need to better develop indigenous industry so as to eliminate the dual economy.

Changes occurring at the local, European and global scale during the late 1980s and early 1990s altered Ireland's position in the world economy, and made it a more attractive location for higher quality investment. Within Ireland, investments in education and a maturing baby boom created a deepening pool of skilled labour. This pool of skilled labour emerged at a time when many multinational corporations centralized their European operations in anticipation of the completion of the Single Market (Breathnach, 1998). While the 'economic planets all came into alignment at the same time' (Haughton, 2000, 44), Ireland took advantage of these factors because its industrial policy adapted pragmatically to the changing international environment. In a sense, the Irish made their own luck. Ireland's success in attracting disproportionate amounts of European-bound inward investment during the late 1980s and early 1990s changed the focus of Irish industrial policy. Whereas unemployment hovered around 20 per cent in the mid-1980s, the subsequent economic growth during the 1990s resulted in a condition of almost full employment (MacSharry and White, 2000). Consequently, full employment allowed Irish industrial policy to move away from its traditional emphasis on employment creation and instead focus more on policies designed to stimulate value enhancement and capture.

Irish policy makers respond to these changing local, regional and global conditions in several specific ways. At the most basic level, the Irish Industrial Development Agency (IDA Ireland) consistently becomes more narrow and selective in the activities and firms targeted for inward investment. Market considerations drive the targeting process at the project level. IDA Ireland first identifies market niches that possess high-growth potential and that are potentially mobile into Ireland. It then assembles information on successful firms, and firms looking to diversify their international production. Next, it initiates contact with the headquarters of these companies, attempting to get the company to visit Ireland to discuss individual projects (Ruane and Görg, 1997). Specific 'Blue Chip' or 'Flagship' investors are pursued with the intention of using these firms to attract other leading firms from the rest of the industry (UNCTAD, 1999). If lead firms prove successful in Ireland, then a 'herd mentality' might emerge throughout the industry with other firms attempting to duplicate the leader's success.

Sectorally, IDA Ireland targets a narrow range of potentially high value-added industries for investment. The evolution of this targeting is illustrated in Figure 9.1, as over time the industries consist increasingly of higher value-

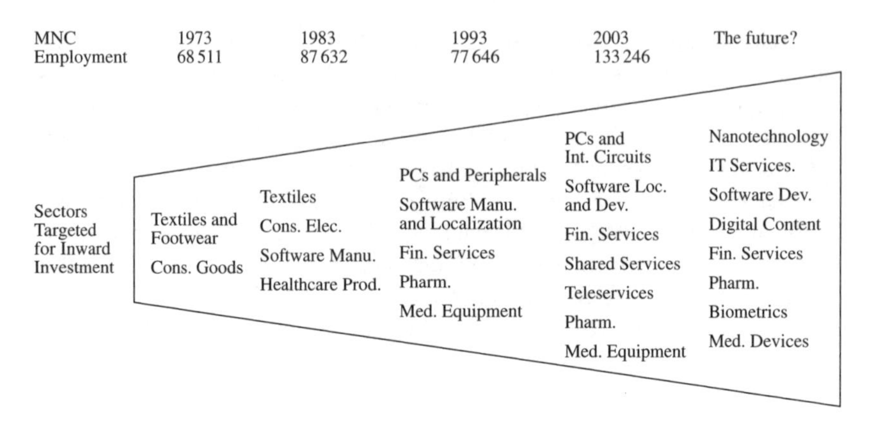

Figure 9.1 Targeted sectors for investment since admission to the EEC

added manufacturing and internationally-traded services. During the economic boom of the 1990s, the industries targeted for investment included electronics (particularly PCs and peripherals), medical devices and pharmaceuticals. IDA Ireland also recognized the growing potential of internationally-traded services (Forfás, 1996). IDA Ireland recognized the potential of internationally-traded services almost twenty years ago when it began targeting software and financial services. But given that most other locations target these same industries (Young et al., 1994), IDA Ireland attempted to stay ahead of the curve by moving into other industries like teleservices and shared services before their competitors (Grimes, 2003).

Attracting higher quality investment remains an important component of value creation, but it does not ensure value capture. Further efforts are now made to emphasize the latter, particularly in light of the declining number of greenfield investments worldwide (UNCTAD, 2003). Therefore in addition to attracting higher quality investments, IDA Ireland attempts to further embed MNC affiliates and win repeat investments. These embedding efforts involve,

> the [development] agencies working closely with local management of overseas companies to secure a wider corporate mandate and to become a vital part of the corporate value chain, thus helping to ensure the long term survival and growth of the company in Ireland....This measure will concentrate on persuading Irish subsidiaries to add strategic functions such as R&D, technical support, software development, logistics and shared services in Ireland in an effort to carve out as much autonomy for the Irish operation as possible and to so structure it within the overall group that it becomes virtually indispensable to the parent (Department of Finance, 2000, 138).

At the most basic level, IDA Ireland encourages local affiliate managers to actively lobby their parent for a wider mandate and more sophisticated activities. Irish managers of MNC affiliates are considered quite entrepreneurial, and almost subversive, in their drive to secure wider affiliate mandates (Delany, 1998). Many in fact see their efforts as contributing to a larger programme of national economic development (O'Riain, 1997). The Irish government further supports these efforts by providing funding for employee training and education, and even going so far as to lobby MNC headquarters on behalf of Irish-based affiliates.

In addition to extracting the maximum benefits from inward investment, Irish policy makers have also responded to the diminishing amount of quality investment by also attempting to enhance the value-creating potential of indigenous industry. Irish firms still trail foreign-owned firms in terms of productivity and exports, but the gap has narrowed and a pronounced dual economy no longer exists. The software and electrical and optical equipment sectors' recent development accounts for much of indigenous industry's improved performance (O'Sullivan, 2000). The emergence of the indigenous software industry garners particular attention, as Ireland now possesses globally competitive niches in activities such as E-learning and Internet security (O'Malley and O'Gorman, 2001). The Irish government actively supports the development of these export-generating activities. Although more developed than in the past, state funds still complement the Irish VC market, as almost 40 per cent of indigenous firms received some financial assistance from the government in the two years prior to 2003 (HotOrigin, 2003). State agencies like Enterprise Ireland further assist Irish companies in finding international partners and commercializing their technologies.

These recent developments leave Ireland in a state of transition, as it becomes less competitive in cost-driven activities and attempts to move into more knowledge-driven activities (Bradley, 2002). The continuous strategic recoupling of regional assets and global demands makes this transition an uneven process over time. At the most basic level, a software development job created in Dublin is not a perfect substitute for a low-skill, assembly job lost in one of Ireland's disadvantaged regions. As a result, Ireland's recent economic development led to a significant degree of social and spatial polarization (Breathnach, 1998). The privileging of skills means that the primary benefactors of Ireland's recent growth are those with the greatest access to education. As a result, the gap between the rich and the poor in Ireland trails only the US amongst OECD countries (*The Irish Times*, 21 August 1997). The demand for skills further concentrates economic activities spatially around Dublin because it possesses the greatest number of skilled workers and universities. Figure 9.2 depicts the spatial unevenness of this growth. Employment in multinationals makes this spatial disparity particularly evident,

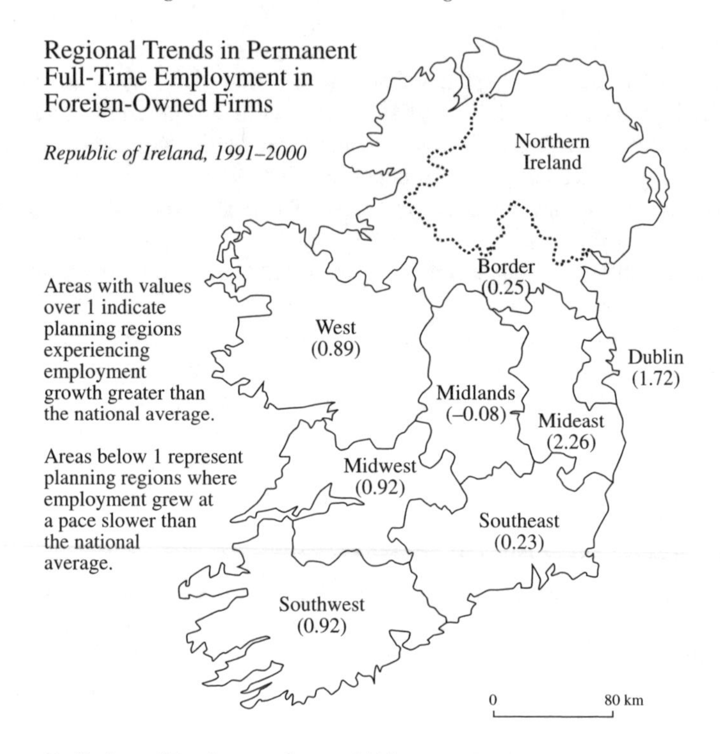

Source: Forfás Annual Employment Survey, 2000.

Figure 9.2 Distribution of employment in foreign-owned enterprises, 1991–2000

as between 1990 and 2000 the Greater Dublin Area's relative share of MNC employment increased 11.2 per cent, from 33.2 per cent in 1990 to 44.4 per cent in 2000. Over the same period, the more disadvantaged BMW (Border, Midlands and West) regions saw their regional share decline by a combined 7 per cent (Forfás, 2000). Albeit uneven, the processes of regional development occurring in Ireland nevertheless altered the country's place in the world economy. Continued regional development will however depend on Ireland's ability to compete in more knowledge-intensive activities. The next section therefore examines several key indicators related to Ireland's current and future capacity to create and capture value.

VALUE CREATION AND CAPTURE

The growing number of people involved in third-level education relates directly to Ireland's enhanced capacity for value creation. During the 1970s, Ireland made significant investments in education while at the same time experiencing a baby boom (Barrett et al., 1999). As a result, the 46 per cent of the population currently under the age of 30 (CSO, 2002) are the first generations to benefit from these earlier investments in education. Figure 9.3 shows the growing participation rates in both second and third level education since 1970. It is worth highlighting that the number of people involved in third level education increased five-fold since 1970. Consequently, Ireland offered a pool of skilled labour at a time when there was a growing global demand for skilled workers.

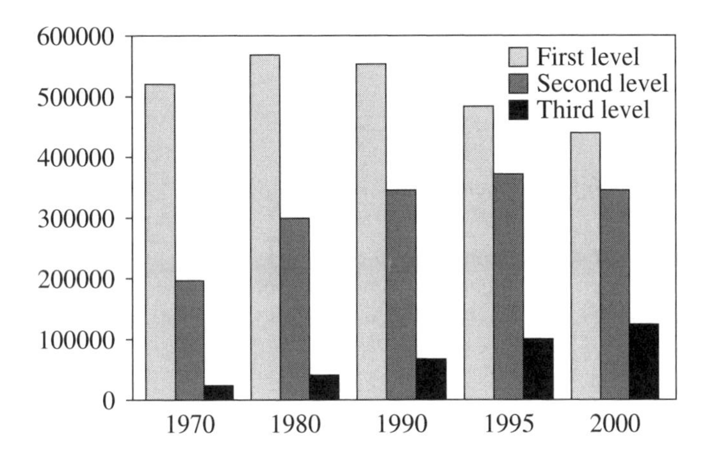

Source: CSO Statistical Yearbook of Ireland 2002.

Figure 9.3 Persons in full-time education, 1970–2000

Returning Irish emigrants together with skilled labour from places like India and Eastern Europe further supplemented Ireland's stock of human capital. Unlike the past, returning Irish emigrants during the 1990s were educated, and after working in places like the UK and US possessed managerial and technical experience. The following numbers reflect the labour quality associated with this influx of people. While 12.7 per cent of the domestic labour force aged 30 to 39 had third-level degrees, 28 per cent of returning emigrants in the same age group were similarly qualified. The corresponding figure for immigrants was even higher at 43.2 per cent (Barrett et al., 2002). This infusion of skills not only deepened Ireland's pool of human capital but also buffered the effects of wage inflation, thereby maintaining some of Ireland's cost competitiveness relative to other locations (FitzGerald, 2000).

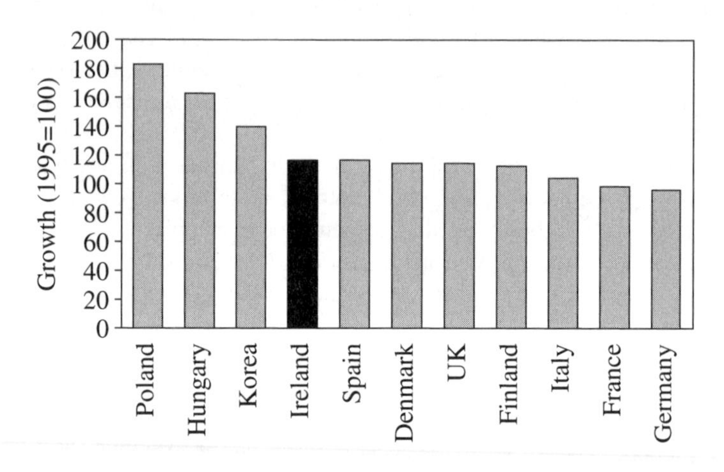

Source: National Competitiveness Council, 2002.

Figure 9.4 Total enrolment in tertiary education growth, 1999

However, these improvements in the stock of human capital are more indicative of a convergence with European averages than a leap ahead. This convergence becomes more evident when comparing Ireland to other places. Figure 9.4 shows that with 29 per cent of people between the ages of 25 and 34 having third level education, Ireland remains in the middle of the pack amongst several other OECD countries. That said, Ireland's position should continue to improve as total enrolment in tertiary education grew by 18 per cent between 1995 and 1999. Of the other countries considered, Irish growth ranked fourth behind Poland, Hungary and South Korea – three other countries in the process of catching up. Ireland also scores particularly well in the number of science graduates produced. In Figure 9.5, Ireland compares favourably with other OECD countries with an average of 2789 science graduates per 100 000 people in the labour force, aged 25 to 34. These figures bode well for future growth in the ICT sector, but recently fewer people are enrolling in science courses and this may pose a direct threat to future competitiveness (National Competitiveness Council, 2002).

While the development of the technological labour pool allows for greater value creation, scepticism remains about Ireland's capacity for value capture. This often revolves around the extent to which the FDI-led development policy leaves Ireland dependent on foreign firms from a limited number of sectors that repatriate most of their profits and create few opportunities for

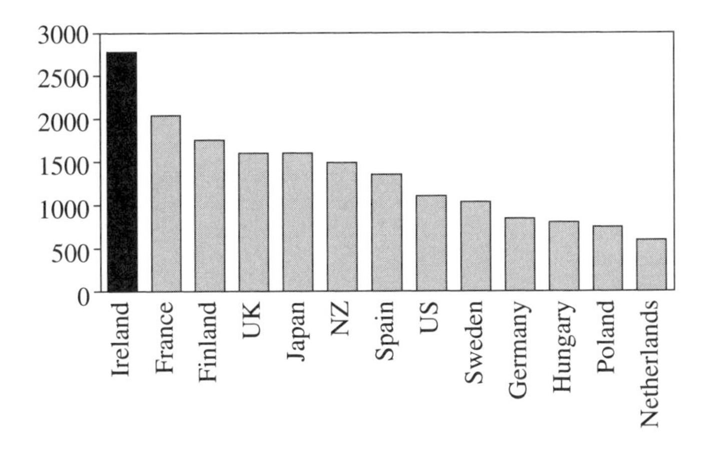

Source: National Competitiveness Council, 2002.

Figure 9.5 Number of science graduates at university level (per 100 000 persons in the labour force aged 25–34)

local linkages (for example Shirlow, 1995; O'Hearn, 1998; 2000). The data presented in Table 9.1 demonstrate that, in a relative sense, Irish Economy Expenditures (IEEs) represent a much smaller proportion of total sales for foreign-owned firms than for Irish-owned firms. Whereas IEEs comprise almost two-thirds of total sales for Irish-owned firms in 2001, they signify only a quarter of total sales for foreign-owned firms. The relative lack of local sourcing may draw criticism, but it may also represent the increased integration of Irish-based affiliates within their wider corporate networks rather than some kind of structural weakness within the local supplier base.

These data are also somewhat misleading about the contributions made by foreign-owned firms. Although IEEs as a percentage of total sales from foreign-owned firms declined steadily from almost 40 per cent in 1995 to 26 per cent in 2001, Table 9.1 also shows that in an absolute sense total IEEs from foreign-owned firms grew by 69 per cent. Multinationals also spend more on wages, even though employing fewer people than indigenous industry. In fact, the average wage in foreign-owned firms is 25 per cent higher than in Irish-owned firms (Barry and Bradley, 1997). While foreign-owned firms also lag behind Irish-owned firms in the volume of Irish raw materials, it is worth noting that expenditures on raw materials more than doubled between 1995 and 2001, thereby reflecting greater levels of local sourcing. This has emerged even though multinational activities are becoming increasingly geared toward services activities and are less material in their output.

Table 9.1 Estimated Irish economy expenditures (€ million)

	1995	1996	1997	1998	1999	2000	2001	% Change 1995–2001
Irish-Owned Firms								
Total Sales	17410	19839	18911	19327	21597	21579	23965	138%
Total Irish Economy Expenditures	13550	15724	14588	14827	16240	13988	15472	114%
Of Which								
Wages & Salaries	2637	2888	3058	3212	3785	3837	4309	163%
Irish Raw Materials	7734	9285	8070	7984	8479	7589	8358	108%
Irish Services	2099	2536	2426	2458	2600	2562	2805	134%
IEE as a percentage of total sales	77.8%	79.3%	77.1%	76.7%	75.2%	64.8%	64.6%	
Foreign-Owned Firms								
Total Sales	27893	32611	38019	43671	51582	66205	72102	258%
Total Irish Economy Expenditures	11011	13251	12908	15154	15914	16915	18579	169%
Of Which								
Wages & Salaries	2869	3166	3391	3785	4252	5470	6120	213%
Irish Raw Materials	3205	3727	3798	4678	5438	6107	6474	202%
Irish Services	4464	5766	5073	5848	5136	5338	5985	134%
IEE as a percentage of total sales	39.5%	40.6%	34.0%	34.7%	30.9%	25.5%	25.8%	

Source: Forfás Annual Reports, various years.

The ICT sector lies at the heart of Ireland's strategy to make the transition into a more knowledge-driven economy, but at present ICT employment constitutes only 4.6 per cent of total business sector employment (National Competitiveness Council, 2002). This puts Ireland behind other European economies noted for their ICT industries like Sweden and Finland (National Competitiveness Council, 2002). Moreover, Ireland imports more technology than it creates. As displayed in Figure 9.6, relative to other OECD countries Ireland runs a significant technology balance of payments deficit. This demonstrates that multinational affiliates overwhelmingly import more technology from their home markets than Irish firms export from Ireland (OECD, 2001). This does not necessarily reflect poor competitiveness, but it does indicate that Ireland remains very much a technology-taker rather than a technology-maker. Ireland's lagging amount of R&D activities highlights these shortcomings. As a percentage of GDP, Ireland ranks 11th out of 16 OECD countries in terms of the Gross Domestic Expenditure on R&D (GERD) (National Competitiveness Council, 2002). That said, with a nearly 15 per cent annual change between 1997 and 2000, Ireland's GERD grew faster than the other countries included in the study (National Competitiveness Council, 2002).

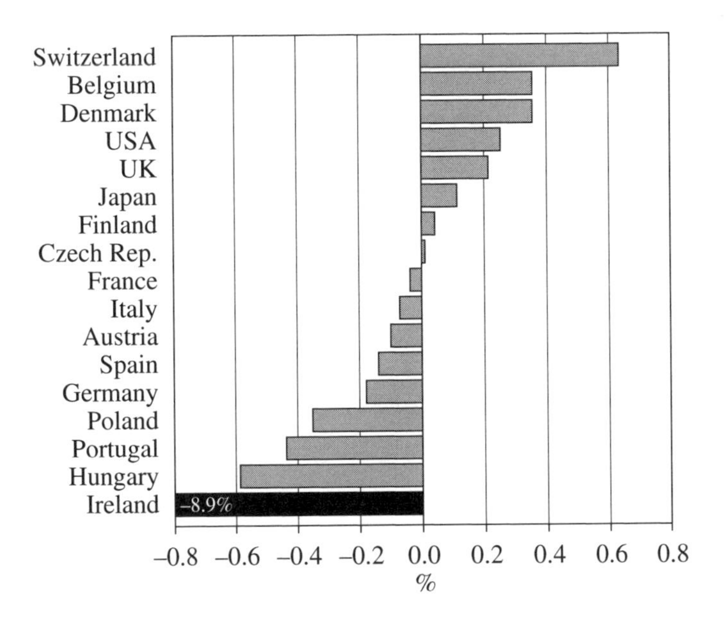

Source: OECD Science, Technology and Industry Scoreboard 2001.

Figure 9.6 Technology balance of payments, 1999

Many of the indicators presented above reflect Ireland's convergence with the rest of the developed world. However, they nevertheless demonstrate that Ireland is becoming better equipped to compete in more knowledge-driven activities. As such, Ireland is better able to extract greater benefits from FDI, and sources of innovation are no longer so heavily skewed toward exogenous sources like multinationals. Even though foreign-owned firms remain more productive than Irish-owned firms (O'Sullivan, 2000), this is no longer true across all sectors. For instance, the indigenous Irish software industry is widely considered to undertake more sophisticated activities than multinational software affiliates located in Ireland (O'Riain, 1997; O'Malley and O'Gorman, 2001). Therefore in spite of criticisms about Ireland's FDI dependence, the FDI-led development policy placed the country in a position to better manage and meet the world economy's changing demands. Twenty years ago Ireland had trouble catching up with the rest of the world, but it is now well set to keep up. What remains in question is the extent to which Ireland will be able to get ahead. Consequently, the next section describes several ways in which policy makers are attempting to establish Ireland as a key location for several emerging technologies.

POSSIBLE FUTURES

FDI continues to serve as one conduit through which Ireland accesses multiple sources of innovation, but as Ireland moves into more knowledge-driven activities FDI cannot sustain continued regional development. As a result, new areas for value creation must meet several criteria. For instance, new niches must provide opportunities for both small Irish firms and large multinationals, with the opportunities for Irish firms not solely dependent on forming a supplier base for the multinationals. New niches must also allow input from multiple sectors to avoid rigidity and buffer against external threats in specific sectors like the global downturn in telecommunications. In addition, entering these markets must occur at a time of significant growth potential and with no imminent substitute in sight. Much like FDI-oriented policies, success requires first-mover advantages in order for Ireland to establish itself as a key site before the sector reaches maturity. Two new niches – Digital Content and Biometrics, illustrate the possibilities of this new avenue for industrial development.

Digital content involves the confluence of previously distinct areas such as media and entertainment, multimedia, software and electronic hardware. It is seen as building on Ireland's existing strengths in software, electronics and telecommunications. As an industry, digital content has yet to reach full maturity with the global market estimated at $178 billion in 2001, but industry analysts expect it to grow at a rate of 30 per cent per annum to reach $434 billion by 2006 (Forfás, 2002). As a result, the growing demand for a wide variety of products and services in areas such as education, entertainment and consumer and business-oriented content presents a window of opportunity for new entrants.

The establishment of the 'Digital Hub' in the Liberties section of Dublin, represents one government programme designed to support the growth of the digital content industry in Ireland. Much like another high profile development project, Dublin's International Financial Services Centre, the Digital Hub, was designed partly to stimulate urban renewal in a previously derelict area but also to create a cluster of related activities (Forfás, 2002). The Digital Hub remains in its infancy and thereby represents more of a policy project than an actual cluster of activity. It does however have a flagship tenant in Media Lab Europe (MLE), a division of MIT's Media Lab. The government hopes that MLE's presence will have a similar effect on other flagship investments such as Microsoft or Intel by serving as a magnet for subsequent investments and lending credibility to the Digital Hub. Several firms now operate out of the Digital Hub, but as currently constituted it represents more of a showcase as the industry remains nascent in character.

Biometrics presents another area with great potential for value creation and capture. Biometrics are automated methods for recognizing and identifying people from physiological characteristics such as fingerprints or voice patterns (*The Irish Times*, 21 July 2003). Much like the digital content industry, biometrics ties into a wide array of other industries like biotechnology and existing Irish specialities like E-security. The industry has yet to reach full maturity with significant growth expected in the near future. Whereas the global market stood at $200 million in 2001, it is estimated to grow to $2 billion in 2006 (Venture Consulting, 2002). Global trends will dictate future demand. For instance, as the US implements new visa, passport and immigration systems, the EU is likely to follow the US lead, thereby creating more opportunities for Irish firms. Already several Irish firms such as Daon and VoiceVault are developing biometric technology. Daon, for instance, already supplies biometric security software to the London City airport (*The Irish Times*, 21 July 2003).

Both emergent niches are in their infancy and will require local institutional support in order to succeed. The Irish state has traditionally acted as a midwife (O'Riain, 2000) aligning local resources to the needs of industry. As Irish industrial policy attempts to foster more sophisticated activities, the coupling of regional assets and global demands has also changed. As these activities become more knowledge-driven then they will benefit increasingly from collaboration with industry researchers. While this collaboration often happens organically, the state encourages more university involvement through institutions like Science Foundation Ireland (SFI). SFI provides the resources for Irish universities to poach globally recognized researchers and bring them to Ireland. The intent is not only to make Ireland a location for cutting edge research, but also to train a new generation of Irish researchers. In addition to augmenting the local skills pool, the government still must put in place the physical infrastructure – notably broadband, necessary to support these industries both in the long-term and in locations beyond selected sites in Dublin. Success for both industry niches depends not only on local supply-side issues, but is also contingent on developments at other scales.

Non-local influences revolve most notably around regulatory issues at the EU level, as well as within the global trade system. For digital content, the drafting of effective intellectual property protection regulation by the Irish government, the EU and the World Trade Organization influences not only industry growth but also the extent to which producers can capably capture value. The implementation of standards and practices in the US and EU markets similarly influences biometrics. The establishment of European standards played important roles in the development of other industries, most notably mobile telephony (Brunn and Leinbach, 2000). For this reason the launch of the European Biometric Forum (EBF) in Dublin further establishes Ireland as a key site for biometrics in Europe (*The Irish Times*, 21 July 2003). In addition to setting and enforcing standards, the EU, through its Research Framework Programme, also represents an important level at which significant funding for advanced research is distributed (Lagendijk and Cornford, 2000). These nascent activities perhaps offer a glimpse of Ireland's future industrial development. Although at their infancy, if they prove successful in delivering each of their constituent parts they will provide significant opportunities not just for value creation, but also for value enhancement and capture. In doing so, they might form the foundation for sustainable development that no longer depends on continually securing new waves of inward investment.

CONCLUSION

Transforming peripheral European regions into dynamic 'learning regions' remains a formidable challenge for policy makers at both the national and EU levels. The confluence of several unique exogenous and endogenous factors led to Ireland's economic turnaround, and their uniqueness somewhat blunts the ability to generalize all elements of the Irish growth phenomenon to other places. While the benefits accrued from investments in education and a pro-business environment are undeniable, two exogenous factors merit further mention. First, the Irish case demonstrates the positive development consequences of being connected to leading technology centres. Ireland enhanced its capacity for value creation by tapping into these innovative milieux through its involvement in GPNs and the attraction of skilled knowledge workers, both foreign and returning Irish emigrants. Second, Ireland's integration in the EU and global markets in general, proved vital in overcoming the small size of its domestic market. For instance, the experience gained by Irish managers working in globally-competitive Irish firms and multinationals, both in Ireland and abroad, better enables them to meet global standards and practices.

Completing the transition into a knowledge-driven economy represents the fundamental challenge currently facing Ireland. Irish policy makers are acutely aware that the country is rapidly losing its relative cost competitiveness. The activities that created the Irish economic boom of the 1990s are not sustainable in the long-term, and as such the development agencies can no longer target cost-driven activities that are merely passing through Ireland on their way to Eastern Europe or Asia. In adjusting to Ireland's new position in the world economy, policy makers now target higher-value added activities that better fit with Ireland's current collection of regional assets. The youthful and increasingly educated workforce has created a track record of success that should enable Ireland to remain competitive both for new greenfield investments and importantly repeat investments. The Irish government is also attempting to support the development of emerging sectors such as biometrics and digital content. By combining the high-tech elements of both Irish firms and multinationals, Ireland hopes to take advantage of global demand expected to undergo exponential growth.

In spite of the promise associated with these developments, the continued development of Ireland's knowledge-driven economy faces several obstacles. At the most basic level, the congestion and rising costs associated with Dublin's rapid development diminish Ireland's attractiveness to inward investors and globally mobile knowledge workers (Ellis and Kim, 2001). The inability to overcome infrastructural deficits rapidly, both in terms of transportation and broadband access, inhibits both future growth and the establishment of more balanced regional development. Nevertheless compared to the poverty and high rates of emigration associated with much of Ireland's economic history, these are good problems to have. Ireland is unlikely to ever again experience growth rates like those of the 1990s, but there is growing confidence that a solid foundation for a knowledge driven economy has been constructed.

BIBLIOGRAPHY

Amin, A., and J. Tomaney (1995), 'The regional dilemma in a neo-liberal Europe', *European Urban and Regional Studies*, **2**(2), 171–88.

Archibugi, D., and A. Coco (2001), 'The globalisation of technology and the European innovation system', in M.M. Fischer and J. Frohlich (eds), *Knowledge, Complexity and Innovation Systems*, Berlin: Springer.

Asheim, B., and M. Dunford (1997), 'Regional Futures', *Regional Studies*, **31** (5), 445–55.

Barrett, A., T. Callan, and B. Nolan (1999), 'Returns to education in the Irish youth labour market', *Journal of Population Economics*, **12**, 313–26.

Barrett, A., J. FitzGerald, and B. Nolan (2002), 'Earning inequality, returns to education and immigration into Ireland', *Labour Economics*, **9**, 665–80.

Barry, F., and J. Bradley (1997), 'FDI and trade: the Irish host-country experience', *The Economic Journal*, **107**, 1798–811.

Bradley, J. (2002), 'The computer sector in Irish manufacturing: past triumphs, present strains, future challenges', *Journal of the Statistical and Social Inquiry Society of Ireland*, **XXXI**, 1–38.

Breathnach, P. (1998), 'Exploring the "Celtic Tiger" phenomenon: causes and consequences of Ireland's economic miracle', *European Urban and Regional Studies*, **5**, 305–16.

Bresnahan, T., A. Gambardella, and A. Saxenian (2001), '"Old Economy" inputs for "New Economy" outcomes: cluster formation in the new Silicon Valleys', *Industrial and Corporate Change*, **10** (4), 835–60.

Brunn, S., and T. Leinbach (2000), 'Nokia as a regional information fountainhead', in J. Wheeler, Y. Aoyama and B. Warf (eds), *Cities in the Telecommunications Age: The Fracturing of Geographies*, New York: Routledge.

Castells, M. (2000), *The Rise of the Network Society*, 2nd edn, Oxford: Blackwell.

Central Statistics Office (2002), *Statistical Yearbook of Ireland 2002*, Dublin: Central Statistics Office.

Cooke, P. (2001), 'New economy innovation systems: biotechnology in Europe and the USA', *Industry and Innovation*, **8** (3), 267–89.

Cooke, P., and K. Morgan (1998), *The Associational Economy: Firms, Regions and Institutions*, Oxford: Oxford University Press.

Culliton, J. (1992), *A Time for Change: Industrial Policy for the 1990s*, report of the Industrial Policy Review Group, Dublin: Stationery Office.

Delany, E. (1998), 'Strategic development of multinational subsidiaries in Ireland', in J. Birkinshaw and N. Hood (eds), *Multinational Corporate Evolution and Subsidiary Development*, London: MacMillan.

Department of Finance (2000), *Ireland National Development Plan, 2000–2006*, Dublin: Stationery Office.

Dicken, P., and A. Malmberg (2001), 'Firms in territories: a relational perspective', *Economic Geography*, **77**, 345–63.

Ellis, G., and J. Kim (2001), 'City profile: Dublin', *Cities*, **18** (5), 355–64.

FitzGerald, J. (2000), 'The story of Ireland's failure – and belated success', in B. Nolan, P. O'Connell and C. Whelan (eds), *Bust to Boom? The Irish Experience of Growth and Inequality*, Dublin: Institute of Public Administration.

Forfás (1996), *Shaping Our Future: A Strategy for Enterprise in Ireland in the 21st Century*, Dublin: Forfás.

Forfás (2000), *Annual Employment Survey 2000*, Dublin: Forfás.

Forfás (2001), *International Trade and Investment Report 2000*, Dublin: Forfás.
Forfás (2002), *A Strategy for the Digital Content Industry in Ireland*, Dublin: Forfás.
Grimes, S. (1993), 'Ireland: the Challenge of Development in the European Periphery', *Geography*, **77** (1), 22–32.
Grimes, S. (2003), 'Ireland's emerging information economy: recent trends and future Prospects', *Regional Studies*, **37** (1), 3–14.
Grimes, S., and P. Collins (2003), 'Building a knowledge economy in Ireland through European research networks', *European Planning Studies*, **11** (4), 395–413.
Haughton, J. (2000), 'The historical background', in J.W. O'Hagan (ed.), *The Economy of Ireland, 8th edition*, Dublin: Gill & MacMillan.
Henderson, D., and K. Morgan (2002), 'Regions as laboratories – the rise of regional experimentalism in Europe', in M. Gertler and D. Wolfe (eds), *Innovation and Social Learning*, Basingstoke: Macmillan.
Henderson, J., P. Dicken, M. Hess, N. Coe, and H.W.C. Yeung (2002), 'Global production networks and the analysis of economic development', *Review of International Political Economy*, **9** (3), 436–64.
HotOrigin (2003), *Ireland's Software Cluster: Winning Sales – Lessons from the Frontline*, Dublin: HotOrigin.
Lagendijk, A. (2001), 'Scaling knowledge production: How significant is the region?', in M.M. Fischer and J. Frohlich (eds), *Knowledge, Complexity and Innovation Systems*, Berlin: Springer.
Lagendijk, A., and J. Cornford (2000), 'Regional institutions and knowledge – tracking new forms of regional development policy', *Geoforum*, **31**, 209–18.
MacSharry, R., and P. White (2000), *The Making of the Celtic Tiger: The Inside Story of Ireland's Boom Economy*, Cork: Mercier Press.
Morgan, K. (1997), 'The learning region: institutions, innovation and regional renewal', *Regional Studies*, **31**, 491–504.
National Competitiveness Council (2002), *Annual Competitiveness Report 2002*, Dublin: Forfás.
OECD (2001), *OECD Science, Technology and Industry Scoreboard 2001*, OECD: Paris.
O'Hearn, D. (1998), *Inside the Celtic Tiger: the Irish economy and the Asian model*, London: Pluto Press.
O'Hearn, D. (2000), 'Globalization, 'New Tigers', and the End of the Developmental State? The Case of the Celtic Tiger', *Politics and Society*, **28** (1), 67–92.
O'Malley, E. and C. O'Gorman (2001), 'Competitive advantage in the Irish indigenous software industry and the role of inward foreign direct investment', *European Planning Studies*, **9** (3), 303–21.
O'Riain, S. (1997), 'An offshore silicon valley? The emerging Irish software industry', *Competition and Change*, **2**, 175–212.
O'Riain, S. (2000), 'The flexible developmental state: globalization, information technology, and the Celtic tiger', *Politics & Society*, **28** (2), 157–93.
O'Sullivan, M. (2000), 'Industrial development: a new beginning?', in J.W. O'Hagan (ed.), *The Economy of Ireland, 8th edition*, Dublin: Gill & MacMillan.
Phelps, N., and C. Fuller (2000), 'Multinationals, intracorporate competition and regional development', *Economic Geography*, **76** (3), 224–43.
Phelps, N., J. Lovering, and K. Morgan (1998), 'Tying the firm to the region or tying the region to the firm? Early observations on the case of LG in South Wales', *European Urban and Regional Studies*, **5** (2), 119–37.
Phelps, N., D. MacKinnon, I. Stone, and P. Braidford, (2003), 'Embedding the

multinationals? Institutions and the development of overseas manufacturing affiliates in Wales and North East England', *Regional Studies*, **37** (1), 27–40.

Porter, M. (1990), *The Competitive Advantage of Nations*, New York: Free Press.

Ruane, F., and H. Görg, (1997), 'The impact of foreign direct investment on sectoral adjustment in the Irish economy', *National Institute Economic Review*, **160**, 76–86.

Ruane, F., and A. McGibney (1991), 'The performance of overseas industry, 1973–1989', in A. Foley and D. McAleese (eds), *Overseas Industry in Ireland*, Dublin: Gill and MacMillan.

Saxenian, A. (2002), 'Transnational communities and the evolution of global production networks: the cases of Taiwan, China and India', *Industry and Innovation*, 9 (3), 183–202.

Scott, A.J. (1998), *Regions and the World Economy: The Coming Shape of Global Production, Competition and Political Order*, Oxford: Blackwell.

Shirlow, P. (1995), 'Transnational corporations in the Republic of Ireland and the illusion of economic well-being', *Regional Studies*, **29** (7), 687–91.

Storper, M. (1997), *The Regional World: Territorial Development in a Global Economy*, New York: Guilford.

Sweeney, P. (1998), *The Celtic Tiger: Ireland's Continuing Economic Miracle*, 2nd edn, Dublin: Oak Tree Press.

Telesis (1982), 'A review of industrial policy', National Economic and Social Council report no. 62, Dublin.

The Irish Times (1997), 'Ireland and US highest in wage inequality, says ESRI', 21 August, accessed at www.ireland.com.

The Irish Times (2003), 'Dublin hosts EU biometric forum', 21 July: p. 16.

UNCTAD (1999), *World Investment Report: Foreign Direct Investment and the Challenge of Development*, New York: United Nations.

UNCTAD (2003), *FDI Policies for Development: National and International Perspectives*, New York: United Nations.

Venture Consulting (2002), 'Converging technologies: pharmaceutical, biotechnology and medical device industries', presentation accessed at www.idaireland.com.

Young, S., N. Hood and A. Wilson (1994), 'Targeting policy as a competitive strategy for inward investment agencies', *European Urban and Regional Studies*, **1** (2), 143–59.

10. The spatial dimension of inter-firm learning: case study and conceptualization

Roel Rutten and Frans Boekema

The aim of this chapter is to contribute to the conceptualizing of the relationship between space and learning. There is room for further theoretical work on this matter as many empirical studies, thus far, have yielded mixed results (for example, Oerlemans et al., 2000 and Smith et al., 2002). The approach followed here is an explorative one, which means that empirical material will be presented first. A theoretical discussion of the empirical results follows in the second part of this chapter. However, the starting point is not completely blank from a theoretical perspective. This chapter follows a knowledge-based perspective (for example, Boekema et al., 2000). Consensus seems to have emerged in the literature that we are now in the knowledge-based economy where knowledge is the most strategic resource and learning the most important process (Morgan, 1997). The question, then, is how the relation between space and learning (or knowledge) can be conceptualized from a knowledge-based perspective. In order to do so, it is necessary to discuss knowledge and learning first. The knowledge-based approach argues that companies create knowledge in order to innovate, that is, to develop new products, services, working practices, and so on. For that purpose, they combine different kinds of knowledge, such as technological knowledge, managerial knowledge, knowledge of markets, which materializes in new products, services, and so on. This is a Schumpeterian view, where innovation should be seen as the making of new combinations of knowledge. Given this dynamic conceptualization of innovation, it makes little sense to distinguish between learning and knowledge creation. In the knowledge-based perspective, learning is a process of knowledge creation, the outcome of which may be innovations, such as new products.

In the knowledge-based economy, companies do not innovate alone. The assumption that networks are important for learning is rarely contested nowadays. Oerlemans et al. (1998), for example, have argued that collaboration with other firms and actors in the innovation process is important for two reasons.

> First, it means that although individual innovating firms are competent in specific areas, their competence is nonetheless limited ... Therefore, they must be able to access and use external knowledge. Second, the multilayered and heterogeneous nature of resource bases makes it necessary to distinguish several actors and institutions inside and outside the firm in which resources are embedded (pp. 300–301).

Similar findings were reported by, among others, Lipparini and Sobrero (1994) and Matthyssens and van den Bulte (1994). Lipparini and Sobrero (1994), for example, in their study on innovation in small-firm networks, argue that 'first, even if in varying degrees, all firms must depend upon their environment for inputs vital to their survival and growth; and second, that technological innovation is increasingly less the result of efforts performed by a single firm' (Lipparini and Sobrero 1994, 126). Moreover, 'Competitiveness emerges as a network-embedded capacity and the coordination among firms, maximizing firm-specific competencies, represents a strategic leverage in accomplishing and maintaining a sustainable competitive advantage' (Lipparini and Sobrero, 1994, 127). Similarly, Matthyssens and van den Bulte studied the relationship between buyers and suppliers and found that in a cooperative model of buyer–supplier relations, it is not lowest prices that are important but the contribution that a supplier can make to long-term strengthening of competitiveness (Matthyssens and van de Bulte, 1994, 74).

The argument, thus, is that companies, even large ones, do not have all the knowledge they need to successfully develop new products and services. They need external knowledge, that is, knowledge that is beyond their hierarchical control, in their innovation process. This not only establishes the need for companies to work together with other companies, but it also creates interdependencies between them. Consequently, knowledge-based exchange relations between companies are not merely casual transactions but the result of a deliberate and strategic choice to engage in a situation of mutual dependence (Best, 1990; 2001). Companies do so because there are important benefits associated with this strategy. It allows companies to innovate more quickly and to develop innovations that are beyond their individual capabilities (Cooke and Morgan, 1998). Moreover, and crucial with respect to competitive advantage, innovations developed in an inter-firm context are based on knowledge from various sources. It is impossible to tell what part of the inter-firm knowledge originates from which company, making this knowledge extremely difficult to copy. A competitor would have to identify the various skills and competences that have contributed to an inter-firm innovation – which are often highly company specific – and find a way to copy them before he could successfully attempt to copy the innovation. Put differently, knowledge creation between organizations adds to the complexity of the outcomes of this process, making it even more difficult for outsiders to recreate. Consequently, network innovations create more durable competitive advantage (cf. Porter, 1998; Teece, 2000).

At this point it is useful to address what knowledge creation, or learning, entails. The work of Nonaka and Takeuchi (1995) can be considered at the basis of the current mainstream literature on knowledge creation, or learning. These authors argue that knowledge has two apparitions, tacit and explicit knowledge. Even more important than the fact that explicit knowledge can be expressed in words, figures, graphs, and so on, and tacit knowledge cannot or only limitedly so, is the acknowledgement that tacit knowledge is wedded to its human and organizational context (cf. Morgan, 1997). That is, tacit knowledge is context-specific – it has value and meaning only within its specific context, be that an individual or a collective, for example a firm or a network. It is this characteristic in particular that makes tacit knowledge a source of sustainable competitive advantage (cf. Porter, 1990 and Maskell, et al., 1998) as competitors must first understand the context before they can copy the knowledge (cf. Rutten, 2003). However, in order to produce innovations, companies are dependent on external knowledge as well, as was just argued. Innovation can thus be seen in Schumpeterian terms as the making of new combinations of knowledge (cf. Schumpeter, 1926 and Rutten, 2003). The difficulty, then, is to make combinations of the different company-specific (that is tacit) 'knowledges' of the companies in a network. This was exactly the challenge of the network, which is the object of inquiry in the next sections.

THE KNOWLEDGE INDUSTRY CLUSTERING (KIC) NETWORK

This empirical section presents data on a regional network in the manufacturing industry. The data were obtained from interviews with 14 suppliers and 14 representatives of the large company in this network. (See Rutten (2003) for a detailed discussion of this case study.)

Discussion of the KIC Network

In the mid-1990s, the Dutch company Océ, manufacturer of copiers and printers, initiated an engineering project to develop a new colour copier together with selected suppliers. In this Knowledge Industry Clustering (KIC) project, which ran from 1994 through 1998, some 40 suppliers participated. As with Océ, all of these suppliers were located in the south-eastern part of the Netherlands, which makes the KIC network a truly regional network. The KIC project itself was organized in approximately 20 clusters. Each cluster consisted of two to four suppliers plus a representative from the Océ R&D department. Some suppliers participated in more than one cluster. Each cluster was given a specific engineering assignment. Suppliers were selected on the basis of relevant competencies for the assignment. The Océ engineer's role was to ensure a continuous flow of knowledge between Océ and the suppliers in his cluster. The advantage of working in clusters is that it allowed engineers from different companies to work in teams, thus bypassing their own companies' hierarchies as well as the hierarchies usually associated with buyer–supplier collaboration. In these teams, or clusters, engineers from different companies worked as colleagues to perform an engineering assignment. Their particular affiliation became incidental. On average, a cluster needed two years to complete its engineering assignment. Consequently, by the time the last clusters were formed, in 1998, the earliest clusters had already been dissolved.

As argued, the KIC project focuses on the engineering phase of the product development process which starts when the functional specifications of a product or module have been determined. For example, the stapler inside the copier has to be able to apply a certain number of staples per minute and must be easy to reach for users when they want to put a new supply of staples in the machine when the old supply is used up. These conditions determine a number of functions and design specifications which are the input for the engineering process. In the KIC project, the engineering was done by teams (or clusters) of suppliers who would work on the engineering of a complete module. Océ's strategy behind this new way of working is very simple. In a broader perspective, Océ wants to become a 'head and tail company' as Océ creates its added value on the head and the tail ends of its value chain. The head in this metaphor is R&D, and the tail is the interaction with customers through sales, after-sales and maintenance of equipment. In R&D, Océ aims to develop new technologies and applications that will offer more value to customers than the products of, for example, Canon and Xerox. Sales, after-sales and maintenance is what customers actually see of Océ. If they are happy on this side, they are more likely to buy other Océ machines in the future. The middle section of the company's value chain, that is, production and the 'easy' part of the engineering process, is left to suppliers. Consequently, Océ chooses to commit its resources to the head and the tail ends of its value chain. The idea behind the KIC project, therefore, was to involve suppliers in that part of the product development process where they can offer most added value because of their specialization. Because clusters were continuously formed and dissolved, a true KIC network never existed. Yet, the term KIC network will still be used to refer to the ensemble of KIC clusters as they shared important organizational characteristics, as is discussed in the following.

Although Océ formally was in charge of the KIC network, it left most of the operational management to the suppliers in their various clusters. The objective was to let the suppliers take the initiative so as to challenge them to use their skills and expertise in the engineering process. This way, Océ could make use of this body of external knowledge. The role of the Océ engineers was to provide the necessary information and knowledge to the clusters. In doing so, Océ tried to be a partner rather than a boss. Océ respondents, for example, argued that they tried to make the relations with the suppliers 'as open as possible' and that lines of communication where short. Moreover, they said that, on the engineering level, there was absolutely no patron/subordinate-like relation between Océ and the suppliers. Formally, such a relation did exist, but in practice there was little sign of it, according to the Océ engineers. In other words, Océ purposely designed the organizational structure of the KIC project in such a way that the suppliers were responsible for the engineering process. This, Océ believed, favoured knowledge creation between the suppliers. As knowledge creation involves communication between the persons involved, the organizational structure has to allow for this communication to take place. The opinions of the suppliers about the organizational structure confirm that it favoured knowledge exchange. In the words of one of them, 'the organizational structure really only had advantages: open communication, knowledge is available in the right places, quick communication, and integration of specialist knowledge in the product'. Several suppliers mentioned that the role of the Océ engineer in their clusters was important as this person 'could get things done within the Océ organization'. Another (lead) supplier observed that he 'made a perfect team' with the Océ engineer in his cluster. In short, the suppliers felt that the boundaries between the partners in a cluster, including Océ, were very flexible and that the organizational structure favoured knowledge creation. One supplier argued, for example, that 'in the clusters, they had the freedom to do what was necessary to achieve the best possible technical result'. Other suppliers, too, argued that 'we had a lot of freedom', and that 'to a large degree, we could make our own decisions'. The suppliers were, of course, aware of the fact that Océ, ultimately, was in charge as Océ was paying them. But they greatly appreciated the fact that 'decisions were made in teams'.

The relations in the clusters involved in this study can thus be characterized as 'open'. Hierarchy played a minor role so as to emphasize the competencies of the companies involved. Lines of communication were short and engineers could interact freely with their colleagues in other companies.

The Space Factor and the Question of Proximity Relations

For Océ, working with regional suppliers on engineering matters is a strategic choice. Océ focuses strongly on regional-based knowledge in the engineering process. Data from Océ's purchasing department confirm this strategic focus. The total purchasing value of Océ increased from 77 million euros in 1988 to 235 million euros in 1996. This confirms the correctness of the move towards involving suppliers more strongly in Océ. Of the purchasing value, 34 per cent (or 26 million euros) was allocated to suppliers in south-east Netherlands in 1988. This regional share increased to 45 per cent (or 105 million euros) in 1996. At the same time, Océ's purchasing value in the rest of the Netherlands remained fairly constant: almost 21 million euros in 1988 versus 23 million euros in 1996. However, in relative terms, the share of the rest of the Netherlands dropped from 27 per cent in 1988 to 10 per cent in 1996. The relative shares of Europe and the rest of the world remained constant. In 1988 Europe accounted for 32 per cent of Océ's purchasing value against 35 per cent in 1996. The figures for the rest of the world were 7 per cent in 1988 and 10 per cent in 1996. These figures show that suppliers in the region have become significantly more important in recent years.

Other data pertaining to the KIC project confirm the importance of proximity with regard to engineering. Respondents found that spatial proximity facilitated the communication between them. The longest distance between any of the companies involved in the KIC project (not just those involved in this study) was 70–75 kilometres (44–46 miles), which corresponds to about one hour's driving time. Therefore, it is justified to say that the relations in the KIC network were proximate relations. As spatial proximity facilitates face-to-face communication it can be an advantage with respect to knowledge creation. Table 10.1 presents these experiences for the respondents in this study. It shows, for example, that all of the 14 Océ respondents found that spatial proximity facilitated communication in the KIC project. Of the suppliers involved in this study, 9 out of 14 (or 64 per cent) also found that spatial proximity facilitated communication. Only one supplier (or 7 per cent) did not have this experience. For 4 suppliers (or 29 per cent) it could not be established how they thought spatial proximity affected communication in the KIC clusters. Taken together, this means that 23 out of 28 respondents in this study (or 82 per cent) found that spatial proximity facilitated communication. Important as they may have found spatial proximity for communication between them, respondents did not think it was necessary. Only 2 out of 28 respondents (or 7 per cent) found that spatial proximity was necessary in engineering projects like KIC, whereas the majority (22 respondents or 79 per cent) felt that, if necessary, communication could also be achieved over long distances. Finally, the respondents were asked whether they felt that face-to-face communication was important. This proved to be the case, as 25 out of 28 respondents (or 89 per cent) found face-to-face communication to be important in the KIC project. The opinion of 3 respondents (or 21 per cent) on this issue could not be established.

Table 10.1 Spatial proximity and face-to-face communication in the KIC network

	Spatial proximity						Face-to-face communication is important		
	facilitates communicaton			is necessary					
	yes	no	n.a.	yes	no	n.a.	yes	no	n.a.
Océ									
N	14	0	0	1	13	0	14	0	0
%	100	0	0	7	93	0	100	0	0
Suppliers									
N	9	1	4	1	9	4	11	0	3
%	64	7	29	7	64	29	79	0	21
Total									
N	23	1	4	2	22	4	25	0	3
%	82	4	14	7	79	14	89	0	11

Note: n.a: not available

However, the respondents did not find that spatial proximity was necessary. Though preferring regional partners, they look for competent partners in the first place. A look at the answers from the respondents during the interviews provides some relevant colouring for these data. Respondents associate spatial proximity with short lines of communication and easier meeting opportunities. But, as the data show, they do not put spatial proximity first. One of the suppliers, for example, argued that 'you have to find a like-minded partner, in which case proximity is of secondary importance'. With regard to face-to-face communication, the respondents argued that modern electronic communication can never replace it because 'you have to look each other in the eye', and 'you have to "taste" a relationship'. In other words, the suppliers valued the short distances as it made the 'social aspects' of the communication easier. It is precisely these social aspects that are crucial to the exchange of tacit knowledge.

THEORETICAL DISCUSSION OF THE KIC NETWORK

The example raises a number of questions that, when answered, can further our understanding of knowledge, networks and space. The first question is why Océ would keep to the background in the particular network? It is not unusual for large companies like Océ to assume a dominant position *vis-à-vis* its suppliers. However, Océ wanted the suppliers to take the lead in the KIC project. Of course, there is more to the power relations in the KIC network than can be discussed in this chapter. Yet it is clear that the suppliers enjoyed a generous degree of discretion. This may have to do with the aim of the KIC network: knowledge creation. The second question is how the importance that respondents attached to spatial proximity can be explained. As the key variable in this matter seems to be (face-to-face) communication, the role of proximity, too, should be explained on that level. That is, the answer, in the first place, should focus on communication, not proximity.

Inter-firm Learning: Lessons from Organization Sociology

As the example of the stapler shows, in the KIC network, inter-firm learning required the marrying of, at least, two different 'pieces' of company-specific knowledge. First, the knowledge of 'motion control', that is the knowledge of moving objects such as a stapler is involved. This was the specialization of a supplier. The second knowledge concerns the knowledge of the paper flow inside a copier, which is the specialization of Océ. The engineering challenge, of course, is to synchronize the stapler and the paper flow. Arguably, this requires considerable exchange of tacit knowledge between the companies involved.

This kind of tacit knowledge exchange is a very social process that depends largely on human interaction (cf. Nonaka and Takeuchi, 1995 and Johannessen et al., 2001). At this point, organizational sociology has some valuable insights to offer. As early as 1961, Burns and Stalker found that organizations with few formalities, 'shallow hierarchy', short lines of communication and delegation of authority to the work place are best suited to perform such social processes. Burns and Stalker (1961) refer to such organizations as 'organic' organizations and the contemporary organizational sociology literature concurs with them as to the importance of organic organization with regard to learning (see Nonaka and Takeuchi, 1995). Hult and Nichols (1996), for example, argue that 'organizational learning manifests itself as degrees of openness and localness'. And, 'Openness ... emerges when ... managers become willing to suspend their certainty when communicating with each other ... [Openness] comprises two constructs: participative and reflective openness. ... Participative openness refers to the freedom to speak one's mind ... Whereas ... reflective openness leads to employees looking inward. [It] is a willingness to challenge our own thinking' (Hult and Nichols, 1996, 202).

> Localness is defined as moving decisions down the organizational hierarchy; designing business units where, to the greatest possible degree, local decision-makers confront the full range of issues and dilemmas intrinsic and growing and sustaining business enterprise. Thus, corporate learning is created by giving employees the freedom to act, to try their own ideas and to be responsible for providing results (Hult and Nichols, 1996, 202–3).

A comprehensive overview of the literature on this point is not feasible here. However, the above findings are supported in numerous other studies such as Judge et al. (1997) and Butler et al. (1998) who argue that organizational slack is an important resource when it comes to learning. Slack, of course, is what one expects to find in organic organizations. A more detailed discussion of the relevant literature can be found in Rutten (2003).

In sum, the organizational characteristics of the KIC network can thus be easily explained. They reflect the characteristics of organic organizations that, according to the contemporary literature on organizational sociology, are the best environment for knowledge creation. As can be observed from the earlier discussion on networks, the characteristics of organic organization apply to both single organizations, such as firms, and networks, the latter, of course, being a form of organization, too – albeit a more complex one (cf. Nohria and Eccles, 1992). A network with organic characteristics, therefore, can rightly be called a knowledge laboratory. The discretion that Océ granted to its suppliers in the KIC network was a price well worth paying as, in return, Océ found access to its suppliers' knowledge that it would have great difficulty to obtain in a traditional hierarchical buyer–supplier network.

Proximity and Learning

Regional economists and economic geographers have successfully demonstrated that space affects economic relations in various ways. Particularly since the early 1990s – in the midst of the globalization debate – this discipline has been revived (see Storper, 1997). The most successful schools in regional economic theory explain the development of regions in terms of their specific economic, social, institutional and cultural characteristics. These characteristics create unique regional capabilities as they, for example, help to generate trust which is indispensable for effective networks, or in that they foster a climate of openness and collaboration which makes it easer to find network partners (Maskell et al., 1998). Just as tacit knowledge is wedded to its human and organizational context, so are these characteristics wedded to a specific regional context. Insiders enjoy its benefits while outsiders, due to a lack of understanding of regional norms, values, culture, and so on will be slower to respond to opportunities that may arise. That is why multinational companies are usually keen to involve local suppliers (cf. Brown, 1998; Chew and Yeung, 2001). Regional characteristics such as the ones mentioned above may also encourage a climate of entrepreneurship and innovation. Being embedded in such a region means having access to its intangible assets that firms in other regions do not have. The literature refers to this mechanism as localized capabilities (Maskell et al., 1998), social capital (for example Morgan, 1997) and untraded interdependencies (Storper, 1997).

In sum, the literature offers ample explanation of why regional networks may enjoy benefits with respect to learning. The problem, however, is that these explanations take the region as a starting-point for their analysis. It is a matter of consistency in the level of analysis of, in this case, the KIC network, which has thus far been the inter-firm knowledge creation effort, that is, the inter-firm level. Finding arguments in favour of regional networks in social capital and untraded interdependencies means changing the level of analysis to the regional level. Of course, the regional level played an important role, too, in the KIC network (cf. Rutten, 2003). If one remains on the network level, however, the spatial proximity of network partners must be explained on the basis of the processes that are going on within the network. As Oerlemans et al. (2000) argue, 'Knowledge and resource flows have to be researched at the micro-level to find out how the proximity effect actually works' (p. 3). When spatial proximity, or the region, is taken as unit of analysis, the behaviour of firms becomes a black box, whereas it is the actual interaction between actors that facilitates or hampers knowledge exchange. Consequently, the question that must be dealt with in the remainder of this section is to the relation between spatial proximity and the process of inter-firm learning. A mechanism that is promising in this respect is that of the 'geography of knowledge'.

The geography of knowledge can be explained using the following quote:

> When the relevant knowledge or skills have cognitive dimensions that are highly specific to the individuals involved, the transaction becomes concrete, and has qualities that cannot be divorced from its existence as a real relation. These relational qualities of transacting may, in some cases, be embedded in large organizations and carried out at great distances. But many, in fact, are highly localized, including those internal to large firms, because their relational content cannot be sustained over large distance (Storper and Scott, 1995: 508).

This quote puts the outcomes of the earlier inter-firm learning discussion in a spatial perspective. It is clear that Storper and Scott are talking about tacit knowledge. Tacit knowledge, it was argued, cannot be removed from its human and organizational context; hence, the exchange of tacit knowledge requires face-to-face communication. That is what Storper and Scott refer to with their 'real relation'. This, it was argued, is the basis under a sustainable competitive advantage. Competitive advantage results from capabilities that, in turn, are created through a process of learning (or knowledge exchange). When these capabilities are based on tacit knowledge, they cannot be easily copied by competitors as they first have to learn to 'understand' the human and organizational context in which the knowledge is embedded. The mechanism works both within and between firms. In other words, creating competitive advantage requires face-to-face communication. The argument that Storper and Scott now propose is that face-to-face communication cannot be sustained over long distances. This can be demonstrated quite easily. Codified knowledge can be sent to any location on earth simply by pressing the 'send' button on a facsimile machine or an e-mail program. In the case of codified knowledge, distance can thus be covered at no additional cost. The exchange of tacit knowledge, however, requires face-to-face communication, which comes at considerable costs if it requires that the actors involved must be transported over long distances. Thus, the adage of the geography of knowledge says that the more embedded the knowledge, the higher the costs of exchange over long distances (cf. Maskell and Malmberg, 1999, 180).

Theoretically sound as it may be, the argument is just too simple and not in touch with reality. The kind of intimate relations through which tacit knowledge is exchanged are found in both proximate and non-proximate relations (Scott, 1998). Consequently, the relation between knowledge exchange and space is more complicated than is suggested by the geography of knowledge. Oinas (2000), too, criticizes what she calls the 'received wisdom' from recent contributions to economic theory made by, among others, the authors discussed above. She argues that 'the case for the association of proximity and learning does not yet seem to have been made very convincingly. It seems possible that this might be related to insufficient awareness of the nature of learning itself' (Oinas, 2000, 62). Oinas suggests that proximity may have a different role in the various stages of the innovation process. The image that emerges is of an hour-glass model where innovation and learning initially take place on a global scale, then narrow down to a local and regional scale in the stages where knowledge of a more applied nature is involved, to widen again to a global scale after the actual product development has been completed (see Sölvell and Bresman (1997) for similar findings). It seems an interesting suggestion that certainly merits further attention, but the present work – as argued – has a different objective.

If anything, it is obvious that the relation between learning and proximity is far from clear. Empirical research from Oerlemans et al. (2000) points in the same direction. In their study, they examined the relation between innovative ties among firms and the spatial embeddedness of these ties. This relation, Oerlemans et al. (2000) conclude, is anything but automatic. Their study confirms the comparative advantages of proximity in relation to learning, but this pattern was not found in every type of relation that Oerlemans et al. (2000) distinguished. They found, for example, that when innovation activities 'exceed a certain level of complexity, it seems that local suppliers are not able anymore to make significant contributions to the innovation process of innovator firms' (p. 17). Some caution is required, though, when interpreting Oerlemans et al.'s (2000) results. They depart from a resource-based perspective where collaboration between firms is explained in terms of gaining access to external resources. The knowledge-based approach of the present study, however, argues that collaboration between firms must be explained in terms of making new and unique combinations of knowledge in order to create a competitive advantage. The difference between the two approaches can be demonstrated through an assumption made by Oerlemans et al. (2000). From their resource-based perspective, they argue that 'more complex processes increase the probability of problems in the innovation process. Confronted with these problems, innovator firms are forced to enter their external environment in order to get access to and obtain necessary complementary resources' (Oerlemans et al., 2000, 7). To their surprise, these authors found their hypothesis rejected in some cases. From a knowledge-based perspective, however, one could argue the opposite. If complexity in the innovation process is related to the development of knowledge of a more fundamental nature, then a company has good reasons not to enter its external environment. After all, fundamental knowledge is connected to a firm's key competences, which are at the heart of its competitive advantage. That is why Océ develops new applications in isolation; they are not particularly charmed by the idea that the external environment can look into its latest inventions and run the risk of this highly sensitive knowledge leaking out to competitors.

A study by Smith et al. (2002), which takes the region as unit of analysis, has difficulties finding a relation between proximity and R&D, too. After analysing quantitative empirical data for Denmark, they conclude that, 'location does not seem to matter systematically to the firms' R&D effort' (Smith et al., 2002, 831). From a knowledge perspective, however, this outcome is not a surprise as the unit of analysis in Smith et al. is wrong. If the process of knowledge creation has a spatial dimension, then, in order to assess this dimension, the unit of analysis must be learning, or knowledge creation, not space.

What then, from an inter-firm learning perspective, characterizes the relation between learning and proximity? The starting-point is the geography of knowledge – this adage is assumed to be correct but subject to modification from two sides: the availability of knowledge and the phase of the innovation process.

- *The availability of knowledge*. The key to understanding the relation between innovation and proximity is not space but knowledge. Companies work together on innovation because they are dependent on each other's knowledge. That is, they select competent rather than proximate partners. However, it pays off to work together in proximate relations, hence the geography of knowledge. Consequently, when firms exchange tacit knowledge with each other, they prefer to do so in proximate relations. Tacit knowledge, as argued, is difficult to sustain over long distances. However, when proximate relations are impossible, tacit knowledge can and will be exchanged over non-proximate relations. The impossibility of using proximate relations can result from the fact that no competent regional partners are available, but it could also be because a company has previous commitments or more trustful relations with non-local companies.
- *The phase of the innovation process*. Because competitive advantage is based on knowledge, it is understandable that companies want to keep outsiders at a distance in some phases of the innovation process. The danger of sensitive knowledge leaking out may be too great, in which case companies will involve no partners at all. Elaborating on the phases that Océ distinguishes in the innovation process, the 'sensitive phase' is where fundamental knowledge is transferred into concepts and applications. In the case of Océ, this is where the competition with companies such as Canon and Xerox takes place. Océ has to develop concepts and applications that offer more value to buyers than those of its competitors. Other companies may label other stages in the innovation process as 'sensitive' and will consequently try to keep outsiders at a distance in these stages. In sum, the geography of knowledge applies only when companies actually seek to involve external knowledge in their innovation process. There is evidence to suggest that, for reasons of secrecy, companies will try to keep outsiders at a distance in the 'sensitive phase' of the innovation process.

The argument thus is that when external tacit knowledge is required, it is easier and cheaper to involve proximate partners. But it is not impossible to exchange tacit knowledge over long distances, and under certain conditions non-proximate relations will prevail over proximate relations. In sum, though desirable, proximity is not necessary to exchange tacit knowledge. This outcome is perfectly in line with the empirical findings in the KIC network (see Table 10.1). Of course, one case study does not prove the geography-of-knowledge argument but the outcomes of the KIC case and the above discussion demonstrate that it is fruitful to explore the relation between proximity and learning along this line.

CONCLUSION

Regional economics has traditionally tried to explain the relation between learning and proximity from the perspective of a region. That is, it has looked at the attributes of a region and from there explained why regional learning may be advantageous to firms. The argument of this article, however, is that the regional perspective, at best, is only half the story. The relation between proximity and learning is a complex one, as the inconclusive outcomes of various empirical studies have shown. The part of the explanation that regional economics has largely left out begins with knowledge creation, or learning, not with regions or proximity. If learning is the objective of a network, proximity can be seen as the outcome of a trade-off between the availability of knowledge and the phase of the innovation process. Proximity certainly facilitates communication and, therefore, knowledge creation – as does the geography-of-knowledge argument. But proximate relations may not always be possible or desirable. Including these arguments in the explanation of the relation between proximity and learning makes our explanations more sophisticated. It draws attention to the (strategic) choices that firms make with regard to learning, networking and proximity. Regional economics can rightly be criticized for largely ignoring this company perspective. This omission is all the more problematic when one realizes that, to a firm, it is not so much the region that is a laboratory of knowledge but the network. After all, knowledge creation takes place in inter-firm relations. These relations may or may not have a regional dimension but it is the network that matters. Consequently, the process of knowledge creation, or learning, and the organizational context in which it takes place, that is the network, should be taken as a starting point for analysis. It places companies at the heart of the argument and it explains why companies organize their networks the way they do and why companies chose in favour or against proximate relations. Following this logic, the KIC network and its spatial dimension could be explained quite easily. So, rather than to look for, for example, a typology of regions, or even networks, regional economics should look at what companies are actually doing, learning in this case, and try to conceptualize the spatial dimension of that particular activity. Arguably, such an approach has a lot to offer in terms of furthering our understanding of how companies innovate in (regional) networks.

REFERENCES

Best, M. (1990), *The New Competition: Institutions of Industrial Restructuring*, Cambridge: Polity Press.

Best, M. (2001), *The New Competitive Advantage: The Renewal of American Industry*, Oxford: Oxford University Press.

Boekema, F., S. Bakkers, K. Morgan, and R. Rutten (eds) (2000), *Knowledge, Innovation and Economic Growth: The Theory and Practice of Learning Regions*, Cheltenham, UK and Northampton, MA, USA: Edward Elgar.

Brown, R. (1998), 'Electronics foreign direct investment in Singapore: a study of local linkages in "Winchester City"', *European Business Review*, **98** (4), 196–210.

Burns, T., and G. Stalker (1961), *The Management of Innovation*, Oxford: Oxford University Press.

Butler, R., D. Price, P. Coates, and R. Pike (1998), 'Organizing for innovation: loose or tight control?', *Long Range Planning*, **31** (5), 775–82.

Chew, Y., and H. Yeung (2001), 'The SME advantage: adding local touch to foreign transnational corporations in Singapore', *Regional Studies*, **35** (5), 431–48.

Cooke, P., and K. Morgan (1998), *The Associational Economy: Firms, Regions, and Innovation*, Oxford: Oxford University Press.

Hult, G., and E. Nichols (1996), 'The organizational buyer behavior learning organization', *Industrial Marketing Management*, **25** (3), 197–207.

Johannessen, J., J. Olaisen, and B. Olsen (2001), 'Mismanagement of tacit knowledge: the importance of tacit knowledge, the danger of information technology, and what to do about it', *International Journal of Information Management*, **21** (1), 3–20.

Judge, W., G. Fryxell, and R. Dooley (1997), 'The new task of R&D management: creating goal directed communities for innovation', *California Management Review*, **39** (3), 72–85.

Lipparini, A., and M. Sobrero (1994), 'The glue and the pieces: entrepreneurship and innovation in small-firm networks', *Journal of Business Venturing*, **9** (2), 125–40.

Maskell, P., and A. Malmberg (1999), 'Localised learning and industrial competitiveness', *Cambridge Journal of Economics*, **23** (2), 167–85.

Maskell, P., H. Eskelinen, I. Hannibalsson, A. Malmberg, and E. Vatne (eds) (1998), *Competitiveness, Localised Learning and Regional Development: Specialisation and Prosperity in Small Open Economies*, London: Routledge.

Matthyssens, P., and Ch. van den Bulte (1994), 'Getting closer and nicer: partnerships in the supply chain', *Long Range Planning*, **27** (1), 72–83.

Morgan, K. (1997), 'The learning region: institutions, innovation and regional renewal', *Regional Studies*, **31** (5), 491–503.

Nohria, N., and R. Eccles (eds) (1992), *Networks and Organizations: Structure, Form, and Action*, Boston, MA: Harvard Business School Press.

Nonaka, I., and H. Takeuchi (1995), *The Knowledge-creating Company: How Japanese Companies Create the Dynamics of Innovation*, Oxford: Oxford University Press.

Oerlemans, L., M. Meeus, and F. Boekema (1998), 'Do networks matter for innovation? The usefulness of the economic network approach in analysing innovation', *Tijdschrift voor Economische en Sociale Geografie*, **89** (3), 298–309.

Oerlemans, L., M. Meeus, and F. Boekema (2000), 'On the spatial embeddedness of innovation networks: an exploration of the proximity effect', paper presented at the 40th Congress of the European Regional Science Association, Barcelona.

Oinas, P. (2000), 'Distance and learning: does proximity matter?', in F. Boekema, K. Morgan, S. Bakkers, and R. Rutten (eds), *Knowledge, Innovation and Economic Growth: The Theory and Practice of Learning Regions*, Cheltenham, UK and Northampton, MA, USA: Edward Elgar.

Porter, M. (1990), *The Competitive Advantage of Nations*, London and Basingstoke: The Macmillan Press.

Porter, M. (1998), 'Clusters and the new economics of competition', *Harvard Business Review*, **76** (6), 77–91.

Rutten, R. (2003), *Knowledge and Innovation in Regional Industry: An Entrepreneurial Coalition*, London: Routledge.

Schumpeter, J. (1926), *Theorie der wirtschaftlichen Entwicklung: eine Untersuchung über Unternehmergewinn, Kapital, Kredit, Zins und Konjunkturzyklus*, Munich and Leipzig: Verlag von Duncker & Humblot.

Scott, R. (1998), *Organizations: Rational, Natural, and Open Systems*, 4th edn, Upper Saddle River, NJ: Prentice Hall.

Smith, V., A. Broberg, and J. Overgaard (2002), 'Does location matter for firms' R&D behaviour? Empirical evidence for Danish firms', *Regional Studies*, **36** (8), 825–32.

Sölvell, Ö., and H. Bresman (1997), 'Local and global forces in the innovation process of the multinational enterprise: an hour-glass model', in H. Eskelinen (ed.), *Regional Specialisation and Local Environment: Learning and Competitiveness*, Nordic Institte of Regional Policy Research (NordREFO), 1997-1, pp. 43–64.

Storper, M. (1997), *The Regional World: Territorial Development in a Global Economy*, London and New York: The Guilford Press.

Storper, M., and A. Scott (1995), 'The wealth of regions: market forces and policy imperatives in local and global context', *Futures*, **27** (5), 505–26.

Teece, D. (2000), 'Strategies for managing knowledge assets: the role of firm structure and industrial context', *Long Range Planning*, **33** (1), 35–54.

11. Knowledge, values and territory: a case study

Goio Etxebarria and Mikel Gómez Uranga

INTRODUCTION

In this chapter, knowledge production and diffusion are understood to be collective tasks and are set up in a framework of inter-agent relationships with certain underlying values. As in any interchange relationship, trust between the parties is required to establish a good relationship. Sharing information and spreading knowledge call for the collaboration of the different agents involved. Therefore, the 'collaboration' value is extremely important in creating and spreading knowledge.

The values mentioned above are useful for firms when managing knowledge. The social capital in the firms' local environment is built on the foundation of values that can be directly used to acquire new business knowledge. The intellectual aptitudes that make up the base of knowledge creation also benefit from the social capital that surrounds them. The values found in a certain local environment help firms located there to obtain a competitive edge. A local economy based on learning shows an ethical dimension (values); it is difficult to conceive organizations based on learning without the presence of certain values (honesty, trust). The foundation of a knowledge economy should include the formation of internalized codes of conduct (Lundvall, 2000).

The case study of the cooperative system based in Mondragon (a small town located in the Basque Country) could illustrate the influence exercised by a culture of local values (trust, collaboration, solidarity, participation) to strengthen learning and knowledge networks, mainly between firms and co-operative organizations. The Mondragon Cooperative Corporation's (MCC) expansion and good results are not different from the development of the 'spirit of enterprise' as a set of values applied to the working of an industrial system based on learning and knowledge.

STAKEHOLDERS AND KNOWLEDGE MANAGEMENT

Capitalist market culture priorities are mainly focused on obtaining profits. Capitalist firms subordinate all of their relationships to the aim for profit. The *stakeholders model* applied to capitalist business organizations calls for a change in conception, in other words, a move from the pure traditional logic of profits to logic in which greater collaboration with agents and the environment is a priority. The shift from logic completely based on profit to greater collaboration with the environment leads us to what some economic currents call *institutional change.*

We must look at this possible route for change in greater depth. A culture of capitalist profit means that the generation of wealth is subordinated to the need to obtain private profits. This signifies that the owners of business organizations are the agents which receive benefit from economic wealth. However, in actual fact, the property system works in a more complex manner, especially in the world of large firms. The managers of firms may carry out strategies which do not necessarily benefit the owners. Evolution of business organizations involves having to reach certain compromises which are often quite problematic as balances between interests are sometimes very different and do not coincide (Evans and Freeman, 1993, 82). Evolution towards a stakeholders model causes the values and objectives pursued by these organizations to become weaker or readapt. This often means weaker ownership and a stronger managerial elite. Managers of business organizations in a knowledge economy may be more interested in integrating in a stakeholders logic, which would give them greater long term stability and also favour the necessary collaboration to achieve better diffusion of information and knowledge.

Initially, a cooperative property organization may find itself in a better position to generate useful values that contribute to achieving an efficient approach in terms of stakeholders as the property is shared by the same employees who make up the business organization. In theory, the managers represent the partners in the cooperative directly and much more closely and, as a result, there is no conflict between ownership and management. However, the Mondragón Group (MCC Corporation), which we will analyse later, becomes a more conventional business group as it goes international. Thus, the question is whether the Mondragón Group's historic know-how places it in a better position to introduce that stakeholders' logic at the international level. Furthermore, we might ask if the Mondragón Group could show management of other international groups how best to develop shared management with other stakeholders.

A stakeholders model is similar to a network pattern endowed with principles such as: trust, reciprocity, the ability to join together and collaboration.

The quality and abundance of the relationships which are set up between the different groups and agents are important in both cases. The spread of knowledge does not mean the mere transmission of information but is a creative process which is made more dynamic through inter-agent relationships in a network model.

Structuring in terms of stakeholders also means structuring shared knowledge. Relationships with stakeholders are associated with the ways knowledge is spread, shared, and partially created. And above all, with the ways that knowledge is used. The bottom line is that good relationships correspond to good knowledge management. Or good knowledge management requires good relationships with stakeholders. There is also an ambivalent conflict of logic in this whole situation; different types of logic coexist. There is a dominant logic, which is what economists and accountants are accustomed to working with. This is the logic of success, which is not only the logic of profits, it is the logic of competition; in other words, the logic that something is right when the situation improves in comparison to one's competitors. In some cases, sometimes the majority of them, that business logic, which is what mainly moves knowledge management, has to be polished by other different types of logic.

We are going to link stakeholders with a way of understanding how a company based on relationships with its environment works. The stakeholders model is like a photograph of the agents and institutions that have relationships with the firm. Understanding the stakeholders model means understanding a wider conception of management of business organizations. In his article, Sirgy (2002) poses the notion of corporate performance: 'The basic notion of corporate performance is effective *management of relationships* with various organizational stakeholders, not only the firm's relationship with the customer stakeholder group, but all relationships with stakeholders (for example, suppliers, distributors, customers, employees, stockholders, labour unions, government, local community, consumer and environmental advocacy stakeholders)' (Sirgy, 2002, 144). Knowledge management is actually management of relationships. For the firm, knowledge management is like generalized marketing. Knowledge management is also management of public relations.

KNOWLEDGE AND LOCAL EMBEDDEDNESS

A network paradigm may be based on values which are useful in achieving a more efficient system. 'Networking makes it possible to valorise knowledge complementarities and hence to access and generate additional knowledge … Networking consists in the systematic and organized sharing of codes of conduct among independent firms, which agree tacitly or explicitly upon knowledge interactions qualified in terms of trust, reciprocity and repetition' (Antonelli, 2003, 601). Antonelli continues, saying that 'location provides a strong basis for networking ... Firms that are co-located are less prone to opportunistic behaviour ... Co-location makes interorganisational coordination in knowledge interactions easier because of the higher levels of commonality in codes, protocols and cultural standards' (Antonelli, 2003, 601).

We can say that the efficiency of the interaction that takes place between the firm and others it cooperates or collaborates with could mean that the firm will locate where its collaborating companies are (Carrincazeaux et al., 2001, 777). The same could be said if the priority for collaboration were, for instance, with the university or with certain centres belonging to the firm itself. Therefore, it is important to know who the firm works with to try to ensure that these more intense relationships with different agents are more appropriate to a locational proximity. Rich relationships, such as personal relationships or exchange of tacit knowledge make localization proximity between agents a priority.

Obviously, in this local proximity culturally shared elements would be created or exist. They would be, above all, linguistic or even other types that would give greater coherence to these relationships. On the other hand, they would also allow the possibility of developing values that are basic to cooperation, such as collaboration and trust. Many studies have shown that localization of activities or local proximity are not only due to strictly cultural reasons but are also due to the type of knowledge that is to be shared. In general, science exercises effects from public scientific research that favour innovation and also favour innovation in private firms, even generating local spillovers. The author Autant-Bernard (2001) shows that public research spills over on innovation. In other words, it makes innovation grow directly or indirectly in private research. All of this is generated from a local or regional effect. When, due to the nature of the knowledge being shared or the research activities that may be shared, firms' private research has very few connections with the university, proximity would not be necessary. We can state that codification is inversely correlated to the need for proximity. In other words, codified knowledge does not demand such close location of the agents that are going to cooperate or collaborate. In contrast, if an industry such as biotechnology, for instance, is very closely linked to university research, then we presume that firms will localize where they can have proximity to universities. In other words, these relationships are preferably local, as can be observed in the study being carried out by Arundel and Geuna (2001).

The conclusion we could reach is that tacit knowledge requires or demands certain proximity and locations, and non-tacit knowledge, however, would be a fundamental element for the development of certain scientific paradigms. In an economy and society where the local and global are constantly mixed, it seems reasonable to think that tacit and standardized knowledge coexist just as these aspects of the local and global coexist.

FIRM'S SOCIAL RESPONSIBILITY

The relationships the firm sets up with its environment, with its stakeholders, are translated in terms of the responsibility the firm contracts with the rest of its partners, institutions and society itself. In this sense, relationships in terms of stakeholders and social responsibility have the same meaning. We could even measure to what degree the firm complies with certain minimums or how it fulfils its role of social responsibility.

'Firms' social responsibility' is a concept which will become widespread in the coming years. Firms enter a certain social environment with which they contract obligations. Fulfilling these obligations legitimizes the firm in its functions while also permitting it to improve results. All the agents that interact with the firm, as well as its own staff, are more motivated to carry out their duties when firms improve the quality of relationships. In the same way, everything linked to the job market, from selection of personnel to internal promotion, may also affect the profits obtained by firms, as we can see from a

> study of high performance work practices (that) was based upon a survey of 700 publicly held corporations (in the United States). The practices covered included personnel selection, job design, information sharing, performance appraisal, promotion systems, attitude assessment, incentive systems, and labour–management participation. The upper quartile of firms – those using the best practices – had a return on capital of 11%, more than twice as high as the remaining firms (Palazzi and Starcher, 2002, 4).

> The social responsibility of firms also includes integration in their local environment, whether it is at the European or world level. Firms contribute to the development of the communities they are part of, above all, local communities as they offer jobs, salaries and benefits and tax income. On the other hand, firms depend on the health, stability and prosperity of the communities where they operate. For instance, most of their contracting is done on the local job market so they are directly interested in having persons with the skills they require in their immediate area. SMEs often find most of their customers in the surrounding zone. A firm's reputation in its area and its image as a business and producer as well as an agent in local life definitely affect its competitiveness (COM, 2001: 11).

The firm's reputation and link with local markets require them to have social responsibility. Big enterprises which are obliged and committed to their interlocutors, stakeholders and partners (OECD, 2001) can contribute to transferring this spirit of cooperation and improvement to SMEs, which also contributes to improved innovative results. On the other hand, big multinationals have greater links with local communities in the sense of respecting certain sustainability of the area where they are located, in other words, respecting, for instance, environmental standards and sometimes even going beyond that to promote sustainable development in those areas.

The firm must contribute to the well-being of the communities or societies where it is located. In other words, these are ways in which firms can foster and contribute to the development of their own employees, firstly, and then to the development of neighbourhoods or cities where the company is located as well. It can encourage investment of a more social nature that supports elements linked to well-being such as educational and social institutions, the fight against joblessness and exclusion, and so on.

Cooperation is exchange, which requires a certain institutional environment. This environment evolves and incorporates values that were outside its limits until just a short time ago. Managers must know and take ethical conduct into account. Just as they must pay their taxes, social security and know the cost of pollution, they must know and deal with these 'ethical costs'. This consists of broadening the logic of what business management means. Competition on today's markets demands it. Knowledge management needs firms to assume a certain ethical conduct. Management of both knowledge and certain codes of conduct involves an organizational learning process; and also means an innovation process (Pedler, 1994). This learning could also take place in the local or regional field (see Cooke, 1998 and Morgan and Nauwelaers, 1998 on learning regions).

Better behaviour of firms concerning better knowledge management must focus special attention on the way the customer is treated. In this case, the very existence of a code of ethics enhances the desire to buy that company's product. Within a framework of competition, this is what we would call the ethics of success.

The ethics of business means that firms are able to mobilize a core of relational/coexistential values. It also means that they learn to bring new values into their existing lot. Just as they have a base of knowledge which allows them to develop production, technological or commercial routines, they must also have a base of values which allows them to lubricate the inner gears of professional, departmental, and in general, human relationships. This stock of values is shaped into behaviour through the development of codes of conduct which spread them throughout the firm by the different types of training structures and expose them to the corresponding social auditing.[1]

It is understood that the firm has a culture based on certain core values. These core values are also formed by a set of beliefs and these values may be the base of certain practices, behaviour and operative routines for the firm.

Developing one's own culture means sharing values, and contrasting with other cultures may mean improving or opening one's culture to other values. In knowledge management, the idea is not only to spread values through the firm itself or through networking but above all to share values, add values and even change some of the values that make up the core. The spread, creation or distribution of knowledge is also linked to the firm introducing a series of instruments or mechanisms to manage this knowledge. Parallel to this process, business strategy includes a series of mechanisms that can mobilize values that accompany knowledge management.[2]

In order to be coherent, these values should take shape as conduct criteria, or ethical behaviour, so that firms institutionalize them in their daily management tasks. This is the only way to adapt this type of conduct to knowledge management and management in general. This point is raised in the Green Paper of the European Commission: 'As issues of corporate social responsibility become an integral part of corporate strategic planning and routine operational performance, managers and employees are required to make business decisions based on additional criteria to those they were traditionally trained to expect' (COM, 2001, 17). Codes would play a role similar to that of other institutions such as: social norms, customs or rituals (Thomsen, 2001, 157). Ethics are a basic component of the environment and socio-political context in which the firm operates (Fernández, 2001).[3]

The more utilitarian the codes of conduct firms develop, and therefore more functional for their management procedures, the more easily and intensely they will integrate in the firm's management strategies. Expressed in other terms, those codes which are less functional, although it may be from the perspective of a higher ethical level, will not adapt as well to the firm's needs and will probably not solve the problems that the firm may run into when designing a knowledge management approach. Therefore, knowledge management is more coherent with functional ethical proposals, that is different from the conventional idea of what ethical is.

In this chapter, we demonstrate how a framework of collaboration based on values favours better knowledge diffusion in a local environment. Firms manage knowledge for mercantile purposes. However, the bases (mostly values) that make it possible to mobilize that knowledge have, above all, a non mercantile nature. For this reason, it is difficult to fully validate the concept of social capital,[4] although from firms' perspective this 'bank of social values' becomes a mine which can be exploited by mercantile interests.[5]

Figure 11.1 shows a graph where knowledge mobilization yields the utilitarian result of greater efficiency. A system in which firms face up to their social responsibilities prompts better quality relationships in stakeholders networks and contributes to improving 'knowledge'.

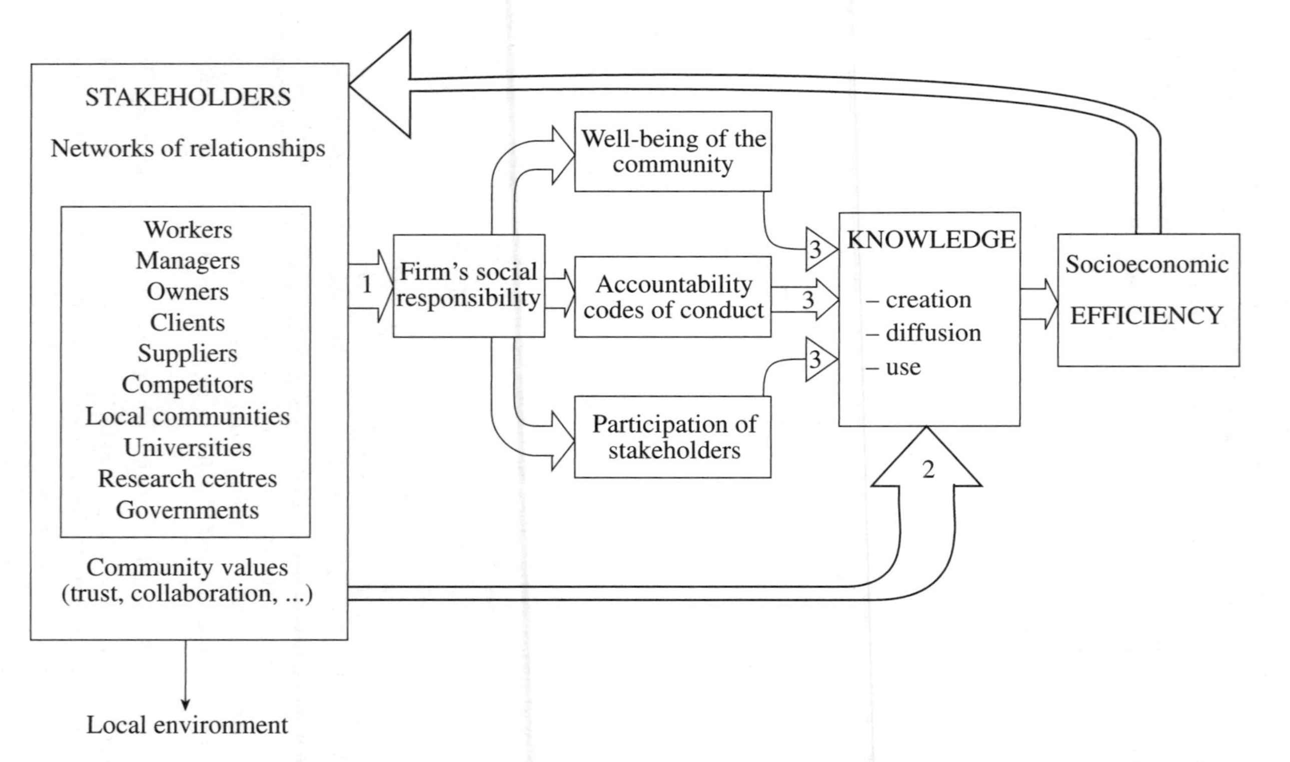

Notes: The firm's social responsibility is practised in a stakeholders' framework (1). Knowledge improves in a stakeholders' and values' framework (2), and develops better in a context of social responsibility (3).

Figure 11.1 Utilitarian conception of business conduct in a stakeholders' framework

We have two meaningful examples about firms' social responsibility: the Japanese company spirit has certain behaviour or cultural schemes for the firm that make it unnecessary to state them explicitly as written codes of conduct. On the other hand, in the case of the Mondragón cooperatives, where there has been both an implicit and explicit framework of values from the beginning, it would be redundant to set down a written code of conduct like other companies have. The problem is that the Mondragón cooperatives would have to write specific codes of conduct when their entrepreneurial expansion pushes them to leave the cooperative property bases.

In the second part, we will examine the case of the Mondragón Cooperative Corporation (MCC). We will analyse how the Mondragón cooperative system has evolved, the effects of the crisis and industrial re-organization, the change in cooperative values, and its effect on knowledge management.

THE MONDRAGÓN COOPERATIVE EXPERIENCE

The Mondragón Cooperative experience has attracted the attention of many researchers through the years. We have chosen this interesting experience as a case study for this chapter because we believe it allows for correct analysis of the relationships between the different stakeholders that take part both on internal and external levels (salaried workers, co-op members, managers, suppliers, customers, policy makers, citizens, ...). It also makes it possible to analyse the principles that inspire these relationships and the flows of information between them, how knowledge is produced and spread amongst these agents within the regional system, how the changes in values which have taken place in the last decade have influenced knowledge management, what role stakeholder embeddedness in society and the region plays in the spread of knowledge, and so on.

Historical Evolution of the 'Mondragón Cooperative Experience'[6]

The origin of the groups goes back to 1956. That year, Ulgor, Mondragón's first worker cooperative, was founded by five scholars from the Professional School[7] and the priest José María Arizmendiarrieta. Since that time, the cooperatives have undergone continuous development, first in Mondragón and the Deba Valley, and later in the rest of the province of Guipuzcoa and the entire Basque Country during the following years, and more recently in Spain and abroad. In 1961, the first industrial complex was created: ULARCO (renamed FAGOR in 1985). The foundation of this first cooperative group set a precedent, and after a few years, the majority of cooperatives joined to form similar groups.

At the end of the 1980s, the co-ops began a re-organization process which led to a new period of pragmatism from 1990–91. In 1989, the solidarity and inter-cooperative training funds were set up. In 1989, the first firms were acquired from outside the group and the first foreign investments were made[8] (Errasti, 2002, 178). However, the greatest change took place in 1991 with the creation of the MCC. This marked a radical change in the structure of the Mondragón Cooperatives. It signified an attempt to improve and strengthen co-ordination between the different co-ops. One of the objectives of creating the MCC was to achieve unity in the cooperative group's management (Bakaikoa et al., 1995, 162).

The MCC was formed in 1991, during the Third Mondragón Group Congress. In 1992, the MCC was organized into three broad groups (see Appendix): Financial, Distribution and Industrial.[9] Among the training centres are: the recently created University of Mondragón (1997), Mondragón Eskola (Teachers' University School) and ETEO (Business studies). Lastly, the research centres include Ikerlan, Ideko (a machine-tool sectorial centre) and the Maier Technology Centre (specializing in thermoplastics R&D).

The Mondragón cooperatives have adapted to the new international conditions better than many capitalist (non-cooperative) firms. The system has survived extremely complicated situations and severe crises which resulted in the destruction of many jobs and firms in numerous industries and industrial areas.[10] Its success was proven by the significant growth levels it reached in terms of jobs, turnover, investment, business abroad, and so on. In addition, we must take into account the embeddedness this experience has had in the Deba Valley where it arose, and which has spread throughout the Basque Country. This special, intense relationship with the territory and region has been maintained for decades, in spite of the group's internationalization.

A significant change took place in the 1990s with the creation of the MCC Corporation as a response to increased economic globalization and an attempt to adapt to new conditions in order to compete on the international market. The creation of the MCC was quite different from the previous experience and signified, in a certain way, a break from the traditional cooperative model. The validity of cooperative principles and values is questioned and debated in a period when neoliberal policies are being imposed and fierce competition is the norm.

The MCC has created a Knowledge Group with the participation of the university and professional schools, technological centres (Ikerlan, Ideko, MTC), and lastly, the consulting and engineering cooperatives. There have been relationship problems between the different groups so the decision was made to first define each group's task and later consider the common activities, thus reaching more integral management. The aim consisted of prompting the different groups to interact and avoid isolated closed actions.

In this way, the MCC has made a commitment to integral knowledge management, including training and learning and innovation in all its aspects (product, process, organizational, and so on). The goal of these processes is to involve the entire group of cooperative firms and workers, although the most active participation has come from certain elite groups of firms, technicians and managers. These internal agents or stakeholders outline and shape the processes of knowledge management. There must be good synergy among these stakeholders for information and knowledge to flow smoothly through the cooperative network. The lasting system of cooperative values which is maintained in the relationships between these stakeholders guarantees the success of strategic activities related to the creation and diffusion of knowledge in the innermost spheres of the cooperative group. We are referring to values such as trust, collaboration, solidarity, intragroup mobility, participation in management, and so on. In spite of the decades that have passed, these values are still ever present in the relationships between key stakeholders involved in the group's most strategic processes such as knowledge management and internationalization strategies.

From its beginnings, the university has played a highly functional role in the cooperative framework. Directed to the world of business, the decision was made to create a small university with very specific studies, mainly engineering and business. At present, studies are being conducted to consider re-defining the role that the University of Mondragón should play. As a result of the qualitative changes taking place in the MCC, largely due to the corporation's growth and internationalization, management has perceived the need for the university to prepare future professionals (engineers, skilled technicians and managers), educating them in the cooperative system of values and principles which the younger generation may find somewhat different from their own. In other words, they realize that the continuity of the cooperative project depends on the persistence of values that must be transmitted to the future managers of the cooperatives. As training becomes a key factor for knowledge creation and diffusion, and ethical values are needed to manage knowledge, we can also affirm that the MCC's efforts to strengthen its traditional values in the sphere of educational training may yield a better culture broth to develop into a knowledge economy. This may also serve to produce and spread knowledge within the group itself.

Financing training (including the university) and research (including technological centres) are strategic features for the MCC. Support and financing for these activities is carried out according to the MCC's accountability to the area where it is located, mainly where the original co-ops were created. This accountability would carry more weight than belonging to the same group or corporation of educational or research bodies. Therefore, the MCC gives greater priority to stakeholders logic (analysed previously) than traditional company logic, thus overcoming a narrow vision focused solely on obtaining profits. This will make a more coherent lasting corporate strategy over time; based largely on knowledge management.

Labour Relations in Cooperative Firms

In view of the democratic representation which functions in cooperative firms, we could ask what the real difference is between a structure like Mondragón's in comparison to any other corporate group where managers hold the real power. In spite of their cooperative rights, blue collar workers have little time or preparation to be informed about the management of the cooperative.[11] There is an obvious 'agency' problem between the management and the cooperative partner due to the existing imbalance of information (in the management's favour).

The cooperative group's culture of lifelong employment is also found in large Japanese business groups where there is another coinciding feature: the almost family-like perception of belonging to the firm; obviously an issue which goes beyond the concept of ownership.

Blue collar workers' mobility between the cooperatives was a vital feature of its solidarity during the worst years of the crisis and industrial re-organization in the 1980s. In effect, this mobility allowed jobs to be maintained in the cooperatives during those hard years when industrial employment dropped considerably on the global level. Mobility of cooperative leaders or managers exercises a greater amount of influence on knowledge management. There is high intragroup mobility amongst managers, which makes it possible to maintain cooperative values and culture on a permanent basis.

We consider that their cooperative values (collaboration, solidarity, flexibility, in the sense of intragroup mobility), together with physical proximity and a common culture (even linguistic and religious) make them better prepared to adapt to new technological and productive changes. Production is increasingly linked to the circulation and management of information, and in consequence, the co-ops' evolution is more coherent with the development of a knowledge economy. This coherence is further strengthened as the Basque Government continues to consolidate modern industrial and technological policy.

Internationalization of the MCC: Problems derived from International Expansion

Nowadays, the Mondragón Cooperative Corporation is an international corporation comprised of cooperative and capitalist (private capital, non-cooperative) firms. The cooperative ownership principle has been pushed aside in the firms the MCC has created or bought to set up production outside its traditional regional scope, the Basque Country. Today, cooperative values and principles are almost only held by members of the central cooperative. This could pose a problem as new stakeholders appear in the cooperatives: temporary employees, workers from MCC subsidiaries located inside the region, workers from subsidiaries located outside (in Spain and abroad), subcontracted workers, and so on. These new stakeholders may not join in these values that are so deeply shared in the cooperative core. Lastly, internationalization of the MCC has created a new reality which is quite similar to that of transnational firms. Thus, traditional cooperative norms and values are no longer shared by all the workers in the cooperatives, nor are they expected to be in the immediate future.

In effect, the firms that the MCC has created abroad and in the region itself (sometimes with other partners, joint ventures) are non-cooperative capitalist firms. These firms are owned by the parent firm (the MCC). Therefore, we find a new dual model: on the one hand, the core formed by cooperative members and firms, and on the other, the outer circle formed by salaried workers and capital firms subordinated to the core (Errasti, 2002, 369–70). The cooperative member takes on a new quality; in addition to being a worker and his own company leader, he becomes a capitalist and company owner. In the entire MCC, fewer than 4 of every 10 employees are co-op members. This tendency has increased and is expected to continue in the medium term (Cancelo, 2000).

This new model has been named *neocooperativism* by some of the heads of the MCC because the new strategic vision tries to combine possiblism and identity (Deia, 1996). Different cultures and company models currently coexist within the MCC; managerial tasks and decision making are different in each case. The workers from MCC's investee firms do not have decision making capacity since this task is in the hands of the cooperative core that exercises ownership. This has given rise to a hierarchical structure in which the MCC's investee firms give greater priority to higher profits than cooperative values. In this sense, the Social Council for Fagor criticized MCC policy. 'Bringing the cooperatives up-to-date in competitiveness is one thing (…) The unnecessary loss of their fundamental character – economic democracy and member participation – is another' (Huet, 1997, 3).

Management's role has been strengthened. The management's responsibilities have increased with internationalization since subsidiaries make decision making more complex. The risk of presenting less transparent information now exists. Before distributing information, managing directors have greater possibilities of monitoring and filtering it. The cooperative framework is increasingly determined by managerial decisions (the decision making process is centralized) while participation from members is significantly lower (Errasti, 2002, 376).

On the other hand, we have to admit that the Mondragón cooperatives have lost important features of internal participatory democracy as they have gone international. This is due, in part, to the elite managerial group centralizing a part of the information. Although it is necessary to share information in knowledge economies, few people actually have the capacity to design business strategies due to the complexity of this knowledge. Therefore, we could say that the deep change in the participative scope of the Mondragón economies was due to the company's strategic need for a few people to control and manage the most sensitive information. It is hard to imagine that highly qualified production technicians might have the skills and qualifications to control increasingly complex financial activities (Huet, 1997).

However, this does not hinder keeping the fundamental traditional cooperative values alive in relationships between managers, highly qualified technicians, engineers and researchers. These values include: trust, involvement in the cooperative business project, intercooperative solidarity, collaboration and work in common. This aspect is very important since these will be the stakeholders that take the most active part in exchanging knowledge and information, in joint and corporate innovation projects, in strategic decisions on knowledge management, in defining strategic plans for internationalization, and so on. The bottom line is that these are the stakeholders that lead the corporation and will enable the cooperatives to be better prepared to adapt to the changes demanded by a knowledge economy. The permanence of these values over time even allows us to state that the industrial division of the Corporation is carrying out efficient knowledge management and diffusion.

There is a break from the traditional cooperative model, which is somewhat worn out. Thus, the cooperatives are put into a new category, that of transnational firms, modifying their operating rules. This gives rise to a dual system, capitalist and cooperative at the same time (Errasti, 2002, 372). Mutation brings about changes in the values system and cultural breaks in the organization, resulting in radical transformations (Val Núñez, 1994, 20). In this sense, the main objective of salaried workers in the outer spheres is keeping the jobs, salaries and the investment capacity of the cooperative core.[12] Furthermore, it is no coincidence that the MCC has gone international in traditional capitalist countries or those in transition where labour is much cheaper, allowing for far lower production costs (Egypt, Morocco, Mexico, Argentina, Thailand and China) (Huet, 1997, 3).

The cooperative firm's need to adapt to international competition leads it to go international and partially abandon certain initial values of the cooperative spirit. Economic utilitarian values are imposed over social values (cooperative ethics) in this new scenario. Internationalization policy has been guided exclusively by the logic of economics.

The culture of cooperative values that runs throughout the Mondragón cooperative movement entered a critical period when growth in the cooperatives' industrial sector inevitably led them to internationalization. It is not possible to remain in industrial clusters at the forefront without launching an industrial strategy of multinationalization. In order to keep up these high levels of competition, it is necessary to branch out and seek new markets. On the other hand, the MCC runs the risk of completely losing its autonomy in a decade like the present when big takeovers are occurring.

Cooperative culture, based not on strictly capitalist values of cooperation and collaboration, allows for some competitive advantages which translate as low transaction costs during stages when the Mondragón industrial group is still small. A small community is better prepared to develop values and behaviour that give it greater internal cohesion. However, as technologies become more complex and are internationalized, along with industrial commodities and consumer markets, there is a tendency to lose that internal cohesion and necessarily to have to join in the culture of values that prevails on international markets.

CONCLUSIONS

Management of knowledge (in the broad sense) is most effectively carried out when it is understood as part of stakeholders logic. Inter-agent collaboration is one of the values that underlies this relational philosophy and is the one that most intensely contributes to the creation and diffusion of knowledge. Knowledge develops better in a framework of social responsibility between firms and the participating agents in a socioeconomic system.

A system of cooperative type organizations from a local culture, like the Mondragón Group, is a good example of how useful certain (cooperative) values are for the development of a competitive industrial economy with high innovation capacity. However, the natural internationalization of the industrial group in a globalized economy does not mean that those cooperative values are spread to other areas (outside the main local area). Setting up codes of conduct for relationships with stakeholders from other countries and locations beyond their borders could be combined with the maintenance of cooperative values in the local area. This mixed model will become more probable with the diffusion of codes, obliging business groups to face up to their social accountability in places which are quite different from their original areas.

NOTES

1. See the Study on 300 firms (BSR, 2002a, 1).
2. 'A 1998 study published in the "CPA Journal" by McMaster University Professor Christopher K. Bart, Ph.D., showed a positive correlation between specific types of corporate statements of mission, vision and/or values and corporate financial performance. Companies' performance was measured by such statistics as return on sales and growth in profits' (BSR, 2002b). Companies that institutionalize a values-based decision-making process can see their profits improve (BSR, 2002b).
3. Most of the codes in the OECD study are applied in main firms (82 per cent), some 50 per cent in contracting firms and only 22 per cent in subcontracting firms (OECD, 1999, 15). This distribution shows that the codes exercise less influence in subcontracting firms, which are smaller and in addition, more firmly rooted to the territory.
4. The concept of social capital brings up two types of problems: a) Technical difficulties, which are related to possibly measuring social capital physically if it is considered as *quasi* physical stock; and b) Those problems stemming from not having taken into account the motivations of participants in social networks, the types of exclusion and power relationships (Markusen, 2003).
5. We find this idea implicitly expressed in a more economic manner in Bourdieu's (1985) notion of social capital and in a more sociological manner in Putnam (1993).
6. A great deal of the information in this section came from Gómez Uranga (2002).
7. The Professional School (Escuela Profesional) – an independent, democratically managed school open to the youth of the region – was founded by Arizmendiarrieta in 1943. Residents, regional small and mid-sized companies and local authorities supported the school's creation. It is currently called the Mondragón Eskola Politeknikoa (Mondragón Polytechnical School).
8. The co-op Fagor Electrodomésticos bought out Fabrelec, SA; Fagor Ederlan bought Victorio Luzuriaga, SA; Copreci signed its first joint venture in Mexico.
9. The Financial Group is comprised of the banking business, social provision, and insurance and leasing. The Industrial Group is made up of seven divisions devoted to industrial production. The Distribution Group includes commercial distribution business and food activity (see Appendix).
10. The cooperatives overcame the crisis of the 1980s without the loss of jobs, in contrast to the high unemployment levels registered in the Basque Country (around 25 per cent). Nor did firms have to go into liquidation or shut down like non-co-op firms in the area. This was largely due to the fact that the cooperative firms shared gains and losses, and surplus workers from one firm were relocated to another which needed cooperative workers. The group's solidarity was a crucial factor in explaining the co-ops' adaptation during a severe industrial crisis.
11. 'A good deal of the frustration that workers feel about information ... can be attributed to their inability to make effective use of it .... all members of the cooperative are given a great deal of information, which they simply cannot get through' (Kasmir, 1996, 137–8).
12. There are cases of cooperative firms in which the costs of the subsidiary (non cooperative) are lower and the subsidiary's productivity is higher. However, when making decisions about the need to adjust production in the parent company (cooperative) and increase production in the subsidiary, the final word rests exclusively with cooperative workers from the head office, which leads to frequent conflicts and contradictions.

REFERENCES

Antonelli, C. (2003), 'Knowledge complementarity and fungeability: implications for regional strategy', *Regional Studies*, **37** (6/7) August/October, 595–606.

Arundel, A., and A. Geuna (2001), 'Does proximity matter for knowledge transfer from public institutes and universities to firms?', SPRU electronic working paper series paper no. 73, October accessed 16 May 2002 at www.sussex.ac.uk/spru/publications/imprint/sewps/index.html

Autant-Bernard, C. (2001), 'Science and knowledge flows: evidence from the French case', *Research Policy*, **30**, 1069–78.

Bakaikoa, B., M. Lierni, M. Merino, P. Rodriguez, and J.M. Perez (1995), *El cooperativismo vasco y el año 2000*, Madrid: Ed. Gezki-Marcial Pons.

Bourdieu, P. (1985), 'The forms of capital', in J. Richardson (ed.), *Handbook of Theory and Research for the Sociology of Education*, New York: Greenwood.

Business for Social Responsibility (BSR) (2002a), 'Business ethics', white paper accessed 16 May 2002 at www.bsi.org/BSRResources/WhitePapersList.cfm?area=2

Business for Social Responsibility (BSR) (2002b), 'Mission, vision, values', white paper accessed 16 May 2002 at www.bsr.org/BSRResources/WhitePaperDetail.cfm. cfm?DocumentID=267

Cancelo, A. (2000), 'Globalizaci6n y señas de identidad', *TU Lankide Review*, **446** (May), Arrasate.

Carrincazeaux, C., Y. Lung, and A. Rallet (2001), 'Proximity and localisation of corporate R&D activities', *Research Policy*, **30**, 777–89.

COM (2001), 'Promoting a European framework for corporate social responsibility', green paper 366 final, 18 July 2001, Brussels.

Cooke, P. (1998), 'Introduction. Origins of the concepts', in H. Braczyk, P. Cooke and M. Heidenreich (eds), *Regional Innovation Systems*, London: UCL Press, pp. 2–25.

Deia (local newspaper), (1996), 28 November.

Errasti, A.M. (2002), 'Kooperatiben garapena globalizazioaren garaian: nazioarteko hedapenaren politika sozioekonomikorako gakoak' (The cooperatives' development in the global era: keys for an international expansion policy), PhD thesis, Donostia (San Sebastián).

Evans, W., and R. Freeman (1993), 'A stakeholder theory of the modern corporation: Kantian capitalism', in T. Beauchamp and N. Bowie (eds), *Ethical Theory and Business*, 4th edn, Englewood Cliffs: Prentice-Hall.

Fernández, J. (ed.) (2001), *La Ética en los Negocios*, Madrid: Ariel Sociedad Econ6mica.

G6mez Uranga, M. (2002), *Basque Economy*, Reno: Center for Basque Studies, University of Nevada.

Huet, T. (1997), 'Can coops go global?', *Dollars and Sense: The Magazine of Economic Justice*, accessed 19 February 2002 at www.dollarsandsense.org/archives/1997/1197huet.html.

Kasmir, S. (1996), *The Myth of Mondrag6n. Cooperatives, Politics and Working-Class Life in a Basque Town*, PhD dissertation, New York: City University of New York.

Lundvall, B.A. (2000), 'The learning economy: some implications for the knowledge base of health and education systems', in *Knowledge Management in the Learning Society*, Paris: OECD, pp. 125–41.

Markusen, A. (2003), 'Fuzzy concepts, scanty evidence, policy distance: the case for rigour and policy relevence in critical regional studies', *Regional Studies*, **37** (6/7), August/October, 701–17.

Morgan, K., and C. Nauwelaers (eds) (1998), *Regional Innovation Strategies: the Challenge for Less Favoured Regions*, London: Jessica Kingsley.

OECD (1999), *Codes of Corporate Conduct: An Inventory*, Paris: OECD.
OECD (2001), *Guidelines for Multinational Enterprises 2001*, annual report, Paris: OECD.
Palazzi, M., and G. Starcher (2002), 'Corporate social responsibility and business success', accessed 3 January 2002 at www.ebbf.org/crswrd.htm.
Pedler, M. (1994), *The Learning Company: A Strategy for Sustainable Development*, London: McGraw-Hill.
Putnam, R. (1993), 'The prosperous community: social capital and public life', *American Prospect*, no. 13, 35–42.
Sirgy, M.J. (2002), 'Measuring corporate performance by building on the stakeholders model of business ethics', *Journal of Business Ethics*, **35**, 143–62.
Thomsen, S. (2001), 'Business ethics as corporate governance', *European Journal of Law and Economics*, **11** (2), 153–64.
Val Nuñez, M. (1994), *Cultura empresarial y estrategia de la empresa en España: su realidad actual y su diseño del cambio*, Madrid: Rialp.

APPENDIX 11A.1: MCC ORGANIZATIONAL STRUCTURE

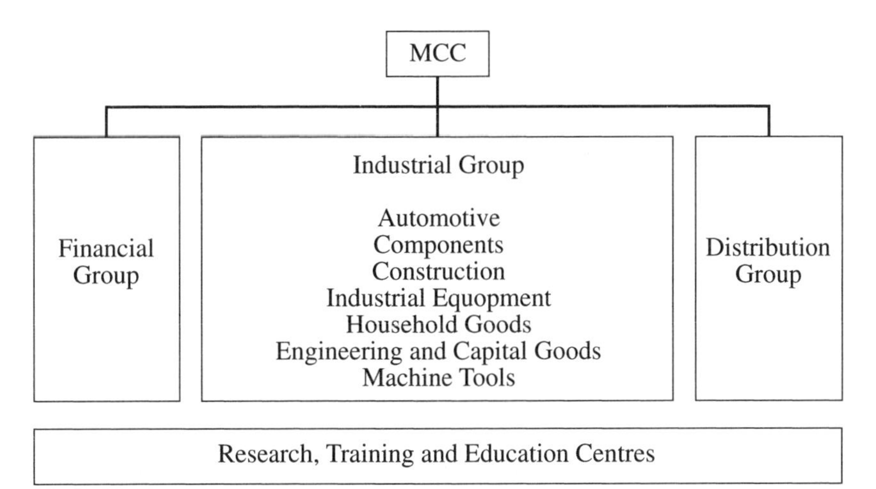

12. The 'knowledge economy': a critical view

Martin Sokol

1. INTRODUCTION

The last decade has seen a remarkable amplification of voices within urban and regional studies literature that places information, knowledge, learning, technology, innovation and institutions at the forefront of their conceptual framework (see Malecki, 2000, for a recent review). Powerful concepts such as 'intelligent region' (Cooke and Morgan, 1994), 'learning region' (Florida, 1995; Asheim, 1996; Morgan, 1997; Boekema et al., 2000), 'innovative cluster' (Porter, 1990; OECD, 2001), 'informational city' (Castells, 1989), 'competitive city' (Simmie, 2002) or 'knowledge-based city' (Simmie and Lever, 2002) have proliferated and dominated urban and regional debate. At the heart of these concepts lies a conviction that knowledge is now the fundamental economic resource, and learning is the most important economic process (Lundvall and Johnson, 1994). More broadly, there is widespread acceptance that society and economy are being transformed into some sort of 'information society' or 'knowledge-driven economy' (Castells, 1996; Giddens, 2000, Leadbeater, 2000; Cooke, 2002). Some commentators go as far as to suggest that the new society emerging from this transformation could be 'post-capitalist' (Drucker, 1993; Leadbeater, 2000; but see also Hodgson, 1999). This, in turn, raises the hopes that within such a society, the old socio-spatial divisions and contradictions of industrial capitalism will fade away as the emerging new 'knowledge age' sets in. Indeed some optimistic voices in economic geography suggest that the new 'knowledge age' offers better prospects for more balanced social and regional development. Morgan (1997), for instance, has argued that within the new economic paradigm, less-favoured regions have better chances to close the gap with the advanced regions. Meanwhile, Florida (1995) suggests that firms are being transformed into 'knowledge-intensive organizations' where teams of R&D scientists, engineers and factory workers are becoming 'collective agents of innovation', and the 'lines between the factory and the laboratory blur' (ibid., 529).

While more harmonious social and regional development could be seen as desirable, the optimism is not universally shared. Indeed, there are doubts whether such goals can be easily achievable within the framework of the 'knowledge economy'. This chapter raises some critical points about the nature of the ongoing socioeconomic transformation and its implications for social and economic cohesion.

2. TRANSFORMATION TO THE 'KNOWLEDGE-DRIVEN ECONOMY'?

Before embarking on a critical analysis of the 'knowledge-driven economy', it is worth noting that the concept appears in literature under various names and guises. The four most influential versions could be identified as the 'post-industrial society', the 'information society', the 'knowledge economy' and the 'learning economy'. While these four concepts could be seen as just the 'tip of the iceberg' of a large and diverse body of literature (see Sokol, 2003a, for a detailed discussion), they encapsulate well the main arguments this literature offers in its various streams. In rather simple terms, the 'post-industrial society' thesis could be seen as an attempt to conceptualize the decline of manufacturing and the perceived growing weight of services in society and economy. It represents an 'original' version of the 'knowledge society' in which knowledge is the 'axial' principle (Bell, 1973). Under the heading of the 'information society', the prominence could be ascribed to Manuel Castells (1996) and his concept of the 'Information Age' that places emphasis on the perceived importance of information and information technology. Meanwhile, perhaps the most vivid and influential account of the 'knowledge economy' has been offered by Leadbeater (2000). Here, the 'knowledge economy' concept is seen to go beyond the preoccupation with 'information' and narrow technological concerns in favour of emphasizing the importance of wider social contexts and more broadly defined 'knowledge'. As such, it nevertheless seems to 'recycle' many of the original 'post-industrialist' ideas. Finally, the notion of the 'learning economy' is associated mainly with the work of Lundvall and Johnson (1994) and represents an attempt to conceptualize the knowledge-intensive economy from the perspective of evolutionary economics.

What is becoming clear from more detailed reviews of these concepts (see Sokol, 2003a, 2003b) is that, despite important differences between them, they also display considerable overlaps. In particular they all seem to perpetuate a widely shared belief that industrial capitalism is undergoing a profound transition towards a new era organized around knowledge, information and technology. Because such an era is supposed to be radically different from the previous forms of (industrial) capitalism, bold claims have been made about its implications for social welfare and regional cohesion. According to Bell (1973), the new 'post-industrial society' would be more prosperous and more equal, not least because technology becomes the engine of rising living standards and reducing inequalities (ibid., 188). For Bell, the 'labour issue' would be *less* important (ibid., 163–4) as the (industrial) working class would shrink if not disappear altogether in the 'post-industrial society' (see ibid., 40, 148–54). This has been echoed by Leadbeater (2000) who has argued that '[o]ne of the most powerful social groups created by the knowledge economy are so-called "knowledge workers"' (ibid., 228). Leadbeater, like Bell, has not denied that the new society will be frictionless. However, he has maintained that new conflicts 'will not be the class tensions of industrial society' (Leadbeater, 2000, 228), because '[w]e are moving into a post-capitalist society' (ibid., 228). Leadbeater also believes that the new global knowledge economy could be harnessed for greater social progress and inclusiveness (see ibid., 235–6) and the reduction of global poverty and inequalities (ibid., 238–9). According to Leadbeater, this can be achieved primarily through a widespread knowledge-sharing process (ibid., 222, 238–9; *inter alia*). Some optimistic voices within economic geography agree that the 'emerging knowledge-based economy represents genuinely new and profound opportunities for endogenous economic development, even for the until now less developed regions and countries' (Maskell et al., 1998, 188). And in a somewhat similar vein, Rutten et al. (2000, 257) suggest that 'all the world's regions have a chance of success in the global [knowledge] economy'.

There is no surprise then that various 'knowledge economy' approaches have gained a very prominent place in policy and strategy documents (see DTI, 1998a; 1998b; EC, 1996; 1997a; 1997b; EU, 2000; OECD, 1996; see also Rodrigues, 2002; *inter alia*). However, these policy documents often seem to overlook fundamental conceptual problems of such approaches.

A Critique of the 'Post-industrial Society'

The critique of the 'post-industrial' thesis has concentrated on the alleged shift from a goods-producing industrial economy to a service-based post-industrial economy. An important challenge to the idea of such a shift was raised long ago by Cohen and Zysman (1987). Focusing on the production side of the economy, they maintained that not only was it the case that 'manufacturing matters'; manufacturing is, they argued, *central* to competitiveness. Furthermore, services and manufacturing are 'tightly linked' and subsequently the succession of manufacturing by services is doubtful. Fundamentally, '[t]here is no such a thing as post-industrial economy' (ibid., 261) insisted Cohen and Zysman. Instead, one could argue that much of the loss of industrial jobs in advanced capitalist countries could be attributed to the 'emigration' of manufacturing to lower factor-cost countries – the process that represented a salient feature of economic restructuring of Western economies at least since the 1970s (see Dicken, 1998; Harvey, 1989, 165). Therefore, taking into consideration a wider global scale, the shift towards tertiarization of the advanced capitalist economies should be seen in conjunction with the emergence of 'newly *industrialized* countries'. Consequently, the phenomenon has perhaps more to do with the continuing processes of redrawing the map of global divisions of labour (see below), than with a fundamental transformation towards a 'post-industrial society' (Sokol, 2002, 92). On the consumption side, a major problem of Bell's account of the 'post-industrial society' is his failure to consider that people might satisfy their service requirements by investing in goods rather than in employing service workers (Webster, 1995, 44). Indeed, following a detailed analysis of consumption patterns, Gershuny (1978) argued that '[i]nstead of buying services, households seem increasingly to be buying...durable goods which allow final consumers to produce services for themselves' (Gershuny, 1978, 8; cited in Webster, 1995, 45). Such a 'self-service economy' amounts to an antithesis of Bell's 'post-industrial service society' (see Webster, 1995, 45).

Meanwhile, contrary to the expectations of the 'post-industrial society' enthusiasts, service employment that *has* been created in the advanced capitalist countries in recent decades is not necessarily of a high-wage, knowledge-intensive, business services or R&D nature (Cohen and Zysman, 1987, 10; Webster, 1995; Sassen, 1994). Quite the opposite, many new service jobs use unqualified/unskilled labour, earning poorer wages than those associated with the skilled labour of the old industrial economy (Sassen, 1994). This signals that the rising living standards posited by Bell (1973) may not be shared across society and that the expected reduction in social inequalities may prove chimerical (see also Castells, 1996; 1997). Further flaws in the 'post-industrial society' thesis were highlighted by Webster (1995) who, after a detailed review, launched an uncompromising attack on Bell's version of such a society. He argued that the rejection of the post-industrial society thesis:

> must be quite sweeping, dismissing everything from Bell's anti-holistic mantra (societies are *not* radically disjuncted, but intricately connected) to his general account of social change as an evolution through stages towards a 'service economy'. His explanation of the emergence of the [post-industrial society] is misconceived, his description of an emergent 'caring' society unconvincing, and his insistence that it is possible to identify separate employment sectors (which are yet causally connected, with services being dependent on the goods-producing level) is incorrect' (ibid, 46).

Various attempts to reincarnate the idea of the 'post-industrial society' – for instance, in the form of the 'information society' – have also faced severe criticisms.

Shortcomings of the 'Information Society' Thesis

It could be pointed out that 'information society' theorists have tried to move beyond the service sector approach typical for writers of the 'post-industrial society' thesis and have focused instead on information and technology that supports the creation, processing and distribution of knowledge. This move, however, has proved to be the source of a major problem, most notably in the form of technological determinism (see critique by Webster and Robins, 1986; Webster, 1995; 1997; May, 2000). Castells' opus on the 'Information Age' is a case in point. Indeed, despite being 'a marvellous work of synthesis' (Webster, 1997, 106) it also contains several fundamental problematic points. Importantly, Webster noted that the 'Information Age' was constructed 'without a really clear idea of what the author means by information, so much so that quite varied information activities and processes were being conflated and confused' (ibid., 120). The second major objection Webster highlighted is that Castells 'shares totally the view that it is changes in the technological system that provide the basis of social advance' (ibid., 109), which makes him 'committed to a technocratic view of development, just as much as is Daniel Bell and, indeed, all other theorists of the "information age"'(ibid., 109). The central belief of such a 'technocratic view' is that 'a certain technological foundation is the prerequisite and determinant of all social and political life' (ibid., 109) which in turn 'subverts all ambitions to bring about profound social and economic change, since always, but always, there must be acknowledged a decisive, if imprecise, level of technological foundationalism to any dreamed of social system' (ibid., 109).

Further critique of various other aspects of the 'information society' concept in general, and the implications of information and communication technology (ICT) in particular has been offered, *inter alia*, by Webster and Robins (1986), Lyon (1988), Tomaney (1994), Webster (1995) and May (2000); (see also Schiller, 1999; McChesney et al., 1998; in particular Hill, 1998; Meiksins, 1998; McChesney, 1998). Meanwhile, the ICT-producing sector (creating technology that is supposed to have benign social impact) is, ironically, itself characterized by a sharp division of labour (Henderson, 1989; Massey, 1995), thus perpetuating rather than mitigating social inequality. Various different versions of the 'information society' have aimed to overcome the obvious technological determinism and other conceptual shortcomings by embracing wider social contexts. These attempts, however, have their own problems, as the subsequent critique of the 'knowledge economy' and 'learning economy' will demonstrate.

Limits to the 'Knowledge Economy' and 'Learning Economy'

A sound critique of the 'knowledge economy' has been offered by Christopher May (2000, 2002). May disputes Leadbeater's 'tone of inevitability' that 'denies human agency to do anything but react to change' (May, 2000, 147). He also challenges the invocation that the 'knowledge economy' is a 'post-capitalist' one (ibid., 147) and provides convincing arguments that the 'logic' of capitalism has not been disrupted by the emerging 'new economy' (cf. Leadbeater, 2000, 228). For May, new modes of economic activity exhibit 'significant continuities' (May, 2002, 1037) with the previous modes of capitalism, primarily because property rights remain a central element of society's legal structure (ibid., 1037). Indeed, May argues, the main problem with Leadbeater's account is its failure to recognize that 'a key element of the knowledge economy has been the largely successful project to render knowledge as property' (May, 2000, 146), not least through internationally enforced *Intellectual Property Rights* (ibid., 147–8). *Intellectual Property Rights* (IPRs) allow commercial exploitation of knowledge, while ensuring that in the 'knowledge economy' (contra Leadbeater) knowledge is *not* freely spread between people, firms, regions or nations. May argues that:

> The rendering of knowledge as property through patents, copyrights, trademarks and other instruments, transforms knowledge that might be regarded as commonly available to everyone into property owned by the few... To enable a price to be taken by capitalists, knowledge must be rendered formally scarce and this is achieved by the legalised limitations of use owners can mandate by utilising IPRs over knowledge of information they wish to control (May, 2002, 1041–2).

For May, this represents a 'continuing commodification' (ibid., 1042) through which 'capitalism has progressively deepened its penetration into previously non-commodified social relations inside and outside the workplace' (ibid., 1043). The latter process includes 'continuing moves to bring information and knowledge to the market as commodities' (ibid., 1043). Following this critique, May moves on to discuss contradictions at the very heart of the 'knowledge economy' by examining the claims that 'knowledge workers' represent a new dramatically different and empowered form of work (cf. Leadbeater, 2000, 1–2, 228). Offering some vivid examples, May (2002) convincingly demonstrates that far from becoming an 'axial principle' in the 'knowledge economy' (as posited by Bell for instance), individual 'knowledge workers' may face 'considerable barriers [in] profiting from the ideas and knowledge they originate' (ibid., 1047). Consequently, more often than not, inventors, creators or performers 'need to be assigned to a large company, who then control those rights for exploitation' (ibid., 1045). Alternatively, they may become 'brains for hire' (ibid., 1045), but in both cases, 'knowledge-worker's output belongs not to them but to their employers' (ibid., 1046). In fact, IPRs can ensure that 'even ideas you have outside the workplace may be owned by your employer' (ibid., 1046). Typical knowledge workers thus cannot wrench themselves free of capitalist social relations. Even the small minority of high-profile knowledge workers with potentially generous contracts, 'seldom retain control of the rights to their intellectual output' (ibid., 1045). This is so, because the 'underlying property relations – those between labour owning and capital owning groups – remain largely unaltered' (ibid., 1044). While it is important to acknowledge that alternative arrangements do exist, it could be argued that the knowledge-related workplace represents a significant continuity in labour relations (ibid., 1047–8).

These points have been echoed by Ray Hudson (1999) in his critique of the 'learning economy'. Hudson starts his critique by asserting that the emphasis on knowledge, learning and innovation is 'hardly novel' (ibid., 59) because 'the creation of knowledge has been integral to the competitive dynamic of capitalist economies since they were first constituted as capitalist' (ibid., 60). Importantly then, current economic transformations should be seen in 'the context of continuities and changes *within* capitalism' (ibid., 59; emphasis added). Consequently, contradictions of capitalist social relations, the class relations between capital and labour, 'can be refashioned but not abolished' (ibid., 66). In turn, these contradictions of capitalism can impose formidable limits to 'learning' that 'learning economy' theorists fail to appreciate. Likewise, the role of power in shaping production and the appropriation of knowledge is overlooked by the 'learning economy' literature. Thus, Hudson has doubts as to what extent the expected benign effects of the 'learning economy' can be realized as far as 'the economy remains a capitalist one' (ibid., 66). Instead he argues that some recent changes in production are in fact 'reproducing in enhanced form the asymmetries of power between capital and labour' (ibid., 66). Hudson (1999) then moves on to demonstrate that the concept of the networked 'learning firm', one of the basic building blocks of the 'learning economy' concept, seems problematic. Indeed, it fails to take into account 'sharp asymmetries of power' (ibid., 67) in inter-firm networks that are increasingly dominated by 'massive transnational corporations' emerging as 'movers and shakers' of the global economy (ibid., 67).

Critical points have also been raised by Jessop (2000) who assesses the globalizing 'knowledge-driven economy' from *Regulation School* positions. Importantly, he does not see the rise of such an economy as a shift beyond capitalism, but rather as a search for 'spatio-temporal fixes' of capitalist contradictions in the post-Fordist era. Jessop argues that far from overcoming old contradictions of capitalist accumulation, the emergence of the 'knowledge economy' means that 'some contradictions have increased in importance and/or acquired new forms' (ibid., 68). He then goes on to argue that '[k]nowledge has always been important economically' (ibid., 65) but that what is novel is 'the increased importance of knowledge as fictitious commodity' (ibid., 65). Transformation of knowledge into such a commodity lies at the very heart of the 'knowledge economy' and can take a form of intellectual property (for example patent, copyright), of wage-labour producing knowledge for the market, or third, of 'the real subsumption of intellectual labour and its products under capitalist control through their commoditisation and integration into a networked, digitised production–consumption process that is controlled by capital' (ibid., 65). A 'fundamental contradiction' arising from such commodification is between the knowledge as intellectual commons (collectively produced) and knowledge as intellectual property (privately appropriated) (see ibid., 65).

Further contradiction, according to Jessop, arises in the globalizing 'knowledge-driven economy' from the conflict between 'hypermobile financial capital' (operating in an abstract space of flows) and 'industrial capital' (still needing to be valorized in place) (ibid., 69). There is also a contradiction between 'short-term economic calculation' (especially in financial flows) and the long-term dynamic of 'real competition' rooted in resources that may take years to create, stabilize and reproduce (ibid., 69). One could add that in consequence, a happy and spontaneous reconciliation between 'financial markets' and 'community' as posited by Leadbeater (2000) may be unrealistic. According to Jessop, a new 'site of problems' also arises from the interaction between 'time–space compression' and 'time–space distantiation'. The latter 'stretches social relations over time and space', the spatial side of which is 'reflected in the growing spatial reach of divisions of labour' (ibid., 70). Thus, instead of a shift towards a 'post-capitalist society' (cf. Drucker, 1993; Leadbeater, 2000), we may be witnessing the *deepening* of the capitalist logic (Castells, 1996, 19; Harvey, 1989, 188; May, 2000, 147).

Such a conclusion in turn casts a shadow not only over the desired outcomes of the transformation to a 'knowledge age', but also over the nature of the 'knowledge-based' or 'knowledge-driven' economy itself. Indeed, if we admit that (even the most advanced) economies have not moved beyond the capitalist market economy, it remains problematic to describe them as *knowledge*-driven. Rather it should be admitted that the market economy remains largely *profit*-driven (cf. Sokol and Tomaney, 2001). Within such an economy, the final goal is not knowledge but profit. In fact, the importance of the market imperative for profit is likely to increase with the advances of neoliberal globalization (see Harvey, 1989; Castells, 1998, 338, 342). This is not to say that knowledge does not play an important role; indeed, knowledge can be a part of a profit-seeking process (and probably always was). But knowledge is neither the only, nor necessarily the most important part of such a process. This point is further emphasized through a critical examination of the knowledge–wealth relationship.

3. CAN AN ECONOMY BE 'KNOWLEDGE-DRIVEN'?

The logic of the 'knowledge economy' is built on the assumption that knowledge is a 'dynamo' of economic growth, that is that there is a firm *causal relation* between knowledge and wealth in a direction that knowledge creates wealth. Knowledge is thus conceptualized as being central to economic success (as the most important if not the only factor of economic development) in virtually all versions of the 'knowledge economy' regardless of their theoretical background.[1] Various approaches may have fundamentally different views on what *form* of knowledge is important for economic development; either tacit (Lundvall and Johnson, 1994; Burton-Jones, 1999) or codified/scientific (Bell, 1973; Leadbeater, 2000), embodied in technology (Castells, 1996) or institutions (Hodgson, 1998; 1999). Various authors may have also different views on *how* and *where* knowledge is produced; in R&D departments and universities (Bell, 1973; Leadbeater, 2000), in and between knowledge firms or knowledge corporations (Burton-Jones, 1999; Bell, 1973), through networks (Castells, 1996) or global trade (Leadbeater, 2000) or via 'organised markets' and government intervention (Lundvall and Johnson, 1994). However, regardless of these differences, the underlying argument firmly enshrined in them is rather clear: in the 'knowledge-driven economy', it is knowledge that drives economic development.

Even critics that question the alleged benign effects of the 'knowledge' or 'learning economy' seem to admit that it 'would of course be futile to deny the significance of knowledge, innovation and learning to economic performance' (Hudson, 1999, 59). Far from disputing this latter statement, it is nevertheless suggested here that the knowledge–wealth relationship needs to be examined in a critical light. The fundamental dilemma (Sokol, 2003a) is whether successful economies are prosperous because they are knowledge-intensive, or whether they are knowledge-intensive because they are prosperous. In other words, the question arises whether the economy is driven by knowledge or whether knowledge creation is driven by the economy.

The answer to this question is far from clear. Jacob Schmookler (1966) for instance studied the relationship between economic development and technological innovation, to conclude that the rates of innovation (considered by many as a vehicle for economic development) may in fact be positively linked to the demand of a given economy, that is, dependent on the economic growth itself. In a similar way, Paterson (1999) challenges a conventional view regarding the relationship between education and economic development. He argues, building on Ashton and Green (1996), that 'there is no convincing research evidence that higher overall levels of education and training really are the cause of more rapid economic growth' (Paterson, 1999, 5). Subsequently, the critical question arises 'whether education is a *cause* or an *effect* of national economic success' (ibid., 5; emphasis added).

One way to resolve the above dilemma would be to argue that instead of a simple unidirectional relationship, knowledge and wealth are engaged in an interactive relationship in a sense that knowledge can create wealth, but also wealth is needed to produce knowledge (be it scientific discovery, technological innovation, or educated individual). Moreover, the relationship between knowledge and wealth may be mutually reinforcing and resulting in a 'virtuous circle' in which investment in knowledge may yield economic benefits that can be reinvested back into the knowledge-base generating further wealth. In other words, a possibility of increasing returns to investment in knowledge should be acknowledged (cf. Solow, 1956; 1957; Arrow, 1962; Kaldor, 1970; Markusen, 1985; Romer, 1986; 1990; Krugman, 1991a; 1991b). Thus, knowledge should be in fact seen as *an integral part* of wealth (capital) accumulation. This puts the proposition that an economy is, or could be, knowledge-driven in a very different light.

The second problem with the knowledge–wealth formula that features at the heart of the 'knowledge-driven economy' concept is its silence over power relations. This is rather disturbing because as Susan Strange puts it '[i]t is impossible to study political economy...without giving close attention to the role of power in economic life' (Strange, 1994, 23). The absence of power in the knowledge–wealth equation thus represents the second fundamental 'omission' of the 'knowledge economy' concept. Indeed, by inserting power into the equation, the picture of a simple, one-directional relation between 'knowledge' and 'wealth' disintegrates, and a more complex (but also more accurate) matrix emerges. This emerging matrix sees 'knowledge', 'wealth' and 'power' as being mutually linked through a web of complex, multidirectional, direct and indirect relations. It is useful to acknowledge that the task of thoroughly defining knowledge, wealth and power and conceptualizing their relationship would be welcome here, but is beyond the scope of this chapter.[2] What is important, however, is that the new emerging matrix (abstract and simplistic as it is) offers an alternative way of looking at economic and social processes. Such insights may be necessary when considering inequalities within and between socioeconomic systems.

Indeed, at the very abstract level, the interplay between knowledge, wealth and power is *unlikely* to result in a sort of equilibrium distribution within and between socioeconomic systems (cf. Cooke, 2002). On the contrary, there are good reasons to expect that this interplay may be patterned by cumulative effects, leading to virtuous/vicious circles from which highly uneven patterns of 'distribution' of knowledge, wealth and power may emerge. On the 'virtuous circle' side, it is not difficult to imagine, for instance, how wealth (economic resources), power (political influence) and knowledge (education, skills, and so on), can reinforce each other to enhance success of individuals or whole social groups. On the adverse side of the process, a 'vicious circle' can develop, where people and social groups can find it difficult to break from poverty, lack of knowledge (education) and the absence of political voice. The likelihood of the virtuous/vicious scenarios resonates with the suggestions by Ferreira (2001) who has argued that initial educational, wealth and political inequalities within society tend to reinforce themselves. Similar conclusions have been drawn by Gunnar Myrdal (1957) a half century ago, advancing the idea of *circular and cumulative causation*.[3] More broadly, such an approach resonates with the disequilibrium economics theories including Keynesianism (cf. Kaldor, 1970).

The possible negative effects of the *circular and cumulative causation* process can be enhanced in the profit-driven economy, in which the differences in power and wealth are further highlighted. Indeed, in the capitalist economy, the ownership of the means of production is in itself a source of considerable power.[4] As seen in the previous section, this logic (typical for industrial capitalism) has not been disrupted in the emerging knowledge-intensive production, courtesy of continuing institution of property rights. Indeed, as May (2002) has demonstrated, even knowledge workers may find that their intellectual output still belongs to the owners of the Intellectual Property Rights. Thus knowledge, far from dramatically transforming the landscapes of capitalism, is itself subjected to the capitalist logic. Consequently, knowledge, in a variety of its forms, is likely to partake in the process of reproducing existing inequalities (Sokol, 2003a). Within such a process, knowledge distribution 'remains patterned by wealth and ownership' (May, 2000, 146).

4. CONCLUSIONS: TOWARDS AN ALTERNATIVE APPROACH

This highlights the need for an alternative conceptualization of the current socioeconomic transformation. Building partly on the strengths of 'institutional/evolutionary' and more 'radical' approaches, such an alternative could start by acknowledging that the economy should be conceptualized as an 'institutionalized social process'. As such, the economy (or rather 'socio-economy' or 'political economy') is shaped by institutions, which can be simultaneously seen as the objects, subjects and outcomes of social struggles over knowledge, wealth and power (Sokol, 2003a). The chapter supports the view that there are important continuities with the past in these struggles and that current socioeconomic transformations in the most advanced market economies are unfolding *within* the framework of the capitalist political economy. Consequently, the institutions of labour, state (local, regional, national, supranational) and capital (productive and financial), seem to have continuing salience in shaping socioeconomic transformations. However, in what appears to be an increasingly neoliberal *profit*-driven economy, it is global capital that is gaining momentum, supported by institutions of global economic governance (perhaps emerging as a category of institution in its own right). Indeed, global capital seems to play a pivotal role in shaping the emerging global 'socio-spatial divisions of labour'[5] accompanied by global 'socio-spatial value chains/networks' (cf. Smith et al., 2002) – two concepts that seem to offer an alternative way of understanding what some observers see as the rise of the 'knowledge economy' (Sokol, 2003a).

Viewed within such an alternative approach, the role of *knowledge* in the economy is indeed changing in that it is increasingly commodified. Thus, rather than dramatically transforming the economic and social landscapes of capitalism, knowledge itself seems to be increasingly subordinated to the 'logic' of the capitalist economy. The commodification of knowledge in turn allows for the emergence of what could be seen as a 'knowledge-intensive sub-economy', but this has to be seen in conjunction with the growing socio-spatial division of labour within the overall *profit*-driven economy framework. Therefore, instead of a widespread knowledge-sharing process, we may witness a process of knowledge accumulation as part of a wider circular and cumulative causation mechanism, in which knowledge, power and wealth reinforce each other with significant social and spatial effects. This in turn casts shadows of doubt over the expected desirable effects that the alleged emergence of the 'knowledge era' is supposed to bring about. These doubts, together with the question marks over the nature of the 'knowledge economy' carry some crucial inferences for concepts in economic geography that take the emergence of the 'knowledge economy' for granted and uncritically embrace the idea that knowledge and learning are the most important factors of economic development. These economic geography concepts thus deserve a critical (re)examination.

NOTES

1. Lundvall and Johnson (1994, p. 23, note 1) have for instance argued that 'knowledge, energy and materials are the basic resources in production rather than labour and capital; knowledge may be regarded as the key resource'.

2. See Bourdieu (1977; 1984) and his concept of 'economic capital', 'political capital' and 'cultural capital' as a possible way forward.
3. Myrdal (1957) originally introduced the idea of *circular and cumulative causation* when studying processes of social exclusion (see ibid., 13–20). Subsequently he applied the principle of such causation into the space-economic context. It is useful to note that Myrdal has argued that the negative effects of the processes of *circular and cumulative causation* can be overcome only when tackled on several or all fronts by intervention from outside.
4. I am thankful to John Tomaney for highlighting this aspect.
5. Cf. the concept of the 'newest international division of labour' of Castells (1996, 106–47).

REFERENCES

Arrow, K. (1962), 'The economic implications of learning by doing', *Review of Economic Studies*, **29** (2), 155–73.

Asheim, B. (1996), 'Industrial districts as "learning regions": a condition for prosperity', *European Planning Studies*, **4** (4), 379–400.

Ashton, D., and F. Green (1996), *Education, Training and the Global Economy*, Cheltenham, UK and Northampton, MA, USA: Edward Elgar.

Bell, D. (1973), *The Coming of Post-Industrial Society: A Venture in Social Forecasting*, New York: Basic Books.

Boekema, F., K. Morgan, S. Bakkers, and R.Rutten (eds) (2000), *Knowledge, Innovation and Economic Growth: The Theory and Practice of Learning Regions*, Cheltenham, UK and Northampton MA, USA: Edward Elgar.

Bourdieu, P. (1977), *Outline of a Theory of Practice*, Cambridge and New York: Cambridge University Press.

Bourdieu, P. (1984), *Distinction: A Social Critique of the Judgement of Taste*, Cambridge, MA: Harvard University Press.

Burton-Jones, A. (1999), *Knowledge Capitalism: Business, Work, and Learning in the New Economy*, Oxford: Oxford University Press.

Castells, M. (1989), *The Informational City: Information Technology, Economic Restructuring and the Urban–Regional Process*, Oxford: Blackwell.

Castells, M. (1996), *The Information Age: Economy, Society and Culture, vol I, The Rise of the Network Society*, Oxford: Blackwell.

Castells, M. (1997), *The Information Age: Economy, Society and Culture, vol II, The Power of Identity*, Oxford: Blackwell.

Castells, M. (1998), *The Information Age: Economy, Society and Culture, vol III, End of Millennium*, Oxford: Blackwell.

Cohen, S., and J. Zysman (1987), *Manufacturing Matters: The Myth of Postindustrial Economy*, New York: Basic Books.

Cooke, P. (2002), *Knowledge Economies: Clusters, Learning and Cooperative Advantage*, London and New York: Routledge.

Cooke, P., and K. Morgan (1994), 'Growth regions under duress: renewal strategies in Baden Wurttemberg and Emilia-Romagna', in A. Amin and N. Thrift (eds), *Globalization, Institutions and Regional Development in Europe*, Oxford: Oxford University Press, pp. 91–117.

Department of Trade and Industry (DTI) (1998a), 'Our competitive future – building the knowledge driven economy', white paper cm 4176, London: DTI.

Department of Trade and Industry (DTI) (1998b), 'Our competitive future – building the knowledge driven economy', analytical report, ; accessed on 28 April 1999 at www.dti.gov.uk/comp/competitive/summary.htm.

Dicken, P. (1998), *Global Shift: Transforming the World Economy* 3rd edn, London: Paul Chapman Publishing.

Drucker, P. (1993), *Post-capitalist Society*, Oxford: Butterworth Heinemenn.

European Commission (EC) (1996), 'Living and working in the information society: people first', green paper COM(96) 389 final, Brussels: EC.

European Commission (EC) (1997a), *Building the European Information Society for us all: Final Policy Report of the High-level Expert Group*, Luxembourg: Office for Official Publications of the European Communities.

European Commission (EC) (1997b), *The first Action Plan for Innovation in Europe*, Brussels: EC.

European Union (EU) (2000), 'Extraordinary European Council presidency conclusions Lisbon, 23 and 24 March accessed 10 June 2000 at europa.eu.int/council/off/conclu/mar2000.

Ferreira, F.H.G. (2001), 'Education for the masses? The interaction between wealth, educational and political inequalities', *Economics of Transition*, **9** (2), 533–52.

Florida, R. (1995), 'Toward the learning region', *Futures*, **27** (5), 527–36.

Gershuny, J. (1978), *After Industrial Society? The Emerging Self-Service Economy*, London: Macmillan.

Giddens, A. (2000), *The Third Way and its Critics*, Cambridge: Polity Press.

Harvey, D. (1989), *The Condition of Postmodernity: An Enquiry into the Origins of Cultural Change*, Oxford: Basil Blackwell.

Henderson, J. (1989), *The Globalisation of High Technology Production: Society, Space and Semiconductors in the Restructuring of the Modern World*, London and New York: Routledge.

Hill, J. (1998), 'US Rules. OK? Telecommunications since the 1940s', in R. McChesney, E. Meiksins-Wood and J. Bellamy-Foster (eds), *Capitalism and the Information Age: The Political Economy of the Global Communication Revolution*, New York: Monthly Review Press, pp. 99–121.

Hodgson, G.M. (1998), 'The approach of institutionalist economics', *Journal of Economic Literature*, **36** (1), 162–92.

Hodgson, G.M. (1999), *Economics and Utopia: Why the Learning Economy is Not the End of History*, London: Routledge.

Hudson, R. (1999), 'The learning economy, the learning firm and the learning region: a sympathetic critique of the limits to learning', *European Urban and Regional Studies*, **6** (1), 59–72.

Jessop, B. (2000), 'The state and the contradictions of the knowledge-driven economy', in J.R. Bryson, P.W. Daniels, N. Henry and J. Pollard (eds), *Knowledge, Space, Economy*, London and New York: Routledge.

Kaldor, N. (1970), 'The case for regional policies', *Scottish Journal of Political Economy*, **17**, 337–45.

Krugman, P. (1991a), 'Increasing returns and economic geography', *Journal of Political Economy*, **99**, 483–99.

Krugman, P. (1991b), *Geography and Trade*, Cambridge, MA: MIT Press.

Leadbeater, C. (2000), *Living on Thin Air: The New Economy*, London: Penguin Books.

Lundvall, B.-Å., and B. Johnson (1994), 'The learning economy', *Journal of Industrial Studies*, **1** (2), 23–42.

Lyon, D. (1988), *The Information Society: Issues and Illusions*, Cambridge: Polity Press.

Malecki, E.J. (2000), 'Creating and sustaining competitiveness: local knowledge and economic geography', in J.R. Bryson, P.W. Daniels, N. Henry, and J. Pollard (eds), *Knowledge, Space, Economy*, London and New York: Routledge, pp. 103–19.

Markusen, A. (1985), *Profit Cycles, Oligopoly, and Regional Development*, Cambridge, MA and London: MIT Press.

Maskell, P., H. Eskelinen, I. Hannibalsson, A. Malmberg, and E. Vatne (1998), *Competitiveness, Localised Learning and Regional Development: Specialisation and Prosperity in Small Open Economies*, London and New York: Routledge.

Massey, D. (1995), *Spatial Divisions of Labour: Social Structures and the Geography of Production (Second Edition)*, London: Macmillan.

May, C. (2000), 'Feature review: living on thin air: the new economy', *New Political Economy*, **5** (1), 145–9.

May, C. (2002), 'Trouble in E-topia: knowledge as intellectual property', *Urban Studies*, **39** (5–6), 1037–49.

McChesney, R. (1998), 'The political economy of global communication', in R. McChesney, E. Meiksins-Wood and J. Bellamy-Foster (eds), *Capitalism and the Information Age: The Political Economy of the Global Communication Revolution*, New York: Monthly Review Press, pp. 1–26.

McChesney, R., E. Meiksins-Wood, and J. Bellamy-Foster (eds) (1998), *Capitalism and the Information Age: The Political Economy of the Global Communication Revolution*, New York: Monthly Review Press.

Meiksins, P. (1998), 'Work, new technology and capitalism', in R. McChesney, E. Meiksins-Wood and J. Bellamy-Foster (eds), *Capitalism and the Information Age: The Political Economy of the Global Communication Revolution*, New York: Monthly Review Press, pp. 151–64.

Morgan, K. (1997), 'The learning region: institutions, innovation and regional renewal', *Regional Studies*, **31** (5), 491–503.

Myrdal, G. (1957), *Economic Theory and Under-Developed Regions*, London: Gerald Duckworth.

OECD (1996), *The Knowledge-Based Economy*, OCDE/DG(96)102, Paris: OECD.

OECD (2001), *Innovative Clusters: Drivers of National Innovation Systems*, Paris: OECD.

Paterson, L. (1999), 'Education, training and the Scottish Parliament', paper presented to the Skills for Scotland Conference, Glasgow, 15 April.

Porter, M.E. (1990), *The Competitive Advantage of Nations*, New York: Free Press.

Rodrigues, M.J. (ed.) (2002), *The New Knowledge Economy in Europe: A Strategy for International Competitiveness and Social Cohesion*, Cheltenham, UK and Northampton, MA, USA: Edward Elgar.

Romer, P.M. (1986), 'Increasing returns and long-run growth', *Journal of Political Economy*, **94**, 1002–37.

Romer, P.M. (1990), 'Endogenous technological change', *Journal of Political Economy*, **98** (October), 71–102.

Rutten, R., S. Bakkers, and F. Boekema (2000), 'The analysis of learning regions: conclusions and research agenda', in F. Boekema, K. Morgan, S. Bakkers, and R. Rutten (eds), *Knowledge, Innovation and Economic Growth: The Theory and Practice of Learning Regions*, Cheltenham, UK and Northampton, MA, USA: Edward Elgar, pp. 245–58.

Sassen, S. (1994), *Cities in A Global Economy*, Thousand Oaks, CA: Pine Forge Press.
Schiller, D. (1999), *Digital Capitalism: Networking the Global Market System*, Cambridge, MA: MIT Press.
Schmookler, J. (1966), *Invention and Economic Growth*, Cambridge, MA and London: Harvard University Press and Oxford University Press.
Simmie, J. (2002), 'Trading places: competitive cities in the global economy', *European Planning Studies*, **10** (2), 201–15.
Simmie, J., and W.F. Lever (2002), 'Introduction: the knowledge-based city', *Urban Studies*, **39** (5–6), 855–7.
Smith, A., A. Rainnie, M. Dunford, J. Hardy, R. Hudson, and D. Sadler (2002), 'Networks of value, commodities and regions: reworking divisions of labour in macro-regional economies', *Progress in Human Geography*, **26** (1), 41–63.
Sokol, M. (2002), 'Poznatkova ekonomika: problemy a vyzvy (Knowledge economy: issues and challenges)', *Ekonomicky casopis* (*Journal of Economics*, Slovak Academic Press), **50** (1), 85–106.
Sokol, M. (2003a), *Regional Dimensions of the Knowledge Economy: Implications for the 'New Europe'*, unpublished Ph.D. thesis, University of Newcastle upon Tyne Centre for Urban and Regional Development Studies.
Sokol, M. (2003b), 'The "knowledge economy": a critical view', paper for the Regional Studies Association International Conference Reinventing Regions in the Global Economy, Pisa, Italy, 12–15 April.
Sokol, M., and J. Tomaney (2001), 'Regionalising the knowledge economy: what's the point?', in A. Maconochie and S. Hardy (eds), *Regionalising the Knowledge Economy (Conference Proceedings of the Regional Studies Association Annual Conference)*, Seaford: RSA, pp. 108–10.
Solow, R.M. (1956), 'A contribution to the theory of economic growth', *Quarterly Journal of Economics*, **70**, 65–94.
Solow, R.M. (1957), 'Technical change and the aggregate production function', *Review of Economics and Statistics*, **39**, 312–20.
Strange, S. (1994), *States and Markets* 2nd edn, London and New York: Pinter.
Tomaney, J. (1994), 'A new paradigm of work organization and technology?', in A. Amin (ed.), *Post-Fordism: A Reader*, Oxford: Blackwell, pp. 157–94.
Webster, F. (1995), *Theories of the Information Society*, London and New York: Routledge.
Webster, F. (1997), 'Information, urbanism and identity: perspectives on the current work of Manuel Castells', *City* (7), 105–27.
Webster, F., and K. Robins (1986), *Information Technology: A Luddite Analysis*, Norwood, NJ: Ablex.

13. Conclusions: regional economies as knowledge laboratories: theories, fashions and future steps

Andrea Piccaluga

INTRODUCTION

If you try an Internet search for books which include the terms 'knowledge regions', 'learning regions', 'knowledge economies' and similar, you will soon realize – even without making accurate comparisons with other comparable concepts – that writing about and discussing this topic is not at all rare. The joint – or better, simultaneous – work of geographers, economists, business scholars, sociologists, and so on – has certainly had the effect of making 'knowledge regions' a popular term in the last twenty years, indeed a hot topic. It is not then surprising any more to find local and regional policy makers, in either central metropolitan areas or peripheral ones, passionately discussing plans for knowledge-based programmes for their areas. That is to say, the fact that – broadly speaking – investing in knowledge (education, R&D, science and technology, and so on) is the current preferred recipe for economic development has become a widespread belief at regional level. In other words, the guardians of regional economies have become pre-disposed to such ambitions as constructing regional advantage through 'knowledge laboratories' in many places. Nonetheless, for a number of reasons, such ambitions are more complicated than they may appear to be. In these concluding remarks an effort is made to say why complexity reigns, and how the contributions in this book help the worlds of policy and academe grapple with it.

REGIONS AND COMPLEXITY

First of all, these concepts have become so diffused and popular that they have sometimes lost much of their impact. In other words, actors talk normatively about knowledge-based processes, including the related territorial dimensions, from such a broad and generalist point of view, that they include almost everything, from support to SMEs involved in manufacturing in mature sectors, to long-term investments in basic research in emerging fields. While it is true that knowledge-based regional development is based on a number of different factors, an excessive variety and elasticity in the terms used in the debate generates, at least, some confusion. This reflects a new 'regional complexity'. *Knowledge laboratories are not the same thing for everyone.*

Second, as a consequence of such richness, complexity – and confusion – in terminology, even the everyday local and regional economic development plan currently says something about knowledge-based processes and the term is so often used that it is not clear any more if it is a fundamental pillar within the plan, or something which has to be added because no plan can currently be written without referring to it, since knowledge-based investments are a sort of 'fashion of the time'. *Knowledge laboratories do attract a lot of attention; sometimes, however, not the right attention.*

This brings along the third aspect – a scale dimension. Not all knowledge-based programmes are identical, and they definitely involve specific investments, strategies and, naturally, outcomes. Too easily the terms 'knowledge regions' and 'knowledge laboratories' are used to refer to areas and situations which differ significantly. These differences are not a problem by themselves; on the contrary, they have to be addressed carefully, in order to personalize and then apply knowledge-based development plans to specific situations. The fact that the label 'knowledge region' is used to describe very different areas has the effect of underestimating the evidence that regions are characterized by different starting points and that for this reason, the recipes must be different, according to what every region can offer, pay and hope for. *Knowledge laboratories are not endowed with the same resources everywhere.*

From a competitive point of view – fourth – the situation is indeed interesting. In fact, knowledge-based strategies are adopted by many regions around the world and it is consequently very hard to emerge in a league where a huge number of teams play (with similar players and similar schemes) and where the threshold of economic resources which are necessary to reach top positions moves further every day. It is rather surprising to observe how the economic and human resources invested by top regions to foster knowledge-based growth processes grow exponentially, generating difficulties for regions unable or unwilling to keep a similar pace. *Knowledge laboratories require relevant investments.*

Fifth, from a social accountability point of view, building knowledge regions poses further difficulties and some opportunities. From the point of view of difficulties, it is often difficult, for policy makers, to obtain wide acceptance for knowledge-based plans. In fact, laid off workers from manufacturing sectors such as steelmaking and automotive, or even service sectors such as airlines or information technology, are much more visible and represent much more immediate issues for politicians, trade unions and citizens, than campaigns to invest in researchers in laboratories or science park facilities, which generally do not generate immediate and visible relevant employment increase. It is certainly not easy for regional administrators to mention Lisbon targets in their documents and support investments in R&D in periods of stagnating economies facing immediate and visible competition (such as in the case of Europe), from the Far East. From the point of view of opportunities, however, the fact that becoming a knowledge region is nowadays a policy imperative often makes it easier for policy makers and administrators to present initiatives they launch as important pieces in the knowledge region mosaic. The paradox is in this extreme case the fact that even initiatives which could encounter intense criticisms are better accepted by local actors if they are presented as part of a wider knowledge-based development programme. *Knowledge laboratories have a role in regional politics.*

Finally, knowledge regions have been sustained by intense marketing actions (see for example the large number of 'valleys' which are now present – and promoted – around the world). It is not so rare to observe that valleys, corridors and technopoles are more convincing in their (virtual) website than on their (concrete) physical site. Nonetheless, from a more virtuous point of view, marketing investments have in a number of cases been very successful in generating enthusiasm and attributing a certain personality to areas where the science and technology base was superior to the perception external and internal actors had about them. *Knowledge laboratories can be supported and sometimes created by marketing actions.*

CONSTRUCTING REGIONAL ADVANTAGE

Along these lines, the fact that regions and even provinces have a 'knowledge valley' within its borders, calls for more adequate and consistent efforts in defining – and especially using – appropriate indicators for regions as knowledge laboratories. In fact, very often regions lack basic indicators, for example with regard to knowledge-related inputs and outputs, which are needed to make comparisons among different cases and medium-term balances about the outcome of specific initiatives. It is well known that spillovers of knowledge-based programmes are very difficult to define and quantify, and that it is not clear which should be the right timescale to consider. Nonetheless, such exercises are not impossible and the difficulties involved are by no means a justification for the many cases in which technopoles, science parks and knowledge laboratories in general are launched and supported for years without rigorous evaluation and benchmarking exercises. As a consequence of this, and following fashion without detailed analyses – often unpopular from a political point of view – it is difficult to distinguish among 'hopeless regions', 'would like to be' knowledge regions, 'fast emerging' ones and 'well consolidated knowledge economies'. It is not a matter of dividing the world into bad and good laboratories, but rather to support future policy actions with adequate empirical evidence about past experiences. For these reasons, despite the abundant literature available on knowledge regions, there is still need for further studies which investigate this topic, crucial not only for developed, but also for developing countries. There is still need for theoretical reasoning as well as practical consideration about cases and strategies.

It has been exactly the aim of this book, which includes works presented for the first time at a Regional Science Association Conference in Pisa, in 2003, to contribute to the better understanding of theories and practices associated with the terms 'knowledge regions' and 'knowledge laboratories'. The 12 contributions cover a variety of approaches, from mainly theoretical ones to those based on detailed case studies; from papers about central, metropolitan areas to those about peripheral regions; from authors who praise the multifaceted virtues of the knowledge economy, to those who are not so optimistic about it or who seek to diminish the emphasis on the regional dimension of innovation processes. *Sotorauta* and *Kosonen* describe the case of South Ostrobothnia, a less favoured region in western Finland. In such a knowledge oriented country, a peripheral and less favoured region runs the risk of being left out of the mainstream investments and growth processes, which take place in central areas. In the described case, the role of the modern university was interpreted innovatively, and research rather than buildings represented the credible core for a wide coalition which managed to collect the economic resources necessary to hire 12 new research professors in emerging fields in both business and technology. The target was ambitious, but it was reached thanks to the coalition which was formed, which succeeded in transmitting a sense of positive urgency to local actors.

Tavoletti addresses a very important topic from a more theoretical point of view. He argues that since the knowledge economy is fully consolidated, it is surprising to observe such a high unemployment rate among people with tertiary education, such as in the case of Italy. His analysis concludes that every effective policy framework for filling the mismatch between higher education and the real economy requires embracing a new concept of knowledge, closer to the Far Eastern tradition. *Frenken and van Oort*'s contribution to a better understanding of regions as knowledge laboratories comes from the perspective of the geography of scientific knowledge production. The authors use data from research collaborations in Europe and the USA in the field of biotechnology, based on comparative empirical research on both continents. Special attention is given to the geography of 'hybrid' collaborations between universities with institutions outside academia, which appears to be geographically more localized than collaborations between universities and than collaborations between extra-academic institutions. The authors conclude that the emphasis on the geography of collaborative networks rather than knowledge production, as the main vehicle of knowledge creation and diffusion, is supported by the fact that collaboration itself is a proliferating phenomenon.

Aslesen argues that economic competitiveness is closely connected to new ways of producing, using and combining diverse types of knowledge and that innovation processes are increasingly the result of cumulative dynamic interaction and learning processes involving many actors. Her analysis is focused on Knowledge Intensive Business Services (KIBS), which play a fundamental role in contributing to regional development through knowledge generation and diffusion. Nonetheless, whereas the diffusion of such services in large cities is rather well consolidated and analysed (Oslo is the case study in this chapter), much less attention has been so far devoted to the diffusion of these services in peripheral areas, where they are nonetheless much needed to foster innovation process.

Lorenzen and *Maskell* present an original theoretical contribution supported by the description of two short case studies. More precisely, discussing knowledge propagation processes in industrial clusters not based on university research, they present the conceptual categories of knowledge creation processes and of inter-firm market relations. The authors describe the cases of the European popular music industry, where inter-firm projects are the main clustering form, and of the European furniture industry, where horizontal knowledge spillovers through weak ties facilitate knowledge creation. Their contribution is that of combining transaction cost and knowledge based explanations about the economic efficiency of industrial clusters.

Poma and *Sacchetti* introduce the new concept of knowledge life cycle, which aims at capturing declining and ascending flows of knowledge. Their main finding, based on empirical researches on manufacturing firms in Emilia Romagna, is that knowledge does not always follow a cumulative process, but it can evolve or stagnate and, if not renewed, it can be subject to a process of decay. The new conceptual category is applied to both local system and firms, and exchange processes between the two are identified and described. Among studies investigating the existence of a 'clustering rationale' which induces independent firms to make identical location choices, *Wolter* analyses the characteristics of a high-tech sector such as biotechnology, using preliminary empirical evidence from Germany. The results further support the hypothesis that firms in this sector agglomerate near the sources of key resources such as knowledge, skilled workers and risk finance providers, although the evidence regarding this last factor is the weakest. The role of universities as part of national industry–science relationships (ISRs) in enhancing regional knowledge economies is the main object of the work by *Kitagawa*. More precisely, she looks at emerging ISRs in Japan and the UK from a comparative institutional perspective, highlighting different processes of regionalization in the two countries. The author examines the evolution of government's science and technology as well as higher education policies in the last decades and argues that regional strategies, policy instruments and indicators are needed in order to put into practice growth processes based on ISRs.

Transforming peripheral European regions into dynamic knowledge regions is the object of the work by *White* and *Grimes*, who analyse in detail the case of the 'Celtic Tiger'. In fact, Ireland achieved near full employment during a period of rapid growth in the 1990s, and a combination of endogenous and exogenous factors and conditions contributed to its emerging knowledge economy. At present the country undoubtedly has several problems still to solve and weaknesses to address, but it seems to possess the solid foundation necessary to compete in the realm of knowledge-based global competition. In particular, despite severe criticisms, Ireland's FDI-led development policy has been oriented towards sectors which have not yet reached maturity, and has put the country in a position to create synergies between foreign and domestic firms. Despite the undisputed importance of regions as knowledge laboratories, *Rutten* and *Boekema* argue that many firms think in terms of networks, and not in terms of regions, when they innovate. The authors try to develop an explanation of when proximity occurs in inter-firm learning and when not. They do so with the help of a case study of a regional network in the manufacturing industry (the Dutch manufacturer of copiers and printers, Océ) and interpretations from an interdisciplinary literature. The chapter offers an original view about regional economics, namely that of firms involved in network creation, which sheds new light on the relation between learning and proximity.

The region may become a particular form of knowledge laboratory in the framework of social responsibility between firms and the participating agents in a socioeconomic system. This is the story behind the case of the Mondragón Cooperative Corporation in the Basque Country, described by *Etxebarria* and *Gómez Uranga* using the stakeholder model. This case study illustrates the influence exercised by a culture of local values – trust, collaboration, solidarity and participation – to strengthen learning and knowledge networks, mainly between firms and cooperative organizations. The authors also describe the evolution of the group, which has progressively abandoned a pure cooperative model, despite the effort to maintain cooperative values at the core of its activities. After a thorough examination of the concepts associated with the transformation towards the knowledge economy, *Sokol* examines the knowledge–wealth relationships from a critical perspective, questioning the capacity of the knowledge economy to reduce existing inequalities. The author argues that the economy should be conceptualized as an 'institutionalised social process', that is shaped by institutions of labour, state and capital. Moreover, these institutions are still operating within the framework of the capitalist political economy, and global capital is particularly gaining momentum. This fact, together with the increasingly commodified role of knowledge, represents the basis of critical views to the approach which takes the emergence of the knowledge economy largely for granted. Altogether, the studies included in the book highlight a series of interesting issues about regions as knowledge laboratories. Perhaps two final considerations might represent further stimuli for future works.

The first one is that, together with more theoretical contributions, there is the need for more 'stories'. However, what we need is a series of nice stories about failures. Usually the people involved in failures are not particularly willing to give information about them, and do not like to be involved in this kind of research. Also, writing the case of a failure does not give scholars much visibility, or popularity, especially if the failure is that of your own area. Nonetheless, it is hard for both practitioners and scholars to learn from a large number of success – or self-defined success – stories, and it would be very useful to learn whatever is to be learnt from a few failures. Second, regional policy makers have made their effort to learn about regions as knowledge laboratories and are trying to apply the recipes as best they can. What they often need is a more accurate description of what the best in class have concretely done in terms of incentives, new actions, collaborations, infrastructures and so on. Information is often anecdotal, rather than detailed, but as we know well, researchers in knowledge laboratories – as in scientific ones – do need detailed and codified procedures in order to try and replicate successful experiments.

Index